NIGHTMARE IN RED

NIGHTMARE IN RED

The McCarthy Era in Perspective

RICHARD M. FRIED

OXFORD UNIVERSITY PRESS
New York   Oxford

Oxford University Press

Oxford   New York   Toronto
Delhi   Bombay   Calcutta   Madras   Karachi
Petaling Jaya   Singapore   Hong Kong   Tokyo
Nairobi   Dar es Salaam   Cape Town
Melbourne   Auckland

and associated companies in
Berlin   Ibadan

First published in 1990 by Oxford University Press, Inc.,

198 Madison Avenue, New York, New York 10016-4314

First issued as an Oxford University Press paperback, 1991

Oxford is a registered trademark of Oxford University Press

Library of Congress Cataloging-in-Publication Data
Fried, Richard M., 1941–
Nightmare in red: the McCarthy era in perspective/ Richard M. Fried.
p.   cm.   Bibliography: p.   Includes index.

1. Anti-Communist movements—United States—History—20th century.
2. McCarthy, Joseph, 1908–1957. 3. United States—Politics and
government—1945–1953. I. Title.
E743.5.F67 1990
973.921—dc20   89-32891   CIP
ISBN-13 978-0-19-504361-7 (PBK.)

For Barbara

Preface

There was far more to the "McCarthy era" than Senator Joseph R. McCarthy. We have sensed this, on one or another level, for some time. In the five years McCarthy bestrode American politics, some of his savvier opponents realized that exaggerated impressions of his importance made their task harder, but the capacity to perceive him on a merely human scale was not altogether commonplace. Although the premise that McCarthy was only part of a larger whole carries a burden of some banality, it is nonetheless crucial to an understanding of anti-communism in mid-twentieth-century America.

In this book, I have sought to place McCarthy and "his" era in perspective. Thus I have attempted to locate him chronologically in the continuum of twentieth-century anti-Communist politics. With deep roots in American culture, anti-communism flourished long before the Senator from Wisconsin adopted the issue in 1950. It was a hardy perennial in American politics before 1947, when historians who blame President Harry S. Truman and the Democratic Party for McCarthyism date the onset of anti-Communist extremism; before 1944, when the presidential campaign gave Americans an early sample of a political style commonly associated with the 1950s; before World War II, when the instrumentalities of the government's later loyalty and security programs were improvised; and even before 1938, when Congressman Martin Dies's Special House Committee on Un-American Activities pioneered techniques that prefigured McCarthy's. Similarly, coverage of anti-communism does not end with McCarthy's censure by the Senate in 1954. Though that event did contribute to anti-communism's decline as a force in American life, the death scene was a lingering one.

In dwelling on the early stages of the development of the anti-Communist impulse, my point is not simply to argue that McCarthyism always existed—a sort of malign Snow White to be awakened by the right demagogue's kiss. Such an explanation risks oversimplification, because extreme anti-communism appeared in different forms at various times. The events of 1950 were not a carbon copy of the Palmer raids of 1919 or the various anti-subversive activities of 1938–40, even though the resemblances are instructive.

I have also sought to put anti-communism in perspective by sketching a crowded canvas, one which contains not only McCarthy but also his predecessors, instructors, and imitators—as well as the targets and victims of these political entrepreneurs. Moreover, I have tried to depict the broader culture of anti-communism of which anti-Communist politics was a part. The variety of anti-communism—the investigations, the accusations, the candidacies, and the other types of exertions—helps to convey its pervasiveness in American life.

To illustrate the origins and consequences of McCarthyism (that imprecise blunderbuss of a word again), I have gratefully used and synthesized the growing body of scholarship on this broad subject. I have endeavored to examine a number of interrelated topics: the role of partisan politics, the Truman Administration, the FBI, and numerous interest groups in elevating the Communist issue to national prominence; the effect of that style of politics upon some of the groups it targeted and upon American life in general; and the waning of McCarthyism. The demands of brevity have forced me at many points to provide only a sampling of issues and events of importance. The desire to write a book of moderate length has also led to a compressed mode of reference notes, which I have used primarily to indicate sources of quotations and particular data. I hope that the bibliographical essay locates the origins of the larger interpretive schemes which inform the book.

I have incurred many scholarly debts in writing this book. A number of fellow historians have shared information and research nuggets with

Preface

me, lent me work in progress, and/or provided useful commentary on fragments of this work in preliminary form. For assisting me in one way or another, I wish to thank James T. Patterson, Alonzo L. Hamby, Thomas C. Reeves, David M. Oshinsky, James L. Baughman, Charles H. McCormick, Justus D. Doenecke, Robert P. Newman, and William F. Vandercook. William E. Leuchtenburg provided a valuable critique of the original proposal for this book, numerous suggestions, and a model in his own scholarship. Thomas Bender and David Reimers first suggested that I write the book and later gave the manuscript two careful readings. Colleagues at the University of Illinois at Chicago, in conversations too casual to be documented, have tolerated my fixations and helped me to rethink aspects of this project. I am grateful to the administration and trustees of the University of Illinois for a sabbatical leave in the early stages of my research and to the Eleanor Roosevelt Institute and Harry S. Truman Library Institute for research grants which expedited it.

I am also beholden to archivists at many libraries and wish to thank in particular the staffs of the Franklin D. Roosevelt Library, the Harry S. Truman Library, the Dwight D. Eisenhower Library, and the State Historical Society of Wisconsin. I owe thanks as well to many staff members at the University Library of the University of Illinois at Chicago, particularly of the Interlibrary Loan Department. The Glen Ellyn Public Library staff was also helpful.

At Oxford University Press, Nancy Lane exhibited saintlike patience and gave good counsel during this book's long gestation. Marion Osmun's editing did much to improve it.

Finally, the members of my family have endured their own bout with the McCarthy era, albeit by distant echo. Though Duffy remained underfoot while the book took form, Rocky and Gail have matured more rapidly and engagingly than the work itself. My mother and my late father instilled in me a taste for history and a distaste for many of the events chronicled in these pages. My wife, Barbara, tolerated years of prattle about the book, the mounds of clutter it generated, and the nomadic research junkets, all the while presiding over an environment that made the work pleasurable. To her this book is dedicated, though words cannot convey the requisite gratitude and love.

Glen Ellyn, Ill.   R.M.F.
June 1989

Contents

1. Two Eras and Some Victims, 3

2. Trojan Horses and Fifth Columns, 37

3. "What Do You Think of Female Chastity?"
Disloyalty in American Politics, 59

4. The Rise of the Communist Issue, 87

5. The Age Finds Its Name, 120

6. "Bitter Days":
The Heyday of Anti-Communism, 144

7. "In Calmer Times. . . .," 171

Epilogue. Where We Came Out, 193

Notes, 203

Bibliographical Essay, 223

Index, 231

NIGHTMARE IN RED

1

Two Eras
and Some Victims

FOR MANY the McCarthy era stands as the grimmest time in recent memory. Beset by Cold War anxieties, Americans developed an obsession with domestic communism that outran the actual threat and gnawed at the tissue of civil liberties. For some politicians, hunting Reds became a passport to fame—or notoriety. It was the focal point of the careers of Wisconsin Senator Joseph R. McCarthy; of Richard Nixon during his tenure as Congressman, Senator, and Vice President of the United States; of several of Nixon's colleagues on the House Committee on Un-American Activities (HUAC); of Senator Pat McCarran and other members of the Senate Internal Security Subcommitteee; and of a phalanx of understudies at the national, state, and local levels.

A new vocabulary entered political discourse. "Are you now or have you ever been a member of the Communist Party?" "I refuse to answer on grounds that the answer may tend to incriminate me." "Fifth-Amendment Communist!" "Soft on communism. . . ." "Witch-hunt!" "McCarthyism!" In the barrage of accusations that rumbled through the late 1940s and early 1950s, reputations were made or ruined, careers blasted or created, lives and families shattered.

It is tempting to locate "McCarthyism" only in the realm of high politics—as the combined sum of national news headlines, noisy rhetoric, and congressional inquiries. Yet it was more than that. The anti-

3

Communist drive touched thousands of lesser figures: a printer in the U.S. Government Printing Office, linguists and engineers at the Voice of America overseas broadcasting service, a Seattle fireman, local public housing officials, janitors, even men's room attendants. Long before the "McCarthy era," loyalty oaths affected teachers. Lawyers, other professionals, and, in Indiana, even wrestlers had to document their loyalty. Colleges policed students' political activities. Labor leaders and unions rose or fell according to their sympathy or hostility toward communism. Entertainers faced a "blacklist." Ordinary people responded to the anti-Communist fervor by reining in their political activities, curbing their talk, and keeping their thoughts to themselves.

Yet paradoxically these bleak years are also remembered as happy times. America emerged from World War II with her continental expanse untouched by the ruin visited on other lands. An "arsenal of democracy," the nation had provided materiel for a global battlefront, food and fiber for friend and conquered foe. The joblessness that haunted the 1930s vanished. Though the postwar economy had its fits and starts, and prosperity did not drizzle on every garden, pessimists were confounded as the good times persisted.

With $140 billion in pent-up wartime savings, Americans went on a buying spree. New autos rolled off assembly lines too slowly to slake demand; some customers bribed dealers in order to buy a car. Freezers, refrigerators, and soon televisions flowed out of factories and into homes. Americans bought 20,000 new TV sets a day in the mid-fifties. By the end of the decade, fifty million televisions were in use. The sprouting forests of antennas snared signals that webbed viewers in every home into the national consumer culture.

The landscape changed beyond recognition as new suburbs sprawled out from the central cities, woven to the workplace by highways. Freshly erected, moderately priced homes—such as the famous Levittown developments—sprang up like new crops in the potato fields they displaced. The family car and single-family home became the norm.

The social landscape changed as well. Though poverty persisted, affluence was far more visible. There were recessions, but no depression. Products found buyers. Buyers had jobs. Thanks to the GI Bill, veterans, many from blue-collar homes, went to college, entered professions, and attained white-collar status. They moved with their families to the thronging new suburbs and became, for good or ill, "organization men," the sociologists' term for those secure and swaddled servants of giant corporations.

For growing numbers life was comfortable. Most lived better and longer, sharing the American dream of homeownership and enjoying the fruits of social mobility. Science and technology promised to eradicate ancient problems. By 1955 Jonas Salk had perfected the vaccine that conquered the dread disease of poliomyelitis, fear of which had for years prompted parents to keep their children indoors away from beaches and crowds during the August heat. No longer.

The spokesmen for corporate America offered a sales message, both for the "free enterprise system" and for its products, that was relentlessly upbeat. "Progress is our most important product," said General Electric's TV commercials. However self-serving such slogans were, the era's prosperity did make converts even of some who had found fault with the economic system in the bleaker 1930s. The era still had its critics, though. Some argued that America's material wealth masked spiritual and civic poverty. Others lamented the tawdriness of mass culture as reflected in the American passion for automobiles—"insolent chariots," one critic called them. As government subsidized highways for autos, public transportation withered. While the family home embodied the American dream, some commentators worried that it bred privatism. On the other hand, William Levitt, pioneer of Levittown developments, ventured that no homeowner could be a Communist. "He has too much to do." Juvenile delinquency was much deplored. Some linked it to communism; others, later, to the newer menace of rock and roll. There were various national scandals. Politicians took deep freezes, vicuña coats, money. College sports and, later, TV quiz shows were blemished by cheating. A deeper blot was the nation's complacency about "race relations."

Some spokesmen thought that the cure for these ills lay in religious renewal. In the 1950s Norman Vincent Peale's *The Power of Positive Thinking* and other books with potent, if not profound, religious messages became bestsellers. The Reverend Billy Graham's monster revival meetings earned him fame and welcome at Dwight D. Eisenhower's White House. Previously unchurched, the President decided that attending Sunday service befitted his role as national leader. Congress stapled the phrase "under God" to the Pledge of Allegiance. Hollywood star Jane Russell claimed that when you get to know God, "you find He's a Livin' Doll."

5

Yet beneath such froth lurked authentic anxieties that the new religiosity was bent on tranquilizing. As the Cold War jelled, particularly after 1949, the prospects of nuclear war grew worrisome. Newspapers published city maps with concentric circles showing levels of destruction expected from a nuclear blast. Schoolchildren learned in drills to crawl under their desks in the event of a bombing. Some were uneasy. In New York, Dr. Peale met a child terrified by the H-bomb. He calmed her with the simple positive thought that God would not let a bomb fall on New York. Popular magazines strove to put the new weapons in a less threatening everyday context. *Look* burbled that the H-bomb—about the size of a living room—was "one of the cheapest forms of destruction known to man."[1]

The pulpit was not the only place, nor theology the only language, for probing flaws in American life. Social scientists sermonized too. Even as Americans enjoyed the bounty produced by the structured, bureaucratic corporate society in which they worked, lived, and consumed, they were its captives—or so they were told. Individual autonomy had become a casualty of the organization, which allegedly drained people's souls and sapped their independence even as it filled their bank accounts. "Organization men" chose security in a corporate womb over entrepreneurial risk, preferred a slot in Personnel ("working with people") to Sales, exalted "teamwork" and "togetherness," and disparaged lone-wolf individualism as antisocial. Lost was the spirit of adventure. Universities graduated and corporations buffed "well-rounded" people who were "other-" rather than "inner-directed" and who were guided by "radar" to pick up cues from peers rather than moved by a "gyroscope" to act according to principles or conscience. Some feared that these corporate clones, dressed alike in gray flannel suits, were dully marching toward a conformist society.

Not everyone accepted the extreme criticisms. Even William F. Whyte, Jr., whose book *The Organization Man* spread much of the critical vocabulary, warned against labeling Americans as conformists. Yet others thought the charge accurate, and many held political forces, particularly "McCarthyism," at least partly to blame for the conformity. If Dwight D. Eisenhower, the genial, grandfatherly "Ike," presided over the era's political imagery, Joseph R. McCarthy, the menacing, barrelchested Wisconsin Senator, was an equally potent symbol. From 1950 through 1954, McCarthy personified the search for Communist influence throughout American life.

6

Two Eras and Some Victims

That charges of selling out to communism should be leveled against President Harry S. Truman seems at first glance bizarre. After all, his administration (with "bipartisan" Republican help) had resisted Soviet expansion; sent help to Greece and Turkey in 1947 in response to the President's enunciation of the "Truman Doctrine" calling for aid to "free peoples who are resisting attempted subjugation by armed minorities or by outside pressures"; framed the Marshall Plan to save Western Europe's frail governments and economies; flown over a Soviet blockade to succor West Berlin in the 1948–49 airlift; restored the draft and joined NATO, an "entangling alliance"; built the H-bomb; planted military bases around the globe; and adopted a loyalty program to guard government from Communist infiltration. These acts, however, did not fully armor Truman and the Democrats from charges of "softness on communism." The rising fear of communism at home intertwined with the growing vexations and complexities of the struggle with communism abroad.

Scholarly debate over the Cold War's origins remains a lively art, but in the 1950s few Americans doubted whom to blame. They saw Communists in East Europe abusing rival political groups; even other leftists mysteriously vanished or were "liquidated." As the Soviets rolled back the Nazis in 1944–45, they treated ruthlessly the goods, governments, and lives of the peoples who lay in their path. Much that was not nailed down—and much that was—became "war booty" shipped back to the USSR. In Rumania, Bulgaria, and Poland, opposition parties were suppressed, civil liberties violated, the press gagged. Stalin ignored a commitment ostensibly made at Yalta to hold free elections in Poland.

Americans had not fought the war out of pure idealism; one thinks of cartoonist Bill Mauldin's weary, stubbled GIs, impatient of cant and seeking only a hot meal and dry socks. Still, a catalog of basic freedoms could be found in documents ranging from the 1941 Atlantic Charter (notably, its endorsement of self-determination, to which the Allies had adhered) to Norman Rockwell's famous *Saturday Evening Post* covers. In Eastern Europe, these basic freedoms crumbled beneath the heel of a boot.

Many historians agree that some menacing Soviet moves came as responses to real or perceived threats by the West. As precedent for its unilateral moves in Rumania, for instance, Russia could cite the West's similar dealings with conquered Italy. Disputes over reparations and Germany's future further complicated relations among the "Big

7

Three"—the U.S., the USSR, and Great Britain. In February 1948, Czech Communists, with Soviet aid, seized control of the government. This event horrified Americans and led to the approval of Marshall Plan aid by Congress, a rearmament program, and a war scare. Yet, some have argued, the Czech coup could be seen as a defensive reaction by the Soviets, who interpreted facets of the West's "containment" policy as hostile.

Whatever the true origins of the Cold War, most Americans came to view the USSR as an aggressive power and threat to peace. Fears of Communist influence at home increasingly counterpointed the rising concern with Soviet aims abroad. Historians of the Cold War have asked whether Stalin's totalitarianism at home necessitated a "totalitarian" foreign policy. Equally one could ask whether the twin development of America's anti-Communist foreign policy and the excesses of its containment of communism at home was preordained or avoidable. It was logical, but was it inevitable?

Although chroniclers grant that the McCarthy era owed much to the Cold War, they agree on little else. Some, like Robert Griffith, in *The Politics of Fear*, have emphasized that members of the right wing of the Republican Party, "as they scrapped and clawed their way toward power," were most responsible for making anti-communism the dominant theme in American politics. These conservatives were moved by a loathing of the New Deal and a frustration at the repeated defeats their party had suffered in national elections, notably Truman's upset victory in 1948. McCarthyism not only thrived on and deepened the conflict between the two parties but also exacerbated the struggle between conservative and moderate factions in the GOP.[2]

On the other hand, some social scientists in the 1950s (and after) attributed the virulence of the anti-Communist upsurge to social strains, to developments that made certain segments of society susceptible to McCarthyism. Some groups (Catholics, Germans, *nouveaux riches*, Texas oilmen) may have supported McCarthy because his attacks on the State Department and other institutions offered vicarious revenge upon an "Establishment" that had long kept them in their place. Or perhaps McCarthy's charges represented a form of "neo-isolationism," a means by which groups such as German- and Irish-Americans could vent their resentments against a generation of Democratic interventionist (and anti-German and pro-British) foreign policies.

More recently, some historians have said that Truman, the Democrats, and the liberals were contributors to McCarthyism, not just its victims. Did not Truman's 1947 federal loyalty program formulate language and methods that, in more extreme form, were taken up by the McCarthyites? (And further, it is suggested, the loyalty order came so soon after his Truman Doctrine address that it appeared to be a means of reinforcing to Congress the gravity of the Communist threat.) Truman and his allies also redbaited Henry A. Wallace and the Progressive Party in 1948, thus—according to the theory—legitimizing a practice that Republicans would turn upon Democrats. And Truman's strident anti-Communist rhetoric on behalf of his foreign policy created an idiom for his critics when that policy met reverses.[3]

This book adheres to the thesis that the origins of McCarthyism lay largely among the grievances and ambitions of conservative politicians (mostly but not solely of the Republican Party). It also shares a recently emergent viewpoint that McCarthyism was a political phenomenon that extended well beyond the antics of Senator McCarthy—indeed, well beyond the boundaries of conventional politics. What gave the "ism" its bite was the political dynamic that obtained at mid-century, accentuated by the anxieties germinated by the Cold War. However, anti-communism derived its persistence from a deeply rooted cluster of values shared by much of American society, a set of views antithetical to Communist doctrines and friendly to private property and political democracy (albeit sometimes oblivious to imperfections in the latter).

The once-popular sociological explanations of McCarthyism do not withstand empirical testing, but they do correctly hint at the *cultural* basis of the mid-century Red Scare. As Seymour Lipset and Earl Raab have argued, McCarthy's anti-communism "was a banner around which various segments of the population could marshal their preservatist discontents and their generalized uneasiness." Many Americans were bewildered by the deep social and political changes at work in the twentieth century. Many such changes occurring in the neighborhood, the nation, and the world could, consistent with the strength of America's anti-Communist consensus, be attributed to Communist scheming.[4]

Thus a profound cultural aversion to communism also underlay McCarthyism. It was this detestation that gave politicians broad leeway to pursue anti-Communist endeavors. A related factor was the nation's underdeveloped appreciation of the importance of civil liberties for repudiated minorities. Public opinion polls gave evidence of the high threshold levels of political intolerance in the 1930s—a time of rising international tension but long before the alarums of the Cold War.

Indeed, to understand the "ism," the Right which gave it birth, and the decade of the 1950s, we must first examine the 1930s, the energetic Left of that decade, and its real and imagined legacies.

IF IN THE 1950s Americans took prosperity as the natural order of things, veterans of the 1930s remembered life as more precarious. That grim decade strongly affected their attitudes and behavior. Some workers who remembered the hard times stuck with unloved jobs because they cherished the security of seniority. Memory prompted Depression survivors to scrimp, to test their ability to do without long after hardship had vanished. They harassed their children to eat every last bite of vegetables. Conversely, others escaped memories of deprivation by piling up material goods or by smothering their children in luxuries.

For many the Depression signaled the final collapse of capitalism that Marx had predicted. By 1932 unemployment gripped almost one-third of the workforce. As jobs were lost, home mortgages were foreclosed, and farms were taken, the Depression seeped upward, eroding the middle class and nibbling at the wealthy. As circles of suffering widened, some doubled up with family; others retreated back to the farm. Sometimes husbands left to scrounge for work or aimlessly tramp across the continent; sometimes women and children rode the boxcars as well. (A few railroads even coupled on extra cars.) There were suicides, but numb despair was more widespread.

The times welcomed radicalism, and homegrown saviors hawked cures. Fascism found a few adherents. Socialism also had advocates. Though not alone on the left end of the spectrum, the most conspicuous agitators for radical change were the Communists. They offered theory from Marx, a blueprint in the successful Bolshevik Revolution, and a commitment to action attractive to those tired of pale reform and empty palaver.

The bankruptcy of the status quo, the obvious need for change, and the Marxists' steely certitude produced a heady elixir. In time of paralysis, communism promised movement. "We had élan," remembered veteran Communist Al Richmond. "We had the exhilarating sense of being on the offensive, ideologically and morally." Sidney Lens, who moved from Trotskyism to independent radicalism, recalled the 1930s as an age when "history was ready for quantum leaps. And in that setting all that was necessary, we felt, was to have the 'correct line.' " Finding it, the tiniest grouplet might hope to ride the wave of the future as had the Bolsheviks in 1917. Their hands, Communists told each other, were on "the throttle of history."

Commitment was reward in itself. One could be part of a greater whole. Even though this doctrine taught atheism, a parallel with the fervor of religion was obvious. Save for the church, wrote novelist Richard Wright, "there was no agency in the world so capable of making men feel the earth and the people upon it as the Communist Party." The Party provided both a politics and a society. "Your life as a Communist was everywhere," said one Party member, "in the shop, at home, at meetings, in the neighborhood. You were always being a Communist." "I felt myself," another recalled, "both as someone living in a small, coherent community and as part of something global."[5]

There were hazards. Marxism-Leninism might mark out history's direction, but perplexing daily developments required constant adjustments. To misread, to adopt the wrong line, was to risk being flattened by history's locomotive. The tight link between theory and action raised the ante for Communists and magnified the importance of disputes over the meaning of events and the proper Party policy. Hence, splits among believers were extraordinarily bitter. Soviet Communists violently fought all heresies, and the struggle was copied by the parties of other nations.

On the American Left, splinter groups formed, divided, subdivided. Thus from the thin ranks of the Trotskyites exited a faction led by Hugo Oehler and Tom Stamm. Then Stamm split with Oehler. Members of one tiny sect picketed its founders' home with signs insisting that "Mr. and Mrs. Field are no longer Fieldites." At its 1940 convention, the main body of American Trotskyites fissioned, the breach dramatically signaled when one leader, James Cannon, warned another: "Very well, Comrade Schachtman, we will seize power without you!" The intensity and the heat of their debates often blinded leftists to the irrelevance (or humor) of their theological disputes.

Though conditions were ripe for radicalism, the early 1930s found the Communist Party (CP or CPUSA) weak and isolated. Two groups inspired by the Bolshevik Revolution had spun out of the Socialist Party in 1919. United in 1921, Communists emerged from underground in battered shape. Their troubles continued as they duplicated the splits that convulsed the Soviet Communist Party. By the mid-1930s, leadership of the CPUSA had passed to Earl Browder, a bland, unfrightening former accountant.

In the 1920s, the CP had had but dim appeal to American workers. It made only a few inroads in the labor movement in mass-production industries (often at the shop level—in automobile plants, for instance) neglected by the craft-oriented American Federation of Labor (AFL). The Party could boast a small, seasoned nucleus of organizers whose day would come when labor grew more militant in the Depression.

But even in the 1930s, much of the Party's growth was of a "revolving door" variety; many who entered stayed only briefly. In the so-called Third Period from 1928 to 1934, the CPUSA assured its isolation by stressing doctrinal purity, assuming the imminent collapse of capitalism and the coming revolution, and disavowing cooperation with others on the Left. The Communists strove to build revolutionary unions to compete with their AFL counterparts. They dismissed Socialists as tools of the class enemy, as "social fascists." They scorned the New Deal, which the Party's veteran leader William Z. Foster described as a "government serving the interests of finance capital and moving toward the fascist suppression of the workers' movement."[6]

In keeping with this strategy, Communists harassed the meetings of left-wing rivals. When Socialists rallied in New York City in 1934 to protest the Austrian government's repression of Vienna's Socialists, Communists threw chairs down from the balcony and broke up the gathering. The same line prevailed in other nations. German Reds took a blasé attitude toward the rise of nazism and shunned alliance with other leftists; their slogan, "After Hitler, us."

This line proved foolhardy, and several Communist parties groped in new directions. In 1935 came the change. The growing threat of nazism prompted the USSR to reorient the world Communist movement. (A joke mocking the CPUSA's dependence on Moscow's orders asked: why is the Communist Party like the Brooklyn Bridge? Answer: both are entirely suspended by cables.) The Communist Third International, the Comintern, laid down a new line—a united front against fascism. Communists would now cooperate with once-despised Socialists, liberals, and other "progressives," including New Dealers.

As a result, the CPUSA's influence increased in the United, or Popular, Front period of 1935–39. Communists played a crucial part in the success of the Congress of Industrial Organizations (CIO).

Since they had always pushed for industrial rather than craft unions, their approach meshed with CIO strategy. John L. Lewis, president of the United Mine Workers and a leader of the CIO, eagerly hired Reds as organizers. (Who got the bird, he asked cynically, "the hunter or the dog?") Courageous, tenacious, and able, they helped build unions like the United Auto Workers and United Electrical Workers. They controlled many CIO locals, dominated such unions as the Mine, Mill and Smelter Workers, and nearly captured the UAW. Though enemies deplored the CP's use of devious organizational tactics, the Communists earned their spurs by being more effective and militant unionists than their rivals, and where they retained power, they often did so because they delivered what the rank and file wanted.

In politics the Communists also abandoned exclusivist purity for a policy of coalition building. They embraced the democratic symbolism of the decade. Earl Browder called communism "the Americanism of the twentieth century." During the time of the Popular Front, the Party enticed intellectuals chiefly by its stalwart anti-fascism. The full employment in the USSR, in contrast to the breadlines in the U.S., impressed some observers, as did the liberal-sounding 1936 Soviet Constitution. To be sure, Stalinist realities—such as the violent collectivization of Soviet agriculture, which led to vast starvation and suffering, and Stalin's bloody and paranoid purge of his party—limited the allure of the "Soviet experiment." Yet through all this, Stalin loomed as the only real counterweight to Hitler.

In 1936 the Spanish Civil War became a burning issue to foes of fascism. Germany and Italy sent soldiers, tanks, and planes to Franco while the democracies pursued a neutrality that crippled the Spanish Republic. Only Russia aided the Loyalists, but not without costs: Soviet commissars subverted the Republic and liquidated leftist rivals. As members of the American Lincoln Brigade, American Communists fought in Spain as well. Many died there.

The democracies also dithered when Italy attacked Ethiopia in 1935 and Japan renewed war in China in 1937. At Munich in 1938, Britain and France appeased Hitler with a generous slice of Czechoslovakia. With some reason, Stalin concluded that the Western powers were more anti-Soviet than anti-Nazi. Since he too could play Realpolitik, he agreed to the Nazi-Soviet Pact in August 1939. Nazism's great foe thus pledged peace and amity with it and, when Hitler invaded Poland to ignite World War II, gobbled up a third of that hapless country.

13

However one rationalized the Nazi-Soviet Pact, it deeply embarrassed the CPUSA and disillusioned many members and fellow travelers. Before the Pact, the Party had steered one of its major front groups, the American League for Peace and Democracy (ALPD), from pacifism to support of collective security. After the Pact, they scuttled the ALPD and set up the American Peace Mobilization to oppose U.S. involvement in the war. One Communist greeted news of the Pact with the cynical remark that "Hitler's a socialist too." On June 21, 1941, the American Peace Mobilization picketed the White House with signs declaiming: "The Yanks are Not Coming." On June 22, Hitler's Panzers rolled into Russia. The front group, swiftly renamed the American People's Mobilization, now clamored for aid to Britain and the USSR. An "imperialist" conflict had become a "People's war."

Communists also flipflopped on labor issues. In 1941 Communist-led unions struck several defense plants. (Though critics claimed the strikes had purely political aims, there were legitimate labor grievances.) Once Russia and America entered the war, unions controlled by Communists eagerly obeyed the no-strike pledge (opposed by most other leftists) and tolerated erosion of labor's hard-won gains. Since black demands for equal treatment in defense plants threatened to slow rearmament, Communists initially opposed A. Philip Randolph's March on Washington Movement, abandoning their role as advocates of racial equality. The *Daily Worker* called Randolph a "fascist helping defeatism."

Despite these bewildering hairpin turns, American entry into World War II rescued the CPUSA. Hitler's invasion of the USSR had galvanized the Left's sympathy. (To playwright Lillian Hellman, the news meant: "The Motherland has been attacked.") Even some on the Right like General Douglas MacArthur were moved by Soviet valor. Yet only the glue of a common enemy held the Soviet-American alliance together. Trust was limited. The Russians had signed one pact with Hitler. Why not again? (They did approach the Germans in 1942.) Conversely, the Soviets were angered by their allies' tardiness in attacking Hitler's forces and wondered if it was part of an attempted sellout or a ploy to make them bear the brunt of the fighting.

Despite such mutual suspicions, Americans knew the Soviet alliance was crucial to victory. The USSR suffered far greater losses than any of its allies: fifteen to twenty million dead, 80 percent of the industrial base of the areas scorched by the war. The Russians also inflicted more damage on the Nazis than did any other nation. At Stalingrad, on the great bend of the Volga where it sweeps toward the Don, the Soviets blunted and smashed Hitler's eastward drive and began grinding up his armies. While the British and Americans faced ten German divisions in Italy, the USSR confronted nearly two hundred.

Pulling out every diplomatic stop to assure victory, Stalin abolished the Comintern in 1943. The American Communist Party dissolved itself into the Communist Political Association in 1944. Earl Browder preached class collaboration, even offering to shake J. P. Morgan's hand if the banker would support Soviet-American amity. Told he would fit in nicely with members of the ultra-conservative National Association of Manufacturers, Browder said, "I'm awfully glad to hear that."

Focused on winning the war, the Communists retreated from previous militant stands. If workers' demands clashed with the war effort, the former must yield. Browder touted "incentive pay" in war industries, the very piecework system against which the CIO had fought. When the Mine Workers struck, *Daily Worker* editor Louis Budenz toured the coal fields to organize back-to-work movements, a campaign usually undertaken by the owners. The convergence of Soviet and U.S. aims enabled the Communists to wrap themselves in the flag and helped them reach a new, albeit short-lived, peak in membership during the war.[7]

Even outside the Party, the war inspired a gush of euphoria about Russia. In his bestselling *Mission to Moscow*, Joseph E. Davies, former U.S. Ambassador to the USSR, sugarcoated unpleasant realities. He described Stalin lyrically: "His brown eye is exceedingly kindly and gentle. A child would like to sit on his lap and a dog would sidle up to him." Similarly, *Life* compared Stalin's dread secret police, the NKVD, to J. Edgar Hoover's storied gangbusters. (After Hoover's secret violations of civil liberties were revealed in the 1970s, the comparison seemed less ludicrous.) The *New York Times* announced that Marxism was out in Russia. "The capitalist system, better described as the competitive system, is back."[8]

Always suspicious of schemes to create "Utopia in a day" and horrified at the human price paid for Soviet progress, President Franklin D. Roosevelt remained skeptical about the Soviet system. Yet he also thought he could deal man to man with Stalin. By offering friendship and yielding to Soviet claims in areas of traditional Russian (and Soviet) national interest in Europe and Asia, he believed he could maintain

Big Three unity and bring the USSR into the postwar system of collective security he sought to build.

Thus, during the war and for a year or so after it, an unstable mix of optimism and antipathy characterized American opinion about Russia. Among policymakers, a comparable balance existed between those hoping for the best from the Soviets and those fearing the worst. After FDR's death in April 1945, the latter group gradually won dominance in the councils of the new President, Harry S. Truman.

As the policy elite's suspicions of the USSR hardened, those of the "man in the street" kept pace. In a September 1945 poll, 39 percent described the USSR as "peaceloving." Two years later, just 12 percent held that view, while the number labeling the Soviets "aggressive" rose from 38 to 66 percent. At one point in the war, 55 percent thought the USSR would cooperate with the United States. In March of 1946, the figure fell to 35 percent; it rebounded to 45 percent in May, sagged to 32 percent in October, then rose to 43 percent the next January. Although clearly public opinion was at times mercurial and contrary, it generally leaned toward increasingly negative perceptions.

Indeed, some historians argue that public opinion is a vaporous commodity that political leaders can and, in the case of Truman and the "Communist threat," did shape. But others assert that it was the politicians who felt pressured by constituents whose views of the Soviets and of American Communists were hardening. Members of Congress, perhaps closer to grassroots opinion and usually more suspicious of Communists at home and abroad, also influenced the stance of the Truman Administration.

In any case, by the late 1940s, politicians, plain folk, and many powerful institutions (the Catholic Church, the U.S. Chamber of Commerce, segments of the labor movement, and numerous others) had coalesced in an anti-Communist consensus. Products of that widely held anti-communism included various applications of the foreign policy of containment and a series of measures against domestic Communist influence. There was some public skepticism about the wisdom of certain foreign policies; there was far less about the need for stringent anti-communism at home.

This consensus served as both cause and effect in the rise of the anti-communism that transfigured public life at mid-century. That politics generated vast amounts of emotion and heat. It also produced a vocabulary, a lore, a set of symbols. The overall phenomenon—

"McCarthyism"—is so often characterized in abstract terms that its meaning remains fuzzy. To sense the emotional bite of the Communist issue and to understand both how it affected life for those who ran afoul of it and how it shaped the nation's political culture, it is useful to look at specific cases.

ALGER HISS was the central symbol in America's struggle over domestic communism. To this day, partisans debate whether he was guilty or not and, if guilty, precisely of what. The Hiss case directly engaged such political leaders as Richard Nixon, J. Edgar Hoover, and Harry S. Truman. Indirectly, it involved many others. On January 21, 1950, a jury found Hiss, an attorney with a once-promising career in the State Department, guilty on two counts of perjury—for having lied about his Communist connections in the 1930s. In the eyes of conservatives, his case and conviction exposed the guilt of the entire New Deal of Franklin D. Roosevelt.

FDR's unprecedented four terms as President attest that the New Deal had many admirers. But it also had foes who resented the bureaucracy it built, its new subsidies, its taxes and regulation of business, its often combative attitude toward entrepreneurs, and its seeming delight in fracturing tradition. To critics on the Right, the New Deal was Communist, Fascist, or both. Some vaguely sensed—or pointedly suspected—that New Dealers collectively or individually were "Communists." The Hiss case confirmed the direst charges of the preceding decade.

Many New Deal loyalists viewed the Hiss verdict with disbelief. At first blush Hiss seemed a far more reliable witness than Whittaker Chambers, his main accuser. His background was respectable, if shabby-genteel. Chambers's was merely shabby. Hiss had excelled at Johns Hopkins and at Harvard Law School; Chambers was kicked out of Columbia University. Hiss won a coveted clerkship with Supreme Court Justice Oliver Wendell Holmes, Jr., while Chambers lived an unstable existence as a writer of some talent but small prospects, drifting in a world of bohemian radicalism.

In 1933 Hiss joined many other young, idealistic, liberally inclined lawyers who filled the bustling agencies of the New Deal. They were energetic, innovative, impatient with the economic orthodoxies that they blamed for the Depression. Some leaned distinctly left, although theirs was usually a radicalism of the parlor. Some were Communists.

Hiss first worked in the Agricultural Adjustment Administration. The AAA was riven by tension between advocates of the agricultural establishment and urban-oriented defenders of consumers and the poorer farmers whom the AAA neglected. Hiss belonged to the second group. George Peek, head of the AAA, had vaguely suspected that some of the leftist urbanites were Reds. Years later, several of Hiss's associates confirmed their own and each other's Communist Party affiliations. In 1935 Secretary of Agriculture Henry A. Wallace reluctantly ousted this group. All were forced to leave—except Hiss, who was then on loan to a Senate investigation into whether U.S. bankers and other "merchants of death" had led the nation into war in 1917.

Hiss eventually landed in the State Department as assistant to the Assistant Secretary of State for the Far East. He earned promotion to positions of increasing responsibility. In February 1945 he went to the Yalta Conference as one of FDR's advisers, though his role was minor. Later that same year he was Secretary General of the San Francisco conference that gave birth to the United Nations. He personally delivered the U.N. charter to President Truman.

But Hiss, according to his accusers, had led a double life in the 1930s. Like others dismayed by the flaws of capitalism that were laid bare by the Depression, Hiss and his wife Priscilla were drawn leftward. The Communist Party tried vigorously to recruit New Dealers, and Hiss was a prize catch. According to his biographer Allen Weinstein, Hiss was wooed by three different Party members. Whittaker Chambers claimed that in the mid-1930s he had collected Party membership dues from both Alger and his wife.

A rumpled, dingy figure, Chambers joined the Party in the 1920s and worked for Communist publications. In 1932 he went "underground," eventually serving as a courier who handed to Soviet spymasters the fruits of espionage gathered in Washington. He not only transmitted materials given him by the Hisses but also became their close friend. Increasingly disillusioned with communism, however, he broke with the Party in 1938, first trying, he said, to convince Hiss to quit too. In 1939, after the ominous Nazi-Soviet Pact, Chambers told part of his story to Adolph A. Berle, an Assistant Secretary of State. The FBI subsequently questioned Chambers several times, but his testimony was not taken very seriously.

Although with some justification he feared for his lfe, Chambers eventually emerged from hiding. He took a job with *Time* magazine, prospering as a writer and editor while Hiss rose in the State Department. Hiss, however, was dogged by others' doubts about his loyalty—doubts that partly originated in Chambers' testimony to the FBI. In May 1946, J. Edgar Hoover wrote a confidant of Truman's that an informant had fingered "an enormous Soviet espionage ring in Washington" seeking to acquire information about atomic energy. Much of Hoover's statement was half-baked and wrong, but his letter showed how prevalent the rumors about Hiss were. In 1945 Secretary of State James F. Byrnes began to edge Hiss out of the Department. A year later, Hiss took the post of executive director of the prestigious Carnegie Endowment for International Peace.

Hiss's career was shattered in 1948, an election year when the Republicans, who controlled Congress, were prospecting for political paydirt. With the Berlin airlift as a grim backdrop, the Cold War had heated up—and with it the Communist issue. In mid-summer a Senate panel and then the House Committee on Un-American Activities heard testimony from so-called "spy queen" Elizabeth Bentley, who identified several New Dealers as members of the spy ring run by her late lover, a Soviet agent. To reinforce her testimony, HUAC also summoned Whittaker Chambers. On August 3, he named eight individuals, including Alger Hiss, as one-time Communists.

Hiss indignantly demanded a chance to refute the charge. On August 5, he denied ever being a Communist, denied knowing Whittaker Chambers. A compelling witness, he made several HUAC members wring their hands in embarrassed despair. One member, however, continued to suspect him. Richard M. Nixon, the freshman Congressman from California, did not operate on mere hunch; he had been thoroughly briefed by Father John Cronin, an expert on communism working for the National Conference on Catholic Welfare. Cronin himself received information from the FBI, which counted him an ally in its campaign against the Red menace. (In 1945 Cronin wrote a report that called Hiss "the most influential Communist" in the State Department.)[9]

Nixon led a subcommittee that heard Chambers describe intimate details of the Hisses' lives in the 1930s. He told of their homes, furnishings, and servants; of a Bokhara rug given them, he said, by a grateful Soviet agent; of a car Hiss had donated to the Party; of the couple's nicknames for each other. He even described a highlight of the couple's birdwatching adventures, their sighting of a prothonotary warbler.

HUAC now recalled Hiss, whose story gradually shifted. Maybe

Chambers was a man he had once known as George Crosley, a mooch with bad teeth who had afflicted the Hisses and then dropped from their lives—but well before 1938, the date Chambers had given for their last contact. The two men confronted each other at a dramatic hearing on August 17, 1948. After inspecting Chambers's teeth and hearing him talk, Hiss said he was prepared to say that his accuser was indeed "Crosley," but he denied involvement in Communist Party activities of any sort.

Chambers had not yet labeled Hiss a spy. He emphasized instead the Communists' goal of infiltrating government councils and influencing policy. Hiss challenged Chambers to repeat his charges outside of Congress, where, without congressional immunity, he could be sued for slander. Chambers complied, stating on "Meet the Press" that Hiss had been a Communist "and may be one now." Hiss sued.

Now Chambers had to prove his claims. From an abandoned dumbwaiter in a cousin's Brooklyn apartment, he removed a packet of materials he had hidden in 1939 as a "life preserver"—evidence that would give pause to any Communist seeking to harm him. Some of these items went before the jury then hearing the Hiss slander case. Behind the scenes a grand jury in Baltimore also looked into the charges against Hiss, but since Chambers's credibility was by no means clear, it was possible that the grand jury would indict him rather than Hiss for perjury. Truman's surprise victory in the November presidential election further complicated prospects for legal action. Chambers was so distraught at these developments that he made a bungled suicide attempt.

In early December 1948, Richard Nixon and a HUAC staff member asked Chambers if he had other incriminating materials. Eventually, Chambers strode to his pumpkin patch and drew from a hollowed-out pumpkin five rolls of microfilm that he had melodramatically hidden inside. He gave these celebrated "pumpkin papers" to HUAC. When developed, they revealed a number of State Department documents, the bulk of which passed through the office in which Hiss had worked. The material was of generally peripheral interest, and none dealt with secrets of cataclysmic importance, but several items were useful to the Soviets.

Various alternative explanations of Chambers's possession of the documents were proposed. Maybe he had stolen them by rummaging through wastebaskets. Or they came from other sources. Most of the microfilmed materials consisted of typed copies of documents. Who had typed them, and on whose machines? So began a race to find an old Hiss family typewriter. FBI agents futilely combed the Eastern seaboard. According to Allen Weinstein, Hiss had known that the typewriter, a Woodstock with serial number N230099, had been given to an old family servant and could be relocated easily enough; only when the investigators found the scent did Hiss produce it. Although no one ever proved conclusively who had typed the documents given to Chambers, the preponderance of expert testimony argued that the Hiss Woodstock had been used.

At two trials, jurors compared Hiss's and Chambers's credibility. The first one produced a hung jury in July 1949. In the second, with looser rules governing admissible evidence, testimony ranged more widely. A psychiatrist friend of Hiss's was brought in to dissect Chambers's mental health. This gambit backfired, particularly when the defense twisted the fact that Chambers had once translated Franz Werfel's *Class Re-union* into English. By a tortured interpretation of the novel's plot, the defense strove to prove that Chambers had hatched a scheme to betray his ex-friend. The prosecution neatly deflated this effort by asking what psychological lesson could be drawn from the fact that Chambers had also translated *Bambi*. "Who's psycho now?" the headlines blared.

Ultimately the documents, microfilms, and Woodstock swung the balance. The documents seemed to show that Hiss passed materials to Chambers and (by their dates) that the two made contact to that end after 1937, when Hiss claimed he had last seen Chambers, thus confirming the two counts of perjury with which Hiss was charged. After Hiss's conviction in January 1950, he and his defenders suggested he had been framed. Perhaps the FBI, working backwards, built a typewriter to match the quirks of typography in the pumpkin papers (perhaps fabricating those too), then planted the machine for Hiss to discover. However, far from carrying on a byzantine plot to create evidence, Hoover was outraged when Hiss's team beat his men to the Woodstock in 1949. The problem with the theories used to buttress Hiss's innocence is that they require greater credulity and imagination than that which underlay the prosecution's case.

Convicted with Hiss were an era, a party, and a political style. Republicans (and some conservative Democrats) had for years inveighed against New Deal "socialism" and "communism"; had lamented the selling of Eastern Europe and China "down the river" to communism by FDR, the "sick man" at Yalta; had resented the smug urbanity of the

New Dealers; and had been willing enough to confound liberals, independent radicals, and Communists. Hiss's guilt permitted a resounding chorus of I-told-you-so's. Karl Mundt, a member of HUAC, could orate after the second Hiss trial that the country "for eighteen years had been run by New Dealers, Fair Dealers, Misdealers and Hiss dealers who have shuttled back and forth between Freedom and Red Fascism like a pendulum on a kukoo clock."

For GOP orators Hiss now served as an unquestionable symbol of betrayal. In 1950 a GOP candidate was asked if he backed McCarthy's methods. He retorted, "Do you favor Alger Hiss?" New York's Republican Senate candidate charged that Democrats were willing to "play along with the Earl Browders and the Alger Hisses." The topic also studded 1952 campaign oratory. Adlai E. Stevenson, the Democratic presidential candidate, was frequently assailed for having given a favorable character deposition for Hiss. "Somebody had to testify for Hiss," Nixon jabbed, "but you don't have to elect him President of the United States." Indiana Senator William Jenner predicted that "if Adlai gets into the White House, Alger gets out of the jail house." McCarthy went about making guffawing references to "Alger—I mean Adlai" Stevenson.[10]

His appeal denied, Hiss spent nearly four years in a federal penitentiary. Mundt and Nixon went on from HUAC to the U.S. Senate, both elected in 1950. They and others profited from a Communist issue now made trump by the Hiss case. Nixon's credentials as an anti-Communist (plus his youth and California residence) made him Eisenhower's runningmate on the 1952 Republican ticket. Facing a crisis triggered by revelations of a "secret fund" anted up for him by wealthy backers, Nixon defended himself in part by suggesting that his attackers had never forgiven his successful pursuit of Hiss.

Nixon would serve two terms as Vice President and then lose narrowly to John F. Kennedy in the 1960 presidential race. In 1968, with the nation and Democratic Party divided over Vietnam, racial tensions, and other issues, he edged out Senator Hubert H. Humphrey to claim the presidency. In 1972 he won reelection by a landslide. Then it all unraveled. The great wave of Watergate, beginning as a "third-rate burglary" of the headquarters of the Democratic National Committee, gathered momentum as Nixon submerged himself in cover-ups and lawbreaking, and finally washed him out of office in 1974.

As Nixon's star dimmed, Hiss's flickered anew. For years Hiss lectured on campuses, a sort of Ancient Mariner contending with the burden of guilt. His visits first raised controversy but later became exercises in nostalgia. After Watergate, the FBI and other intelligence agencies were found to have perpetrated "dirty tricks" and violated the civil liberties of many adversaries. In this atmosphere, theories that Nixon, Hoover, and others had conspired to frame Hiss became less fantastic. Hiss's popularity on the lecture circuit grew; his credibility rose as Nixon's plummeted. He regained the right to practice law. His defenders sought but failed to have his conviction overturned on the basis that the prosecution had not entered court with "clean hands." Notwithstanding the flaws that cropped up in Chambers's testimony and despite the dirty tricks employed by Hiss's pursuers, the preponderance of evidence still points to Hiss's guilt.

To some, his guilt remains unproven. As new evidence obtained under the Freedom of Information Act emerges from FBI files, as the case stirs continued debate, the sides resemble the line-ups of 1948. Conservatives and Cold War liberals tend to affirm Hiss's guilt; those who dissent from the Cold War orthodoxy tend to be skeptical. His case once served as a touchstone for controversies agitating American politics in the 1950s. It continues as a symbol of betrayal now laden with the issues of the age of Vietnam and Watergate.

THE STORY of how Esther Caukin Brunauer became one of Joe McCarthy's victims contains elements of both the inevitable and the unpredictable. Born in 1901, Esther Caukin grew up in California, graduated from Mills College, and earned an M.A. and Ph.D. from Stanford. She devoted her entire career to educational pursuits, including work with the American Association of University Women (AAUW), a group that fostered continuing education among women college graduates. For seventeen years she guided the AAUW's extensive program in international education.

In 1931 she married Stephen Brunauer, a poor immigrant from Hungary who would attain international repute as a chemist. As a student he belonged briefly to the Young Workers' League, a Communist front. He wrote a few radical pieces for its newspaper but joined mainly to seek companionship. Increasingly critical of communism, he quit the League in 1927. His and Esther's politics eventually matured into a liberal anti-communism (deepened when the Communists

23

seized Hungary), but their youthful associations would return to haunt them.

In Germany on fellowships in 1933, the Brunauers saw the Nazis seize power. (Esther even interviewed Hitler.) Returning to the States, Esther spoke and wrote of the looming threat of fascism. At a time when many noted pacifists were women, she consistently advocated collective security. After she led a study of national defense and published it in 1937, the Chief of Naval Operations told her the book "was largely responsible for converting various pacifistic organizations in this country and thus making possible an immediate program of rearmament." She joined groups working to relax the Neutrality Acts to mobilize U.S. aid to the foes and victims of aggressor nations.

In 1944 Dr. Brunauer took a post at the State Department, helping to plan and carry out programs for the international organizations on which many pinned their hopes for postwar peace. She advised the U.S. delegation at the U.N. founding conference in 1945. She represented her country at international conferences of the United Nations Educational, Scientific and Cultural Organization (UNESCO), achieving the diplomatic rank of minister. Her deft opposition to the schemes of Communist delegations won kudos from several observers.

The war boosted her husband's career too. After working for the Agriculture Department, in 1942 he moved to the Navy's Bureau of Ordinance, became an authority on explosives, and stayed on after the war, retaining the rank of Commander in the Naval Reserve. In 1946 he performed "technical intelligence" in his native land, checking on wartime scientific developments there and helping several Hungarian scientists to emigrate. He also did sensitive work in connection with America's postwar atom bomb tests at Bikini.

Despite the rapid upward arc of their careers, the descent was fast approaching. Both Brunauers had ill-wishers. Esther's internationalist activities had not endeared her to isolationists. J. B. Matthews, a noted fellow traveler in the 1930s who was reborn as an expert on communism, had once belonged to an International Friendship Club with the Brunauers. He apparently supplied early and fanciful reports about them—not the first time a soured ex-radical informed inaccurately on one-time associates. Moreover, for years the FBI, local police, naval and military intelligence, and other enemies of radicalism had routinely recorded leftist comings and goings. The subjects of such bureaucratic records thus became hostages to their files' hidden contents—and to politics.

Trouble appeared in 1947. Illinois Congressman Fred Busbey attacked Esther and other "pro-Communist fellow travelers and muddle heads" in the State Department's information and cultural division. He misinterpreted a speech of hers as "echoing Soviet progaganda." Busbey himself often echoed the isolationist *Chicago Tribune*, which had assailed her foreign-policy views as early as 1941. Her husband also encountered a problem: the Atomic Energy Commission denied him clearance to attend a meeting because his link with the Young Workers' League.

Even *anti*-communism could occasion mischief. In 1947 Stephen incurred a Hungarian diplomat's wrath by refusing to help obtain foundation money for Hungarian science. "That incident," his wife suspected, "and what came later, point to a deliberate effort by someone, somewhere in the background, to punish my husband for his contributions to the fight against Communism and Soviet imperialism." His activities in Hungary had prompted its Communist regime to call him a "spy." In those years the possibility of insinuations of disloyalty from such sources was never discounted.

These first charges did no obvious immediate damage. Stephen's superiors assured him of their trust. In 1948 Esther's loyalty was investigated but affirmed. Though HUAC paid them passing attention in 1947, the Brunauers went about their business until Joe McCarthy discovered them in 1950.

McCarthy first named Esther Brunauer off-the-record to reporters while on the trip that launched his anti-Red crusade. Later, she was number forty-seven of the eighty-one unnamed State Department employees whose loyalty he questioned in a speech of February 20, 1950. On March 13, before a subcommittee chaired by Senator Millard Tydings, he shifted ground. Unable to name his eighty-one cases, he listed only nine, including Esther Brunauer.

Most of McCarthy's charges were flimsy—those against Esther Brunauer especially so. He claimed she steered the AAUW toward pro-Communist consumer activities. Yet she never handled consumer issues. He called her Alger Hiss's "first assistant" at San Francisco in 1945. She was no such thing. He said she chaired a 1936 meeting sponsored by a body later listed as a Communist front. She had, but she was not a member; presiding at such functions fell within her AAUW duties. She once signed a "call" to a meeting of a Communist-captured group, but so had 110 others, including prominent public officials. He alleged that in the 1930s she joined a Communist-led organization advocating collective security. In fact, he confused two such advocacy groups—she had belonged to the other, which was non-Communist.

Esther Brunauer also shared in her husband's troubles. McCarthy asserted that two committees of Congress had evidence tying the couple to the Communist Party. He claimed that for ten years Stephen had been constantly investigated by federal agencies; had been "a close friend and collaborator" of Noel Field, who had fled to Czechoslovakia; and had admitted Party membership. The investigations may have taken place; the connection with Field was not intimate, recent, or compromising; Brunauer never admitted CP membership.

Esther Brunauer answered McCarthy's charges crisply. She also noted the emotional toll they exacted. One paper had run her picture with the caption "Top Red?" Then there were the anonymous phone calls—with threats, obscenities, and such advice as "Get out of this neighborhood, you Communists, or you will be carried out in a box." She feared that news disproving the charges "may never catch up with the accusation" in the press.

In July 1950, the Tydings Committee's Democratic majority blasted McCarthy and exonerated Esther Brunauer. Yet their report, undercut by partisanship and grim war news from Korea, neither persuaded the public nor rehabilitated McCarthy's victims. However flimsy, the charges acquired a momentum that damaged all of McCarthy's targets. During the Tydings probe, President Truman ordered the Loyalty Review Board (the loyalty program's highest tribunal) to reopen the case of anyone McCarthy accused. The Brunauers were thus pitched once more into the loyalty-security maze. When Mrs. Brunauer's name was removed from the delegate roster for a UNESCO conference, her superiors told her little but conveyed a sense that they were "sitting, waiting for the lightning to strike again."

It struck on April 10, 1951. The Navy suspended Stephen on security grounds; because of that action, the State Department simultaneously suspended Esther Brunauer. The procedure was traumatic: his files were sealed, his building pass confiscated, his parking sticker scraped off. She was the subject of a humiliating State Department press release that was rushed to reporters to preempt something "much more embarrassing" which McCarthy might issue. The charges against Stephen rehashed old ones. Esther's problem was simple: she was his wife. As a further complication, the standards of the loyalty program were tightened in 1951, prompting yet another loyalty inquiry for the Brunauers.

Stephen Brunauer readied his defense, but learning that the Secretary of the Navy was determined to fire him, he yielded to the inevitable, resigning in June. His wife persisted, but her hearing before the State Department's Loyalty-Security Board in July was not encouraging. She was, most importantly, accused of "close and habitual association" with her husband. One informant reasoned that her decision to marry a foreigner and presumed radical warranted suspicion. Trying to help, one panel member suggested that perhaps she wed him as a reclamation project. She declined this gambit. No evidence reflecting on the performance of her duties was offered.

Ten months later, the Loyalty-Security Board found her loyal but judged her a security risk. She appealed. Though she was not told the specifics of the evidence against her, clearly the problem was her husband. In June 1952, her ouster from the State Department was affirmed. Left in "no-man's-land," she felt "caught in a nightmare from which there is no awakening." Especially frustrating was her failure to convince the hearing panel of the ability, discretion, and loyalty so clear to the many friends and colleagues who had rallied to her defense.

Though their careers had been mangled, the Brunauers made the best of it. Stephen went to work for the Portland Cement Association in the Chicago area and discovered that his security dismissal did not hound him that far away from Washington. Esther worked briefly at the Library of Congress—one newspaper protested her hiring—before joining Stephen in Illinois. There she found editorial work at two publishing houses. She died in June 1959.

One wonders about the role of gender in her case. Was there a particular "McCarthy era" for women? Esther Brunauer was not the only woman accused of communism; there were plenty of female Communists, radicals, and liberals to assail. Since "women's sphere" had long included such causes as peace and social reform, which came naturally under conservative attack, it was no surprise that many women became targets of the red scares that followed both world wars. Those who fought to enforce traditional roles for women used redbaiting as a weapon.

Did some men resent her successful career? She wondered about the thinking of the all-male panel that heard her appeal. "Either their opinion of the reliability of women in professional positions was very low, or else they knew of many men who shared State Department secrets with their wives, and thought that a woman . . . must behave the same way." One finds slight hints of condescension in the handling of her case. Senator Tydings asked McCarthy how old she was. Would he have asked a male suspect's age? Shrugging, McCarthy suggested that maybe "some of the ladies do not give their age in their biographical sketches." Conversely, most of the thirty-six testimonials offered on her behalf stressed her loyalty and professionalism in genderless terms. (The exceptions were her family doctor, who called her an "intelligent and loving mother," and two others who lauded her family life.)

Esther Brunauer's main problem was a quite traditional marital link. Moreover, though she achieved success in the State Department, an old-line male "club," UNESCO's educational, social, and cultural focus did not remove her from "women's sphere." There are no studies to indicate whether wives of suspicious characters were more harshly treated than husbands. On balance the injustice done to Esther Brunauer stemmed only marginally from "male chauvinism."

To the many colleagues and friends who eagerly vouched for them, the Brunauers' loyalty was manifest. Former Minnesota Senator Joseph Ball termed Stephen Brunauer "perhaps the most violently anti-Communist person I know." Doubts about the couple were confined to the pages of anonymously rendered "evidence" in their loyalty-security files and to partisans of the far Right. Even McCarthy's staunch defenders, William F. Buckley and L. Brent Bozell, found his evidence mostly "weak and inconclusive."

Still, the loyalty-security apparatus did its damage. At the time, most liberals agreed on the need for precautions against real Reds. Yet they were frustrated when liberal anti-communism like the Brunauers' did not inoculate against more primitive forms of anti-communism. This trauma appeared to have no cure. Liberals searched for a middle path that would guard against Communist subversion yet protect individual liberties, but moderation had a limited appeal in an atmosphere pregnant with fear of communism. The argument of those on the Right, that there should be no compromise in the war against communism, easily prevailed.

On the other hand, New Left historians have claimed that Cold War liberals have conceded, in the rhetoric and procedures of the loyalty program, too many right-wing premises. By trying to perfect a moderate anti-communism, liberals paved the way for the more extreme McCarthyite version. This criticism implies that no halfway position can preserve civil liberties and that to proscribe one group as disloyal only legitimizes clumsier efforts by zealots with less precise definitions of subversion.

Such critiques touch the dilemma of Cold War liberalism. Was the balance the liberals struck between national security and individual rights tenable? One could argue that the equilibrium worked out at the height of the Cold War did too little to preserve tolerance of political dissent. But by the same token, one could counter that civil-libertarian absolutists were unrealistic about both the nature of communism and the balance of political forces in the United States. Though the dilemma of liberty versus security was not successfully resolved and led to hardship and even tragedy, it is not self-evident that a more purist answer to the hard choices of that day would have brought better results.

Thus cases like the Brunauers' defined the boundaries of McCarthyism as fully as did the Alger Hiss controversy, showing how even anti-Communists sometimes suffered injury. Esther Brunauer hoped that her performance of duty, her friends' testimony, and the reign of common sense would see her through. They did not. McCarthy never proved his case, but ultimately the State Department saw her as a necessary sacrifice to appease its critics. Before the Tydings Committee she had supported the loyalty program, but later she reconsidered: might she have been wiser, when summoned to her 1948 loyalty hearing, to have resigned then, assailing the "dangers inherent in the system" and the "un-American procedure"? Instead, she assumed, too optimistically, "that truth and justice would prevail." Ultimately the force of McCarthyism proved too strong.[11]

THE MID-CENTURY Red Scare targeted ideas as well as people. Critics feared that it had spawned "thought control" and conformity and fed deep springs of anti-intellectualism. Commentator Elmer Davis warned that many "local movements" constituted a nationwide "general attack not only on schools and colleges and libraries, on teachers and textbooks, but on all people who think and write . . . in short, on the freedom of the mind." Many purveyors of ideas were charged with having Communist or front connections, indoctrinating the young with alien principles, or holding views that aided the Communist cause or contributed to forms of moral decay associated with the advance of communism. As part of this counteroffensive, many Americans labored to eliminate noxious sorts of entertainment, thought, or culture—and thinkers and performers.

Modern art offers a case in point. Though the art world was less battered than the Hollywood movie or New York entertainment industries, it too became entangled in Cold War politics. Many artists—including some actual Communists—who roved on the Left in the 1930s (and after) now found themselves listed in HUAC reports and berated by guardians of the nation's libraries and museums. Art itself was vulnerable. Some styles were labeled subversive. Conservatives condemned the social realists for painting American society with too many warts. Many viewers found nonrepresentational art—especially abstract expressionism—jarring, discordant, and if comprehensible at all, subversive.

Professional jealousies and rivalries deepened these quarrels. Traditional "academic" sculptors and painters seethed when critics and collectors lionized the avant-garde, especially if the government was the buyer. Aggrieved artists, particularly those of the American Artists Professional League (AAPL), often advised politicians otherwise untutored in art and, with patriotic groups, stoked the attack on modern art. Redbaiting in the art world thus served economic (and psychic) as well as ideological interests.

But political assaults on art or literature were old hat. In 1939 John Steinbeck's *The Grapes of Wrath* was labeled pro-Communist. So was the New Deal's Federal Arts Project, which became a casualty of the conservative reaction against the New Deal. A member of the House Committee on Un-American Activities claimed that the Federal Theatre Project only put on plays "containing Communistic or New Deal theories." That committee also charged that guidebooks published by the Federal Writers Project purveyed Red propaganda. Art beyond the New Deal's embrace felt the ax too. In 1933, when Diego Rivera refused to remove a heroic depiction of Lenin from his anti-capitalist murals at New York's Rockefeller Center, they were destroyed. José Clemente Orozco's 1930 murals on "social revolutions astir in the world," which were on display at the New School for Social Research in New York, roused such controversy in the Cold War era that in 1953 authorities put a curtain in front of the offending portion that depicted Lenin and Stalin.

In paradoxical contrast to these intrusions, it was frequently argued during the Cold War that culture offered a way to refute claims that America was a crude and materialistic society. The State Department sponsored international exchanges of culture and information. Books, art, and music ranging from longhair to Louis Armstrong's jazz exhibited American cultural vitality abroad. Even the CIA promoted culture, covertly funding intellectual and student activities. In 1952 it paid the Boston Symphony's way to Paris (to avoid the vexing security clearances that went with funding from other sources).

It was ironic that abstract expressionism, in which the United States had seized postwar hegemony, stirred so much outrage, for while American rightists labeled such art "Communist" and degenerate, commissars of Soviet culture condemned it as representing bourgeois decadence. Yet abstract expressionism embodied the individualism characteristic of a free society. Sophisticated cold warriors sought to exploit this fact even as their right-wing countrymen strove to discredit such art. [12]

The traveling show "Advancing American Art" unleashed a storm that signaled the cultural impact of Cold War anti-communism. In 1947 the State Department mounted the show for Europe and Latin America with over one hundred modernist works. Artists in the modern classicist tradition, whose work had been ignored, protested that the show reflected subversive, decadent, and alien modernist trends. Hearst newspapers and rightist politicos took up the cry. The paintings were "Communist caricatures" meant to "mislead the rest of the world as to what America is like," said Congressman John Rankin.

George Dondero, a conservative Michigan Republican who received backstage coaching from the AAPL, led the fight in Congress. In 1949 he explained that expressionism, abstractionism, futurism, dadaism, and cubism were the same subversion-on-canvas used to sap Russia's old regime and now plied by Lenin's heirs against other nations. All these foreign "isms" were "instruments and weapons of destruction." Modern art was Communist "because it does not glorify our beautiful country, our cheerful and smiling people, and our great material progress. Art which does not portray our beautiful country in plain, simple terms that everyone can understand breeds dissatisfaction." Its creators and promoters "are our enemies."

The State Department, no stranger to acrimony, now found its taste in art questioned. A House committee teased William Benton, Assistant Secretary for cultural affairs. Brandishing copies of works in the show, the committee chairman challenged Benton to explain them. When Benton declined to describe the first picture, its cost of $700 was duly noted. Of one abstract painting a lawmaker asked: "Are you holding it up straight?" Benton suggested that it resembled "many things that are not fit to mention before this committee." And so it went.

Thinking to cut its losses, the State Department sped the exhibits home (and sold them for a song). Yet the show in Prague so discomfited the Soviets that they hastily slapped up one of their own and showered free tickets over the city from an airplane.[13] For a time the gun-shy federal government stayed clear of left-wing and modern artists. The scene of battle shifted to the localities, but the arguments were familiar.

In some cities, art lovers and libertarians combined to hold off the anti-modernists. The Los Angeles city council sponsored an exhibit of modern art in 1951. Artists who had been snubbed for their traditional bent protested the show's content and the artists' affiliations. Three council members warned that "ultramodern artists are unconsciously used as tools of the Kremlin" and that some abstract paintings might actually reveal secrets of U.S. defense installations. At length the city council voted that modern art was not subversive. In 1952 the Diego Rivera murals at Detroit's Art Institute drew fire from a right-wing city council member who wanted this display of "pure Communist symbolism" torn down or concealed. Again, libertarians and connoisseurs prevailed: the Detroit Art Commission urged that the murals remain, and so they did.

Anton Refregier's murals for a San Francisco post office raised a bigger ruckus. What local veterans and patriotic groups wanted was commemoration; what he provided was quite different. Completed in 1949, the murals blended modernist techniques and social realist concerns. A panel depicting the 1934 waterfront strike showed a striker in a VFW cap. When the Veterans of Foreign Wars protested, federal officials made Refregier remove the hat. A scene of earlier labor protest enraged conservatives, some of whom picketed Refregier as he worked. The signs in this section were also painted out. Others faulted his obese and unflattering portraits of the Spanish priests who founded California's missions. The padres were slimmed down.

Critics multiplied. Several conservative groups and even San Francisco's Young Democrats called for scrapping the murals altogether.

Local Congressman Hubert Scudder assailed the work's accuracy and spirit, attacked Refregier's leftism, and held hearings in 1953. However, local and national art circles mobilized in defense. Experts vouched for Refregier's reading of the past and likened the proposed censorship to Soviet behavior. Artistic expression won out; the resolution to remove the murals was pigeonholed.

In Dallas, foes of "Sport in Art," an exhibit mounted by the United States Information Agency (USIA), triumphed. After touring America, the show was to go to Australia for the 1956 Olympics, but a coalition of Dallas patrioteers and traditional artists waylaid it. The art was uncontroversial, but the left-wing ties of four artists were not. An alliance of Dallas fraternal, veterans, and patriotic groups and traditionalist art clubs established a Communism in Art Committee. It charged that Red artists used their money and prestige to aid Red causes; a "well-organized apparatus" conspired to foster art by Communists, "however inferior," over that of others, "however superior." The Dallas Art Museum resisted demands to close the local show, but the USIA timidly canceled the trip to Australia.

In 1959 another USIA exhibit, this one slated for Moscow, kindled outrage anew. HUAC Chairman Francis Walter, angry that twenty-two of the sixty-nine artists had long leftist records, held hearings. One witness, the president of the AAPL, warned that a "cabal" of critics, jurors, and "museum boys" connived to promote only the "sinister and disturbing social realist protest and destructionist 'ism' schools" and had cut off old-line artists from the public with a "paper curtain." He critiqued the assembled art, including a depressing slum scene, which left "the impression that that is all we have." The attempt to halt the show failed, however, thanks to several circumstances: the waning of HUAC's authority by the late 1950s, President Dwight D. Eisenhower's disinclination (despite his own traditionalist aesthetic) to weigh in against the exhibit, the vigor of the advocates of artistic freedom, and the now-strong position of avant-garde art.[14]

The HUAC hearings thus marked the decline in the potency of anti-communism leagued with artistic traditionalism as a force in the art world. And yet this was not the last time that politics muscled in on taste. The Vietnam War, for instance, would prompt efforts to crimp the careers of dissenters like Jane Fonda and folksinger Pete Seeger (who had earlier tangled with HUAC).

The anti-Communist politics of the 1950s also targeted the literary world for attack, as in Senator McCarthy's 1953 assault upon the International Information Agency's (IIA) overseas libraries. As McCarthy grilled leftist authors and harried officials in charge of bookbuying, worried IIA employees stripped the shelves of books that had been—or might be—attacked. Purged volumes included Dashiel Hammett mysteries, Howard Fast novels, even works by historian Foster Rhea Dulles, the Secretary of State's cousin.

Smaller but equally absurd dramas were played out in many communities. Rightists often protested "internationalist" or "socialist" textbooks. Yet they did not always triumph. In one notorious instance, an Indiana woman crusaded to suppress the story of Robin Hood because of its subversive message—rob from the rich, give to the poor. The current sheriff of Nottingham, no less, protested the smear on Robin's good name. A study of sixty Ohio public libraries turned up only four that were pressured to censor books and only one that yielded. The more outrageous cases often rallied opposition, as did McCarthy's vandalizing of IIA libraries.

To say that evidence of suppression is mixed is not to dismiss the power of the censors. Even their failures daunted librarians weighing purchase of controversial books, school officials selecting texts, or just plain citizens choosing what to read or say. Discourse was constrained. Once police were summoned to a Houston restaurant to arrest two diners for "talking communist." (They had alluded critically to Jiang Jieshi's regime in China.) Similarly, in Wheeling, West Virginia, city fathers flew to arms at the first inkling of a plot against the loyalty of its youth. The latter were buying penny candies whose wrappers depicted countries of the world and gave a few pertinent facts. Some gum pictured the Soviet Union.

The impress of anti-communism upon the culture extended beyond highbrow art. Thus baseball bore a heavy symbolic and moral burden in these years. The national pastime defined America as it wished to be seen. Not coincidentally, the American Legion plowed resources into both "Americanism" and a vast baseball program for teenagers. From another perspective, Harold Taylor, president of Sarah Lawrence College, once waspishly defined an American patriot as "one who tells all his secrets without being asked, believes we should go to war with Russia," and favors "peace, universal military training, brotherhood, and baseball." Briefly Cincinnati renamed its team the Redlegs, to avoid homonymous confusion with any other "Reds." Later they reclaimed the original name—they, after all, had had it first.

In 1952, in a fit of Cold War bragging, a Soviet magazine claimed that "beizbol" (which cruelly exploited its players) derived from an old Russian game. Tongue in cheek, *Saturday Review* printed a reply by Eddie Stanky, the feisty ex-second baseman then managing the St. Louis Cardinals. Stanky insisted Russians could not master baseball, a game of "give and take. The Russians like to dish it out, but they can't take it." With its rhubarbs, sportsmanship, double-play teamwork, and "opportunities for little men," baseball "is the big game of a free people."[15]

In some of these episodes, anti-Communist rhetoric stemmed from ideological concerns (as in the defense of baseball) or, in less rational interludes such as the Wheeling candy plot, from simple fear. In others, it was more functional. Congressman Dondero's approach to modern art was ideologically rooted, but the artists who seconded him yoked philosophical with practical interests. A similar mix of ideological and functional considerations motivated both anti-Communists in the labor movement and those in management who used anti-communism as an anti-union weapon.

In a sense, all anti-communism was "functional." Even true-believing politicians could build careers on it, but the blend of conviction and utilitarianism varied from case to case. Some critics of the emergent anti-communism saw deeply sinister motives. A leftist union warned of a "conspiracy . . . to identify as Communist or Communistic" anyone daring "to assert independence in thought." The "great industrial and financial monopolists" aimed to "control the economy of the United States in the interests of a few at the expense of the many, to swell profits and to beat down wages."[16] Such goals might explain the enthusiasm of West Coast economic interests for the early efforts to deport Harry Bridges, leader of the left-wing International Longshoremen's and Warehousemen's Union (ILWU). Economics account less well for the persistence of federal officials in harassing him.

Similarly, if the thrust of Joe McCarthy's crusade had been economically oriented, he would have aimed more often at targets of directly economic rather than symbolic importance. Foreign policy can involve heavy economic stakes, but McCarthy certainly took the long way around. (If, as some historians argue, the fate of Vietnam concerned the future of American capitalism, McCarthy missed the point:

in the spring of 1954, as Ho Chi Minh's forces sprang the trap at Dienbienphu, the Senator was bewitched by the question of who had promoted a Communist Army dentist.) Indeed, his critics often questioned the effectiveness of his anti-communism, though such rejoinders failed to stop him.

One might ask whether the potency of anti-communism stemmed mainly from the manipulation of public opinion by political leaders, or whether the public's latent anti-communism formed a consensus in which the elites operated and with which, in order to survive, they had to conform? Here, too, evidence is mixed. One finds labor leaders using anti-communism against union rivals (or rival unions) or corporate management happily exploiting the carnage left in the wake of inquiries by Congress. Yet the anti-communism of many unionists and politicians appears to have been ideological.

Perhaps the essential point is that there existed in Cold War America a broad anti-Communist consensus shared and seldom questioned by most liberals as well as conservatives, by intellectuals as well as plain folk, by union members as well as "bosses." This defining reality of the period, together with the weak and undeveloped civil-libertarian consciousness of most Americans, explains the ease with which anti-communism came to dominate the political scene. These circumstances were endemic. They were present even before the Cold War fixed itself upon the world. Combined with a chain of threatening developments in the Cold War and the partisan dynamic that obtained at mid-century, they were responsible for the onset of McCarthyism.

2

Trojan Horses and
Fifth Columns

AMERICA has a fabled radical tradition, but its anti-radical tradition runs at least as deep, and conflict has persisted. In the 1790s, the Federalists tried to shield the nation from French revolutionary turmoil by resorting to the Alien and Sedition Acts, but this bout with repression ended in victory for their opponents. Similarly, though the anti-slavery view prevailed, it took decades to do so, during which mobs dealt violently with abolitionists, anti-slavery literature was banned from the mails, and Congress imposed a "gag rule" against anti-slavery petitions. Later, industrialists waged war on labor unions with court injunctions, vigilante action, and the deployment of federal and state troops, private armies, and police. Not until the 1930s did unions secure legitimacy.

The essential American freedoms appear with grandeur in the Bill of Rights and the syllabi of civics classes, but those rights, ever tested and redefined, have been challenged more often than conceded. Thus, that basic First Amendment freedoms were at risk from 1945 to 1955, at the peak of Cold War tension, should come as no surprise. A nation created by acts of will and peopled by newcomers from divergent backgrounds, the United States has found it harder to define nationhood and citizenship than have many older societies with longer traditions. Americans have sought mightily to articulate and instill "Americanism." (In the McCarthy era, critics of such efforts noted that France or Britain had nothing so gauche as a committee on un-French or un-British activities.)

In a nation groping for identity, opponents of radicalism naturally sought to curb immigration, on the theory that immigrants carried dangerous ideas. (In fact, most were profoundly conservative.) Partly to block radical ideas from France, the Federalists nearly tripled the term of residency required to become a citizen. (The shorter period was reinstated in 1802.) In the nineteenth century, restrictionism made scant headway, but after President William McKinley was assassinated, Congress passed a law excluding alien anarchists in 1903. Defenders of order also urged literacy tests for all immigrants; in 1917 their wish became law.

In the early twentieth century, the Industrial Workers of the World (IWW) became the main target of anti-radicalism. Known as "Wobblies," the IWW plagued the West Coast, organizing lumbermen and farm workers and preaching from soapboxes about the inevitable conflict of capital and labor. When they were arrested, other Wobblies flocked in to fill the jails in the famous IWW free speech fights. In 1912 Immigration officials in the Pacific Northwest began to deport foreign-born Wobblies. Since precedent held that deportation was not a criminal punishment, Immigration officers had broad authority to oust aliens. These officials, along with local economic interests, implored the national government to take stronger action.

American entry into World War I spurred a federal crackdown against the IWW's ongoing agitation in the forests, farms, and mines. The Army raided IWW offices, arrested Wobblies and their associates, guarded IWW-infected job sites, and even created the Loyal Legion of Loggers and Lumbermen, a bizarre union consisting of 10,000 soldiers who produced lumber for the war. In Bisbee, Arizona, vigilantes rounded up 1,200 Wobblies, suspects, and sympathizers, loaded them on a train, and dumped them in the desert, where many were held for two months. Meanwhile, the Post Office suppressed IWW literature. The Justice Department, lacking overt acts for which to prosecute IWW leaders, compiled every incendiary Wobbly utterance since the organization's founding in 1905, arguing that the IWW itself amounted to an unlawful conspiracy. One hundred sixty-six IWW leaders were thus tried under the 1917 Espionage Act, as were leading Socialists. In addition, the 1917

Immigration Act authorized the deportation of aliens who advocated unlawful property destruction. This law proved immediately useful.

In the winter of 1917, the cutting season over, lumbermen streamed into Seattle, and city authorities and local immigration officials panicked. In January 1918, the latter packed some one hundred foreigners off to jail. Even the Fire Department arrested fishy-looking aliens. The Immigration Bureau proposed to use the 1917 Immigration Act to deport alien Wobblies by equating membership in or support of the IWW with advocacy of property destruction. A few deportations were carried out; only Secretary of Labor William B. Wilson's last-minute intervention prevented wholesale expulsions. This anti-IWW campaign offered a model for the more virulent anti-communism of 1919–20.

The Bolsheviks' 1917 seizure of power in Russia sparked new antiradical hysteria. Russia's withdrawal from World War I convinced many that the October Revolution was a Hunnish plot. Moreover, Lenin's program horrified all who cherished private property, democracy, and pluralism. Soviet reality was grim enough, but many Americans acquired a fanciful view of events there. Some newspapers wrote that Russian women had been "nationalized." Fear abounded that Russia might export its revolution. Short-lived Soviet regimes sprang up in Bavaria and Hungary; a leftist revolt convulsed Berlin. In March 1919, the Bolsheviks established the Third International, the Comintern, to promote revolution around the world.

This external menace, plus turmoil at home, stoked anxieties that culminated in America's first Red Scare. There were economic hardships—postwar unemployment, then runaway inflation that rasped at the middle classes. In industry after industry, workers battled these economic riptides, trying to preserve wartime gains in wages and bargaining status. On their part, owners and managers strove to crush unions and restore the open shop; they labeled union demands for anything more as Bolshevist.

These forces produced much homegrown unrest. In February 1919, an already spooked Seattle faced a general strike. Called by local AFL unions, the strike had conventional trade union goals, but alarmed conservatives cried revolution. Vowing to crush anarchy, Seattle Mayor Ole Hanson called in troops. Opposed by public opinion and by the national AFL, the strike gave out after four days. A Seattle paper hailed the end of "this Bolshevik-sired nightmare." A Senator exclaimed that "from Russia" the strike leaders had come "and to Russia they should be made to go." Now a hero, Hanson embarked on a national lecture tour and announced he would run for President—early evidence of anti-radicalism's political dividends.

More dire events followed the Seattle strike. A bomb was mailed to Mayor Hanson in April. A parcel exploded at a U.S. Senator's home, maiming a servant. An alert postal clerk recalled setting aside similar packages: bombs had been mailed to thirty-six prominent politicians and businessmen. May Day 1919 brought rioting to several cities and clashes between parading leftists and their foes. Bombs blew up at the homes of Cleveland's mayor, of judges in Boston and New York, and elsewhere. The most publicized bombing damaged the home of Attorney General A. Mitchell Palmer. The explosions seem to have been the work of anarchists, but no one was ever caught (the bomber of Palmer's house was himself blown to bits). The public was now ready to lash out indiscriminately against the Left in general.

Although the Bolshevik seizure of power in Russia had electrified U.S. radicals, America's newborn Communist movement was divided and weak. The left-wing majority of the Socialist Party (already enfeebled by wartime suppression) wanted to emulate Lenin's triumph, but it was expelled by the right wing. The outcasts split into the rival Communist and Communist Labor parties. On Moscow's order, they united, but battered by the Red Scare, their combined membership fell below 10,000.

Thus, in the United States, radicals posed a threat mostly in their enemies' and their own imaginations. True, a self-styled "Soldiers', Sailors' and Workers' Council" ran a Butte, Montana, miners' strike in 1919. In Portland, Oregon, a "Council of Workers, Soldiers and Sailors" or "Soviet" proposed to "strike the final blow against the capitalist class." And yet these posturings were frightening beyond their merits only because they took place in turbulent times.

A radical triumph was therefore unlikely, but labor unrest was real. In February 1919 occurred the Seattle general strike, the Butte walkout, and a Lawrence, Massachusetts, textile strike. From March through August, over 1,800 strikes erupted. In September Boston's police walked off the beat. Troops were mustered to restore order; three people died in the turmoil. Next a quarter-million steelworkers left the mills. In November miners launched a coal strike.

In each case, labor's opponents found redbaiting useful. A newspaper termed Boston's rioting and petty looting a "Bolshevist nightmare." "Lenin and Trotsky are on their way," said the *Wall Street Journal*. Management used the Communist bogey in the steel strike too—with help from the strike's leaders. The strike's goals were not extreme, but William Z. Foster, a chief organizer, was a radical and ex-Wobbly. (Though working for the AFL, Foster stood far to that body's left. He eventually became a top Communist leader.) Similarly, one paper claimed that many striking coal miners were "red-soaked in the doctrines of Bolshevism." Four million workers walked out in 1919, but sensationalist reactions by politicians and the press obscured their usually moderate goals.

The Left's posturings, the Right's self-interest and fear, and a general public unease inflated the Red Scare. By the war's end, many Americans had been wrenched by the flux of urban growth, immigration, and industrialization. Economic, social, and cultural changes had altered the individual's relation with government, society, employer, and neighbor. Out of the turmoil arose several movements to restore tranquility, old-fashioned ways, old-time religion, undiluted patriotism, and unhyphenated Americanism. The Ku Klux Klan's rise, cultural and religious fundamentalism, and the drive to curb immigration all expressed anxieties of citizens resisting the tow of rapid change. Patriotic groups like the American Defense Society, National Security League, and American Legion worked to enforce "100-Percent Americanism."

The man about whom these currents swirled was A. Mitchell Palmer, Attorney General of the United States. A progressive Democrat, Palmer joined the Cabinet in March 1919. As chief law enforcer he had both the task of solving several vexing problems and the chance to pursue his political ambitions. On him rained demands that the hoarding of scarce goods like sugar and meat be ended, that galloping inflation be halted, and above all that the bombings cease and the radicals be put down.

Palmer moved only as fast as public opinion pushed. Finally he named William J. Flynn, former chief of the Secret Service, to head the Bureau of Investigation. A Radical Division (renamed the General Intelligence Division in 1920) was created to study the radical threat; chosen to head it was a young law-school graduate John Edgar (later known as J. Edgar) Hoover, who soon compiled a card file index on

60,000 radicals. But these steps did not appease Congress: the Senate unanimously demanded that Palmer report if he had acted against those seeking to overthrow the government, and "if not, why not."

The answer was swift. On November 7, 1919, Palmer launched raids in twelve cities against offices of the radical Union of Russian Workers. Three hundred people were arrested. Some were beaten up and many tossed in jail. On December 21, 199 aliens rounded up in the raids, plus fifty others (including renowned anarchist Emma Goldman), were herded aboard the *Buford* for deportation to the Soviet Union. Most were guilty only of radical views.

Buoyed by the favorable reaction, Palmer widened his nets. On January 2, 1920, his agents swept into Communist and Communist Labor Party meeting halls in thirty-three cities and arrested—often without warrants—over 4,000 suspected members. Those seized were denied counsel; some were manhandled. Many of those arrested had no ties to communism. One man was detained for asking about the uproar; another, because he "looked like a radical." U.S. citizens caught in the raids were turned over to the states for prosecution under state sedition laws. Aliens were held for deportation.

Eventually these excesses awakened concern in another segment of government. The Bureau of Immigration had cooperated with Palmer to accelerate the deportations, but as protests poured into the Labor Department (which housed the Immigration Bureau), Assistant Labor Secretary Louis F. Post carefully reviewed each case. When proof of crime was lacking, he held up deportations and canceled 2,200 arrest warrants. In his tussle with Palmer and his allies, Post had the support of his boss, Secretary of Labor William Wilson, and managed to parry impeachment proceedings in Congress. Of those arrested in the "Red raids," 591 were finally deported—far fewer than Palmer had confidently promised to expel.

The Red Scare soon subsided. Palmer was embarrassed when the massive violence he predicted for May Day 1920 failed to materialize. His candidacy for the Democratic presidential nomination sagged, fear of the Red menace waned, and anti-radical excesses came into disrepute. Even conservatives rebuked the New York State Assembly for unseating five duly elected Socialists.

One might dismiss the 1919–20 Red Scare as the long-ago product of departed men, extraordinary world events, and gullible citizens—as an excess attributable to unique circumstances without relevance to more recent times. Yet the first Red Scare prefigured later outbreaks. Like them, it combined activities by extremists and by cynical exploiters of fear with concerns of the truly fearful and the play of bureaucratic interests. The Red Scare and later counterparts grew from both actions by the central government and pressures from below—state and local government, economic interests, and grassroots fears. Modes of repression were similar too. The Wobblies' deporters applied the theory that joining a subversive organization was on its face a crime, that founding it constituted conspiracy. The prosecutors of the Communist Party's leaders in 1949 offered a similar thesis. In both periods, aliens ran greater risks than citizens, but xenophobia was more potent in the earlier outbreak. Dissimilarities outweigh the similarities, but the parallels are instructive and sometimes daunting.[1]

IN KEEPING WITH the idea of "normalcy," Warren Harding avowed: "Too much has been said about Bolshevism in America." Though J. Edgar Hoover continued to stress the Red menace (as did Naval and Military Intelligence), the Justice Department's anti-radical efforts were sharply crimped in 1924, when it was learned that Flynn's Bureau of Investigation had been spying on several prominent politicians. President Calvin Coolidge halted these doings and Flynn was fired. Taking his place, Hoover agreed to end political snooping. The General Intelligence Division was abolished. However, local Bureau offices apparently continued their surveillance of radical activities.

Despite communism's feebleness, its opponents did not rest. Foes of reform found anti-communism too useful. Critics reviled as a Red plot the child labor amendment that Congress passed in 1924. One group warned that it would nationalize children. It was even claimed that Lenin's mistress first proposed the idea. Such arguments helped to block ratification. Similarly, business spokesmen labeled the closed shop (in which, to obtain a job, one had to belong to the union) an un-American invention. A 1924 proposal to recognize the Soviet Union was buried amid a vehement anti-Communist outcry.

Feminist causes were also slathered with a red brush. The National Association Opposed to Woman Suffrage, which led the fight against the Nineteenth Amendment, argued that bolshevism inspired the unnatural pursuits of feminist reformers. Renamed the Women Patriots, the group continued to resist various women's reform causes in the

1920s. Because many feminists were active pacifists, the Army also joined the fray. Its Military Intelligence Division busily filled dossiers on radicals of either sex. A War Department librarian drew up a chart in the form of a spider web to trace the alleged links between bolshevism and noted women reformers like Jane Addams. Variations of this spider-web chart were widely published even after the Army, following public outcry, withdrew the original from circulation. Thus was born an important anti-Communist metaphor.

In that era's conservative climate, when reforms traveled rough pavement in any case, redbaiting often seemed an excessive touch. It owed much of its persistence as a political artform to conservative AFL labor chieftains, to the National Civic Federation (NCF), and to patriotic organizations. Since several prominent AFL leaders belonged to the NCF as well, cooperation between the AFL and the Civic Federation was often close.[2]

But if the 1920s proved inhospitable to American Communists, the 1930s offered them new vistas. As the nation sank into depression after 1929, with America's vaunted economic promise now a grim joke, the old political orthodoxy and the elites that defended it had become vulnerable. Radical cures attained a hearing. In 1932 fifty-three noted writers and artists, dismissing the old parties and system as bankrupt, endorsed the Communist ticket.

The Communists earned some support at street level for their labor activities and agitation for relief. They tried, with modest results, to build industrial unions. In many cities, they fought evictions. When the sheriff dumped a family's furniture in the street for not paying the rent, a Communist-led Unemployed Council often moved it back. Unemployed Councils also marched for jobs and relief. The Workers Alliance agitated for higher relief payments, sometimes holding sit-ins at relief offices. At some homes electricians reconnected power after the electric company cut it off.

Such activities vexed conservatives. Several state legislatures mounted investigations of radical troublemakers in the 1930s. The "Red squads" of many city police forces infiltrated radical groups and kept Communists under close watch. In 1932 a ragtag Bonus Army assembled in Washington to petition Congress for early payment of a bonus due some years later to World War veterans. Army Chief of Staff Douglas MacArthur convinced President Herbert Hoover that Communists were at work. With horses, tanks, and tear gas, MacArthur routed the veterans from their tent city. That mob, he said, "was animated with the essence of revolution."

Herbert Hoover resisted calls to crack down on radicals, but others wanted action. Ralph Easley, secretary of the National Civic Federation and committed anti-Communist, persuaded New York Representative Hamilton Fish to call for an inquiry into Red activities. Scion of an aristocratic family, a tackle on Walter Camp's first All-America football team, leader of an all-black regiment in World War I, and a founder of an American Legion, Fish had thick credentials as an Americanist. In May 1930, he got the go-ahead.

Fish's panel heard federal officials (including J. Edgar Hoover), AFL chiefs, professional patriots, and police officials. Many witnesses stressed that Communist ideas appealed little to native Americans—only to aliens. The hearings were seldom dramatic. Testimony depicted Communists as noxious but uninfluential. Alarmed that the Justice Department had since 1924 lacked funds and authority to surveil Reds, the Fish Committee advocated strengthening the Bureau of Investigation. It also wanted the CP outlawed and—Fish's favorite recommendation—Communist aliens deported or barred from entry, but facing deeper, Depression-born woes, Congress did not act.[3]

The New Deal's advent in 1933 created an altered context for the Communist issue. In FDR's first months in power, a warlike emergency atmosphere prevailed, and the public accepted bold experiments in federal intervention. However, as the sense of urgency ebbed, protests arose from those wounded by the new programs or disturbed by government's vastly expanded role. Some claimed to see the hidden hand of communism at work.

A smattering of Communists had New Deal jobs, notably in the Agricultural Adjustment Administration and National Labor Relations Board, but the CP had no real strategy to penetrate government. Critics later cited FDR's diplomatic recognition of the USSR in 1933 as the first of many pro-Communist steps, but at the time it was a popular move. At the first Soviet Embassy ball, Daughters of the American Revolution waltzed alongside old Bolsheviks.

The first loud cry of communism in the New Deal arose in 1934 congressional hearings on a bill to police the stock market. A critic called the measure a step toward communism and said that Dr. William Wirt could pinpoint sinister forces within the New Deal. The superintendent of schools in Gary, Indiana, Wirt spun a strange tale before a House committee. He stated that in 1933 he attended a party whose guests included minor New Dealers and a correspondent for the Soviet news agency Tass. Talk turned to communism. To Wirt's alarm, other guests welcomed it as the New Deal's logical outcome. The man from Tass allegedly referred meaningfully to FDR as the unknowing cat's paw of America's coming revolution. Other guests denied the charges, recalling that it was Wirt who monopolized the conversation. The frailty of Wirt's story and the Democrats' control of the inquiry brought a harmless end to the probe and made Wirt a laughing stock. The New Deal survived its first bout with redbaiting, but it would soon face other similar attacks.[4]

In 1934 the House of Representatives launched another probe of subversion—this time led by New Dealers. Liberal Democrat Samuel Dickstein came from a heavily Jewish Manhattan district in which pro-Nazi hooligans harassed his constituents in the streets. In January 1934, he proposed to investigate Nazis and other subversive propagandists. The inquiry was approved, but Dickstein was appointed as vice chairman only; Boston Congressman John McCormack was the chairman.

The McCormack-Dickstein panel held hearings in the summer and fall of 1934. McCormack conducted most of them in low-key executive sessions, but the excitable Dickstein, whose chief concern was Nazi activities, led hearings that degenerated into shouting matches. One ended with a crowd of pro-Germans snapping off Nazi salutes and yelling "Heil Hitler." The probe was naive and halfhearted. The committee's West Coast investigator carried out his duty simply by wandering into Communist headquarters to see what was up.

Dickstein had viewed the inquest into Communist activities as mere public-relations ballast for his concern with the Nazis, but the committee's 1935 report reflected more of McCormack's deep anti-communism than of Dickstein's views. It noted pro-Fascist, pro-Nazi and anti-Semitic activities. It labeled the Communist Party a tool of the Third International and stressed that the USSR was violating the pledge it had made in 1933, in exchange for diplomatic recognition, not to encourage subversive activities in the United States. McCormack proposed to require agents who spread propaganda on behalf of a foreign power to register with the government. A 1938 law fulfilled his suggestion.[5]

A New Deal loyalist, McCormack blocked efforts to extend the inquiry. Until 1938 Red-hunters only operated sporadically, on the floor of Congress. Yet the McCormack-Dickstein inquiry, despite its restraint, set a pattern of some portent. Conservatives pushed hardest to investigate radicalism and pass restrictive laws, but many liberals also accepted the premise that the subversive menace required both investigation and action.

In the 1930s, the menace indeed existed, as Hitler's war machine gained momentum and as the Soviet Union, on one side or the other, asserted its interests. But the liberals and moderates, no less than the conservatives, may have reacted to these threats with an imprecise diagnosis and clumsy touch, making it easier for those on the Right to inflate the rhetoric and apparatus of national security to the point of endangering American liberties.

Anti-communism's pivotal year was 1938. FDR's ill-advised (and unsuccessful) court-packing plan and the unruly sit-down strikes of 1937 had angered conservatives and split Democratic ranks in Congress. Out of these events and the 1937–38 economic recession emerged a conservative coalition in Congress, an informal alliance of Republicans and (mostly) Southern Democrats who blocked liberal measures. The New Deal had for practical purposes ended, its demise both marked and hurried by the creation of the Special House Committee on Un-American Activities, chaired by Texas Congressman Martin Dies. Ironically, liberal Sam Dickstein had called for another probe of subversive—mostly right-wing—activities, but his proposal foundered. Still, the idea of studying radicalism was popular, even if Dickstein was not, and in May 1938 Dies, backed by House Democratic leaders, won authority to investigate "subversive and un-American propaganda." Dies would pioneer in the methods of defamation and self-promotion for which Senator McCarthy later received credit.

The Texas Congressman had once lauded FDR as "the Jefferson and Jackson of the Twentieth Century," but Dies's phobias overpowered his New Dealism. New Deal liberalism had rasped his South Texas sensibilities. The sit-down strikes, which reflected the militance of unions established by the CIO, had been the last straw; Dies had always scorned urban and "foreign" influences. Even in his New Deal period, he had urged nativist answers to current problems. In 1935 he had charged that one million aliens were benefiting from relief or public works; six million held jobs "Americans should have." The cure? Halt all immigration and deport the aliens—pronto.[6]

Dies first had his committee glance at the pro-Nazi German-American Bund, but more indicative of his tendencies was his next

47

project. An AFL official charged that the rival CIO crawled with Reds, who had instigated the sit-downs. The Dies Committee's chief investigator blamed ILWU leader Harry Bridges for labor turmoil on the West Coast and claimed that the Labor Department was shielding him from deportation. When Labor Secretary Frances Perkins postponed a hearing on Bridges's status pending a parallel case's outcome, the Dies panel proposed her impeachment.

The committee added professional gloss by naming J. B. Matthews to its staff. A missionary and preacher, Matthews had journeyed from Methodism's reformist Social Gospel to membership in numerous front groups manipulated by the Communists. In the late 1930s, he moved rightward with equal speed. He brought with him a huge set of files and left-wing letterheads that would occupy the Dies Committee for years to come.

Dies soon assaulted the Federal Theatre Project, which employed jobless actors and theatre people. Like other projects of the Works Progress Administration and in accord with the era's artistic trends, its shows spotlighted "social" themes. Conservatives were peeved at propaganda they considered New Dealish or even radical. Indeed, Communists did gain entrée to payrolls of the federal arts projects and sometimes used them to further their aims, but even without the radicals, conservatives in Congress would have disliked the theatre program's liberal-to-left hue. Roosevelt jettisoned the politically vulnerable Theatre Project in 1939.

The Dies Committee attacked the New Deal on other fronts as well, focusing on several states just prior to the 1938 election. For example, it showcased charges of coddling communism against Michigan's Governor Frank Murphy, who had outraged conservatives by refusing to evict sit-down strikers at General Motors. FDR's complaint of "flagrantly unfair and un-American" meddling did not save Murphy from defeat at the polls.

In the 1938 elections, the New Deal also suffered sharp losses. Although the Dies Committee's electoral impact is not clear, it had struck a resonance among the American public. Post-election Gallup polls found that 74 percent of those who knew of the committee thought its life should be extended. Though many of those interviewed had no knowledge, no opinion, or only a vague notion of the Dies group's activities, substantial pluralities in several polls supported or approved its continuation.

Certainly Americans shared Dies's distaste for Reds. In a 1939 poll, a majority of respondents thought the CPUSA took orders from Russia; only 9 percent believed it operated independently. In June 1940, during the Nazi-Soviet Pact and the CP's antiwar phase, the public wanted drastic action against Communists. Some 26 percent would deport them; 2 percent backed capital punishment; 3 percent would jail or intern them; 13 percent would "find some way of getting rid of them." Eight percent favored registration or other control or denying them any political rights. A mere 4 percent would "teach them democracy" or remove the causes of communism; 11 percent would leave them alone.

By 1939 Dies was riding high. "Martin Dies could beat me right now in my own district," said fellow Texan Sam Rayburn.[7] Though unhappy with Dies, Roosevelt felt he had to pull his punches. He told Frank Murphy, now Attorney General, to have the Justice Department check out the various charges made by Dies's committee. He did not reappoint to the National Labor Relations Board a member whom Dies had assailed. Meanwhile, Dies continued to snipe at the New Deal and the unions; he warned against the peace movement, youth groups, and occasionally pro-Fascist groups as well. Each year his mandate to investigate was renewed and a substantial appropriation was voted.

DIES'S FEARS were widely shared, even among government officials, liberals included. This convergence of concern was accentuated in 1939–41, during the Nazi-Soviet Pact, when pro-Communists and pro-Fascists jointly opposed FDR's efforts to step up defense preparedness and to aid Hitler's enemies. Not without some justification, Americans had grown jumpy about foreign threats.

Events of the decade gave color to those fears. Both liberals and conservatives fretted about the "fifth column," a term born of the Spanish Civil War. One of Franco's generals was asked which of his four columns advancing on Madrid would take the city; none of them, he replied, but rather the fifth column already inside the gates. Connoting political sabotage that weakened an enemy from within, the phrase soon studded American political discourse—especially after the fall of France in 1940. A man wrote to warn Roosevelt of an innocuous-sounding radio show, "Professor Quiz." Contestants had to name their town, its landmarks, and chief products, thus perhaps conveying valuable data to the "fifth column." A group called Hoboes of America pledged to use their peculiar vantage point to guard against "fifth column stuff."

Despite a 3,000-mile ocean frontier, many Americans dreaded Europe's new forms of statecraft. The notion of enemies within grew less fantastic as marching boots, shrilling divebombers, and wailing air-raid sirens heralded a grim new decade's arrival. Once-fashionable pacifism yielded to calls for armed readiness, social discipline, and watchfulness. In *Zero Hour* (1940), poet Steven Vincent Benet admonished: "Democracy can be betrayed. Democracy can be chained. Democracy can be killed." Lewis Mumford warned that too great a concern for civil liberties risked the whole of democracy to save a mere part. He called for vast sacrifices in the coming struggle—perhaps even turning New York City's West Side subway into an airdrome and leveling nearby apartment houses to provide for a landing field.[8]

By the late 1930s, the images of communism and fascism had blurred. Under both "isms" thrived repression, terror, and one-party, single-leader totalitarian states. American journalists cited the symmetry between Hitler's violent purges and Stalin's. The Nazi-Soviet Pact and the sack of Poland signaled further convergence. After the latter, the *New York Times* declared: "Hitlerism is brown communism, Stalinism is red fascism." After 1945 the phrase "red fascism" became popular, but it had already gained currency in the 1930s.[9] FDR too found the comparison apt. He labeled the USSR "a dictatorship as absolute as any other dictatorship in the world." Like Dies, he decried the "Trojan Horse." After Germany invaded the Low Countries and France, he warned of "new methods of attack. The Trojan Horse. The Fifth Column that betrays a nation unprepared for treachery. Spies, saboteurs and traitors are the actors in this new strategy."

The fifth-column threat was not empty. A Nazi spy ring was uncovered in New York in 1938. German agents meddled in American politics—in 1940 the German chargé in Washington paid travel expenses for twenty-two Congressmen to lobby at the Republican Convention for an isolationist foreign policy. Communists were busy too. During the Nazi-Soviet honeymoon, their intelligence services cooperated, a fact which might have chagrined those Americans who passed data to Soviet agents in hopes of halting fascism.

At times Roosevelt exaggerated the fifth-column menace, used it against opponents, and set dangerous patterns of political repression. The Federal Bureau of Investigation (as the Bureau was renamed in

1935) began broadly violating liberties; for this trend FDR bears much blame. He breezily widened the FBI's role, first to combat crime in the early 1930s, then to scotch intrigues hatched abroad. J. Edgar Hoover launched a public-relations program to trumpet FBI triumphs over famous gangsters, thus enhancing his reputation, appropriations, and power. In 1934 Roosevelt asked Hoover to track Nazi schemes, ending the 1924 ban on FBI political involvement. In 1936 he told Hoover to monitor "subversive activities . . . particularly Fascism and Communism." The FBI simply expanded ongoing efforts. A 1939 executive order assigned countering espionage and sabotage to the FBI.

But Hoover stretched every authorization to the ripping point. In 1939 his newly revived General Intelligence Division began drafting lists of those engaged in subversion, espionage, or other activities "possibly detrimental" to internal security. This Custodial Detention Index included leaders of the Communist Party and the German-American Bund, some to be rounded up immediately in a crisis, others to be "watched carefully." By 1940 the FBI had assembled "suspect lists" of thousands of Americans who might be detained "in the event of greater emergency or . . . additional legislation."

The index had no statutory basis, so Hoover coyly asked Attorney General Robert Jackson whether one was needed. It is not clear how much he told Jackson or what FDR knew, but procedures and plans were drawn up. When Jackson's successor, Francis Biddle, ordered the Custodial Detention Index scrapped, Hoover slyly evaded the edict by renaming it the "Security Index," then keeping all information about it secret—from Biddle. Under friendlier Attorneys General, Hoover regained approval for and kept on expanding the detention program.

FDR much enjoyed the tidbits of information Hoover had fed him since 1933. Having infiltrated the CP, Hoover could report on its schemes, though much of the news, such as the CP's desire to abolish the Dies Committee, was hardly jolting. Roosevelt himself asked the FBI to watch the far Left and the far and not-so-far Right. He told Hoover it was "a pious idea to put one of your men at Palm Beach" in the winter of 1940–41 "to cover 'friends and enemies'!" (One of them may have been Joseph P. Kennedy.) In 1942 the FBI passed on word that Kennedy's eldest son was "intimate" with a newspaperwoman who had ties to prominent Nazis. (Actually Jack, not Joe Kennedy, Jr., dated her.) At times FDR blurred the line between national security and his own political well-being.[10]

51

Clearly FDR was no fanatic civil libertarian. In 1936 the American Civil Liberties Union asked him to make Naval Intelligence cease listing supposedly pro-Communist groups (including the ACLU). Citing national-security needs, FDR refused; he would not agree "never to look into the affairs of any organization," for a few extremist groups "sometimes disseminate false information and false teachings which are contrary to our democratic ideas and the objectives of a republican form of government."[11]

During this time of crisis, conservative sniping at the New Deal, and liberal concession of a fifth-column threat, much of the legal and administrative groundwork of the "McCarthy era" was laid. In 1938, when the Dies Committee was born, Congress also passed the Foreign Agents Registration Act, sponsored by John McCormack, which required anyone issuing political propaganda on behalf of a foreign nation to register with the State Department. In 1940 the Voorhis Act (its sponsor Jerry Voorhis, a devout liberal) mandated that all groups with foreign affiliations must register with the government. In 1939 Congress passed the Hatch Act, whose Section 9A denied federal jobs to members of any organization or party that advocated overthrowing the government. In endorsing 9A, Attorney General Frank Murphy commented that "no man can serve two masters." The Civil Service Commission soon applied Section 9A to the Communist Party, the Bund, "or any other Communist, Nazi, or Fascist organization."

In 1941 Congress voted the FBI $100,000 to investigate federal employees or applicants who came under Section 9A. (Some liberals hoped that expanding the FBI's role might upwind Dies and thought a little political surveillance better than extremist legislation.) For the armed services, stronger measures were mandated: the secretaries of War and the Navy were authorized to dismiss summarily any worker whose continued employment was deemed contrary to national security. Thus began the security program, which was substantially broadened after World War II.

In the late 1930s, nativism and fear of subversion strongly reinforced each other. In 1939–40 Congress considered over forty alien and sedition bills. The fifth-column menace vexed politicians already alert to claims that aliens absorbed scarce jobs and relief funds. Proposed remedies included limiting immigration, suspending it for up to ten years, denying aliens relief or public-works jobs, excluding them from some professions (like optometry and cabaret singing), or even deporting those who did not declare their intent to become citizens within as little as a month after entry.

After 1945 a hastening process of assimilation would smooth a few of the jagged edges of ethnic differences, alleviating some of the strains in American society and making the earlier anti-alien zeal seem antic and bizarre. Yet in 1940 galaxies of ethnic enclaves still dotted the cities, and over a thousand foreign-language publications reached almost seven million readers. Officially the country was "urban" (any town of 2,500 so qualified), but a small-town WASP political culture still prevailed. Despite recent political gains by urban, ethnic Americans, in Congress lawyers from middling towns in the heartland still dictated the tone.

These tensions welled up in Congress. A Wisconsin Congressman told colleagues who lauded aliens, "You can have them if you want them"; his constituents did not. Tempers flared as New York's Emanuel Celler warned that a bill to deport aliens who owned illegal weapons might entrap innocent hunters. As colleagues guffawed, John Robsion of Kentucky allowed that "perhaps in New York City they do hunt with machine guns and sawed-off shotguns." Celler said he knew "how they hunt in Harlan County, Ky." (Striking miners had met violence there some years earlier.) Robsion retorted that if Kentucky had "as many gang murders, bank hold-ups, kidnapings, and gang killings" or "anarchists and Communists" as New York, he would keep mum about Harlan.

Passage of the Smith Act showed the resiliency of the notion that communism was a preferred ideology among aliens and city folk. The Smith Act required that all resident aliens register with the government and be fingerprinted. Title I of the act grated harshly upon alien and citizen alike. It made it a crime to interfere with or impair the loyalty, morale, or discipline of the armed services. It also outlawed teaching or advocating the "duty, necessity, desirability or propriety of overthrowing or destroying any government in the United States by force or violence," or organizing or belonging to a group with that aim.

Nativist anxieties simmered during debate on the Smith Act. In 1939 one solon remarked that the current mood would permit repeal of the Ten Commandments if it were linked to an anti-alien bill. When the bill came up again in 1940, nativism had deepened. Even Emanuel Celler, who had previously blamed the bill on "anti-alien hysteria," now endorsed the act for fear that a worse measure would pass. In June

1940, the House passed the bill with only four nay votes; the Senate approved it without a rollcall. Debate dwelt mostly on the law's impact on aliens. The provision making it a crime to advocate the violent overthrow of government or to conspire to do so drew less scrutiny. Noting that few opposed the bill, several departments favored it, and some hoped it "might serve to curb certain fifth column activities," FDR signed the Smith Act.[12]

During the Nazi-Soviet Pact, government hit hard at domestic Reds, punishing transgressions that before had been little noticed. In their goings and comings, Communists often ran afoul of passport and immigration laws. Indicted with other Party chiefs for passport fraud in 1940, Earl Browder received an unusually stiff jail term. William Schneiderman, another Party leader, was denaturalized for having been a Communist when he became a citizen. The Roosevelt Administration also reacted sharply to strikes staged in defense industries by Communist-influenced unions. In June 1940, the Army was sent to break a strike at North American Aviation. When told that their countries of origin would not accept certain deportable "labor agitators," FDR suggested that some be put on ships and left "on some foreign beach with just enough supplies to carry them for a while." Thirteen states arrested over 350 Communists on a wide range of charges.[13]

Hitler's attack on Russia in June 1941 rescued America's Communists from this growing repression. Staunch patriots now, they called for aid in the fight against Hitler. The USSR's role as an ally was reflected in its enhanced status in popular opinion and the media. *Collier's* even suggested that communism was on the way out, that Russia was a "modified capitalist set-up." In 1942 FDR commuted Earl Browder's jail term to foster "national unity," and Wendell Willkie, the GOP's 1940 presidential nominee, argued before the Supreme Court that William Schneiderman should not lose his citizenship.[14]

Communists adjusted dexterously to the new wartime unity. They cheered the Smith Act indictments of eighteen members of the tiny anti-Stalinist Socialist Workers Party. Americans, declared the *Daily Worker*, had "no objection to the destruction of the Fifth Column in this country. On the contrary, they insist on it." The Party also applauded use of the Smith Act against twenty-six shrill "native fascists" and right-wing foes of the war.

Still harried by the Right, the Roosevelt Administration elaborated procedures during the war to winnow out disloyal federal employees.

The Navy and Army summarily ousted 359 employees as security risks. Under the Hatch Act, the Civil Service Commission began to sift the loyalty of federal jobseekers; it handled over a quarter-million cases during the war. In 1942 it tightened its standards; if a "reasonable doubt" of his loyalty existed, an applicant was disqualified. By April 1944, some 1,000 jobseekers were found ineligible.

The Justice Department checked incumbent employees accused of disloyalty. Initially a complaint (from the Dies panel, for example) went to the jobholder's agency; an inquiry was begun only if the agency head asked for it. Since few investigations thus resulted, in October 1941, FDR ordered the FBI independently to check out all charges; it sent its findings to the employee's department, which made the decision for retention or dismissal.

Since many department heads were unsure how to handle FBI reports, in 1942 the Attorney General named an Interdepartmental Committee on Investigations to provide advice and assure uniform procedures. On request, the committee reviewed a case, but its opinion was only advisory. This panel also distributed the names of organizations whose members warranted inquiry. The twelve groups so designated were the germ of what later became the Attorney General's list. By mid-1942 the list numbered forty-seven groups. Front group affiliations were not declared proof per se of disloyalty but were to be weighed along with all relevant data.[15]

In 1943 FDR created a new advisory body, the Interdepartmental Committee on Employee Investigations (ICEI). Like its predecessor, it tried to balance employee rights and government security, but slowly the pendulum moved toward the latter. The ICEI conceded that those who had belonged briefly to subversive groups might be loyal, but it was their duty to prove that they had broken from their dangerous liaison. In the ICEI's first year, it exonerated 141 employees and discharged only five. A year and a half later, the clearances stood at 394, the dismissals at twenty-four.

FDR's loyalty program remained genteel, however much New Dealers resented it. Treasury Secretary Henry Morgenthau, Jr., fumed at the quizzing of two women in Internal Revenue who were alleged to be Communists. The inquisitors were not "the kind of fellows that represent me or represent the New Deal." The two interdepartmental committees were lukewarm about their task. The first concluded that "sweeping charges of disloyalty in the Federal service have not been substantiated"; the results of their labors had been "utterly disproportion-ate to the resources expended." The ICEI's chairman suggested that it could be disbanded without danger to the republic.

Nevertheless, mainly out of fear of congressional wrath, the Roose-velt Administration kept the FBI scouting for the disloyal. As Attorney General Biddle confided, "We're very much afraid of what's going on in Congress. Apparently those boys—the Dies crowd—are just waiting for a chance to crack down hard." The administration was setting backfires to halt the flames before they got out of hand, a tactic which remained the chief rationale for the Executive Branch's spreading efforts to assure the loyalty of its employees—and for the extremes these measures reached during the Cold War.[16]

The cure may not have worked, but Biddle's diagnosis was valid. Anti-New Dealers in Congress kept up a drumbeat of charges of Com-munist subversion. Indeed, the Dies Committee kept the FBI busy. The $100,000 appropriated in 1941 was mostly spent running down charges Dies had made against 1,121 federal workers. Dies also found numerous targets among employees of the new war agencies. On Febru-ary 1, 1943, he named thirty-nine "irresponsible, unrepresentative, radical and crackpot" federal employees and said that if they were not fired, funds would not be voted to pay them.

Congress had grown so surly that Democratic leaders named a spe-cial subcommittee to review Dies's charges. It recommended that two men with the Federal Communications Commission and one in the Interior Department be dismissed for associations and utterances that, while not Communist, offended congressional sensibilities. Their sins included joining Communist fronts, aiding causes like Spanish Loyalist relief and the Harry Bridges Defense Fund, and saying things nice about the USSR or critical of capitalism. In May 1943, a House-passed appropriation rider forbade any payment to the three men. The Senate rejected the rider three times but then accepted a compromise; FDR grudgingly went along. The three men sued for lost pay and won. In 1946 the Supreme Court termed the rider a bill of attainder—a finding of guilt without a trial or appropriate law—which the Constitution expressly forbids. The episode highlighted the anti-administration ran-cor in Congress that Dies had tapped.

Redbaiting flourished in the 1944 presidential campaign, during which Republicans zestfully linked FDR, labor, and communism. Re-publicans were scandalized by labor's growing political role, especially that of the CIO's Political Action Committee. Endlessly they sang the refrain, "Clear it with Sidney," referring to FDR's supposed instruction to have Sidney Hillman, chief of the CIO-PAC and the Amalgamated Clothing Workers, clear Roosevelt's proposed nominee for Vice President. Jewish, foreign-born, a founder of the CIO, Hillman became a choice target. Rhymed one anti-Roosevelt newspaper:

> Clear everything with Sidney,
> And when they pass the hat,
> Drop in a buck for Sidney,
> The Commydemocrat.

During the campaign, conservatives also fell into a lather over FDR's commutation of Earl Browder's jail term two years earlier. Republican vice-presidential candidate John Bricker cried that Browder had been sprung from jail to line up Communists behind what was now "the Hillman-Browder communistic party with Franklin Roosevelt as the front." GOP presidential nominee Thomas E. Dewey called FDR "indispensable" to both Browder and Hillman. When FDR angrily denied seeking Communist aid, Dewey termed this a "soft disclaimer." Separating allies from subversives, he said, "In Russia, a communist is a man who supports his Government. In America a communist supports the fourth term so our form of government may more easily be changed." An Illinois Congressman mailed handbills warning: "Browder, Hillman, and the Communists will vote. Will you?"

Democrats replied in kind. Interior Secretary Harold Ickes, deriding slurs at the "foreign-born" Hillman, found it "better to be a foreign born American than an American born foreigner" like the isolationists behind Dewey. A star-studded, party-sponsored radio show developed the premise that Hitler would vote Republican. Said Orson Welles: "The enemy seems very anxious for Dewey to be president. There must be a reason." The Nazis "rose to power by the same lies" as those men "who use Communism as a word to smear liberalism." He even suggested that "the Deweyites might attempt their own equivalent of the Reichstag fire. I don't know—I'm just asking." On another show Humphrey Bogart, Jimmy Cagney, Judy Garland, and Jimmy Durante ridiculed redbaiting by crooning: "The old red herring, the old red herring, it looks like Hitler and it smells like Goering."[17]

It is unclear whether election campaigns leave lasting scars or persist in the collective political memory. If the effects do linger, 1944 was an important rehearsal for conservatives in applying the red brush to the Left and for liberals in using the "brown brush" and charges of "isolationism" against the Right. The comity Americans like to think of as characterizing their politics was sorely lacking in this election.

The United States entered the postwar, post-FDR era with a recent history of rough political rhetoric. It had also established a tradition of basing fitness for a government job on the holder's "loyalty"—and a modest vocabulary and bureaucracy for making such judgments. Thus much of the machinery and the discourse of "McCarthyism" was in place before the Cold War or McCarthy's advent.

The main impetus behind this development came from conservatives of both parties, but especially Republicans, who deplored the New Deal and the changes it brought to American life. Yet to some extent the conservatives' targets shared their language and methodology. Liberals had accepted the notion of the "fifth column." They usually dreaded its entrance from the Right—Nazis, Fascists, and their isolationist "allies"—but sometimes they feared Communists as well. The experiences of those embittered by Communist duplicity in the 1930s would put them among the leaders of the movement to exclude Communists from the forum of political legitimacy after the war.

One hesitates to blame "McCarthyism" on a group that itself became a victim of that peril. Nonetheless, Arthur M. Schlesinger, Jr., a leader of the new anti-Communist Left, warned his fellows that New Deal liberals, not just their foes, had used some of the weapons that they now themselves faced in the late 1940s. Lamenting the new politics of loyalty, Schlesinger noted that attention had shifted "from *acts* to *thoughts*" and that "people who hounded the intellectual fellow travelers of fascism must not be surprised to find other people invoking the same principles in order to hound the intellectual fellow travelers of Communism."[18] The trials of the McCarthy era were aggravated by the fact that so few of the participants entered them with hands entirely clean.

3

"What Do You Think of Female Chastity?"

Disloyalty in American Politics

WITH THE ONSET of the Cold War came a heightened anxiety over the Communist threat at home. Some revisionist historians have argued that the Truman Administration, by aim and/or ineptness, paved the way for the second Red Scare. Confrontational foreign-policy rhetoric converged with increasingly harsh treatment of domestic Communists to nudge public opinion toward anti-communism. Promises of "absolute security" against subversion undid the administration when later revelations of Communist infiltration of the federal government prompted public backlash. Some historians have also argued that Truman's 1947 loyalty program prefigured McCarthyism by inventing many of its premises. Since he announced this program only nine days after he proposed the Truman Doctrine to aid regimes beset by Communist-led opposition forces, might the timing have flowed from strategem, not mere coincidence?[1]

It would be naive to dismiss the possibility of such ulterior aims; and no matter what his motives were, Truman's internal-security policies warrant criticism. Yet the darker accusations overreach the evidence and misgauge public opinion. Popular anti-communism was more formed and less plastic than these explanations imply. Public attitudes were molded by the political elites, but they were already strongly anti-Communist. They may have lacked a clear focus on policy, but few citizens doubted that communism was an alien presence and a threat to the "American way of life."

The earliest public opinion polls indicate how tightly anti-communism was stitched into the American fabric. A 1937 Gallup poll found that 54 percent favored a law to allow police to "padlock places printing Communist literature." In 1939 pollsters found that many respondents—even 40 percent of CIO members, whose unions the Communists had helped build—favored "drastic measures" against Communists.

The war improved the CP's standing. Support for destroying the Party declined from prewar figures of about 70 percent to lows of 49 and 44 percent in 1946—yet this was hardly a vote of confidence. In 1946, 36 percent of those polled urged harsh measures ("Get rid of them, deport them, jail them, shoot them"), while 16 percent would ban them from public office or "make it hard for them to be active." Seven percent thought it enough merely to keep watch over them; 16 percent, to do nothing. By a 69 to 17 percent margin, Americans would deny Communists government jobs. In 1947, 61 percent would outlaw membership in the CP. By May 1948, 77 percent would make Communists register with the government. These levels of loathing had little to do with administration rhetoric.

In fact, Americans sensed a more than speculative Communist threat. In June 1946, 57 percent suspected there were "a great many" Communists in the U.S.; 28 percent thought there were "a few." Another poll in 1946 discovered that 19 percent believed "a good many" labor leaders were Reds, while 6 percent distrusted government employees, 4 percent, schoolteachers, and 3 percent, journalists. By a two-to-one ratio, Americans thought Communists were loyal to the USSR rather than to the United States.[2]

Events piled up to reinforce this suspicion. One was the 1945 *Amerasia* episode. A low-circulation, left-wing journal of Asian affairs, *Amerasia* was published by Philip Jaffe, a businessman close to the CP. In 1945 an Office of Strategic Services (OSS) analyst saw an article in the magazine that aped parts of a top-secret memo that the analyst himself had written. OSS agents broke into *Amerasia*'s office and found hundreds more government documents, many highly classified. The FBI sought further evidence through surveillance, bugging, and illegal entries. On June 6, six people were arrested for conspiring to commit espionage. Among the six were Jaffe; Emmanuel Larsen, a minor State Department employee who had given materials to *Amerasia*; and John Stewart Service, a diplomat.

Service was one of several "China Hands"—Foreign Service officers in China who witnessed the decay of Jiang Jieshi's Nationalist regime and the rise of Mao Zedong's Chinese Communist Party. Worrying that, in supporting the Nationalists, America had tied itself to the losing side, the China Hands urged policymakers in Washington to reduce the U.S. commitment to Jiang. But Jiang had vast political leverage in Washington. Moreover, General Patrick J. Hurley, America's flamboyant wartime Ambassador to China, rejected his staff's views and demanded that Service, who had drafted the China Hands' message urging a policy shift, be recalled to Washington. In April 1945, Service met Jaffe (then under an FBI tail), discussed China with him, and gave him personal copies of his own reports. Service was quite patently leaking stories critical of the Nationalists, but these contacts signaled indiscretion, not pro-communism.

With the help of Tommy Corcoran, the Truman Administration successfully averted the political embarrassment that Service's indictment would bring. An ex-New Dealer and political fixer, Corcoran worked, ironically, for the Nationalists, who also feared political repercussions from a noisy trial. The grand jury no-billed Service and two others. The case against the rest soon came unglued. Larsen learned that the FBI had entered his apartment illegally; his lawyer demanded that his indictment be quashed. Lest Jaffe learn and exploit this news, the prosecutors agreed to let him off with a fine if he pled guilty to possession of the documents.

For years Republicans cried foul. Given *Amerasia*'s huge store of documents and elaborate photocopying gear, espionage was naturally suspected. (Jaffe, a friend of Earl Browder, had also had contacts with Soviets.) Evidence, however, was never obtained. Conservative suspicions of a high-level fix were correct. Tommy Corcoran dealt with Attorney General Tom Clark and one of his top aides in the Justice Department to make sure that Service was treated gently during his grand jury appearance. (Corcoran's role came to light four decades later, when records of the FBI's tap on his telephone, undertaken at Truman's direction, were revealed.) A House subcommittee probed the case briefly in 1946, but this inquiry only stirred charges of whitewash.

That same year Service was cleared by a departmental loyalty inquiry, but his days were numbered. He remained anathema to Jiang's supporters and would become an early target of Joe McCarthy.[3]

In September 1945, events in Canada reaffirmed fears of espionage. Igor Gouzenko, a code clerk in the Soviet embassy in Ottawa, sought asylum. In revealing a major Soviet spy ring, the Gouzenko case eventually helped lead to the unmasking in 1950 of Klaus Fuchs, a German refugee scientist who, working for the Soviets, had spied on the Manhattan Project's effort to develop the atomic bomb; from Fuchs the trail led to the arrest of Julius and Ethel Rosenberg.

More immediately, however, Gouzenko stated that he had been told that an aide to the American Secretary of State was a Soviet agent. Fitting this piece to the puzzle of information supplied earlier by Whittaker Chambers, the FBI concluded that the man was Alger Hiss. These suspicions were confirmed by Elizabeth Bentley, a former espionage courier who went to the FBI with her story in 1945. Soon the FBI tapped Hiss's phone, tracked his movements, and mentioned him prominently in a report to President Truman on Soviet espionage.

Hiss's continued presence caused growing unease at the State Department; Secretary of State James F. Byrnes wanted him out. His desk calendar was watched, his access to secret papers crimped. Outside pressures mounted. From Congress issued scattered accusations. The FBI leaked data about Hiss to potent allies. Hiss was given to realize that his career prospects in the State Department were blighted by suspicion. In 1946 he exited gracefully to the Carnegie Endowment.

Throughout 1946 questions about the loyalty of its personnel buzzed around the State Department. The closing down of wartime agencies complicated the problem as some four thousand of their employees were dispatched to the State Department. Several of the defunct agencies, notably the OSS, had willingly hired leftists (whose talents were useful for some wartime missions and whose political antennae were well tuned). The influx of new personnel overtaxed the State Department's inadequate security machinery.

Congress worried the issue. In 1946, with the "McCarran rider," it empowered the Secretary of State summarily to fire anyone whose ouster he deemed "necessary or advisable in the interests of the United States." Several lawmakers pressed for the rider's prompt use. Delegated by the House Foreign Affairs Committee to look into the loyalty issue, Congressman Bartel Jonkman opined that employees should be fired even on mere hearsay evidence. A House Civil Service subcommittee also briefly canvassed the loyalty problem. The subcommittee's two Democrats recommended that the President appoint a commission to design a uniform system from the existing crazyquilt; the lone Republican urged more drastic action. A State Department official warned: "the sentiment clearly seems to be—'What is Jimmy Byrnes waiting for?'" Responding to the pressure, in July 1946 Byrnes appointed a secret Advisory Committee on Personnel Security. The State Department also tightened security in the broader sense, installing locks on file cabinets and instituting a system of passes with photographs.

Amid these moves emerged the case of Carl Marzani, which revealed much about the new Cold War political landscape. A graphic display specialist, Marzani had come to the State Department from the OSS. A wartime loyalty board had exonerated him of charges that he was a Communist, but suspicion dogged him. Thinking it politic to remove him swiftly, but lacking proof, the State Department investigated. In the files of the New York City Police Anti-Subversive Squad, it struck paydirt. An NYPD detective identified Marzani as a Communist who used the Party name of "Tony Whales." Marzani was dismissed in December 1946 under the McCarran rider and convicted on eleven counts of fraud in concealing his Party past.[4]

The 1946 Congressional election kept the Communist issue bubbling. Calling the campaign a fight "basically between communism and republicanism," Congressman B. Carroll Reece warned that "alien-minded radicals" had seized control of the Democratic Party. House Minority Leader Joe Martin urged voters to elect a GOP Congress to halt "boring from within by subversionists high up in government." As in the 1944 presidential campaign, the CIO-PAC became once again a prominent Republican target.

The Communist issue aided Richard Nixon, then a young lawyer and Navy vet contesting the California congressional seat of liberal Democrat Jerry Voorhis. GOP ads touted a vote for Nixon as "a vote against the Communist-dominated PAC and its gigantic slush fund." In a debate, when Voorhis denied he had CIO-PAC's support, Nixon retorted that Voorhis nevertheless had the support of a local unit of the National Citizens Political Action Committee, a more left-wing group than the CIO-PAC. Voorhis disavowed NCPAC; he even rejected the aid of California's CIO, for there was "at least a grave question" that the Communists exercised "inordinate if not decisive influence over state and county organizations." But backpedaling did not save Voorhis, and Nixon went to Congress.

So it went in many campaigns. An aide to William F. Knowland, GOP candidate for Senator in California, announced that Communist Party chief William Z. Foster had come to the state to line up his minions against the Republican campaign. In another Senate campaign, Governor Edward Martin flailed against what one wag termed "the threat of a Soviet Pennsylvania." Missouri Representative Claude Bakewell labeled his foe a "stooge" of the "Moscow-inspired" CIO-PAC. Congressman Jennings Randolph of West Virginia had worked to tighten loyalty standards for federal employees, but his GOP opponent called his efforts "belated."

The Democrats tried to counter. Senate Majority Leader Alben Barkley derided charges of pro-communism as "a political scarecrow erected by the Republican leaders." Party Chairman Robert Hannegan advised the Communists to support Republicans—their real allies since they would bring the "chaos" on which communism thrived. A few Democrats even plied the Communist issue against fellow Democrats. In Washington state, Howard Costigan belabored incumbent Congressman Hugh DeLacy as the candidate of the pro-Communist Left. In Wisconsin, after Edmund V. Bobrowicz, a Fur and Leather Workers Union organizer, won a Democratic congressional nomination from the arch-conservative incumbent, the *Milwaukee Journal* launched an exposé. "In thought and action he has shown himself to be a communist, spelled with a small 'c.' " State and national Democratic leaders disavowed Bobrowicz as the party's nominee.

Republicans sensed the Communist issue's potency. Materials on communism sent out by the National Committee in 1944 had been ignored, a Midwestern Republican recalled, but "this year we used them and we think they are having effect." With a smashing victory in 1946, Republicans won control of Congress for the first time in sixteen years and with it, they assumed, a mandate to sweep Reds out of government. Incoming Speaker of the House Joe Martin declared open season: "They should be—they must be—removed."[5]

BY LATE 1946, as lines hardened between the United States and the Soviet Union, so they rigidified between anti-Communists and their foes in the orbit of American liberalism. In the Democratic Party, in the unions, and in other liberal institutions, the pivotal question of the proper orientation toward communism, foreign and domestic, was debated and resolved.

One side held peace with Russia to be the crying issue and chiefly blamed American policy for worsening relations. Holding attitudes prevalent in Popular Front days of 1935–39, this group deplored all anti-communism as "redbaiting" that only weakened "progressive" forces, and it seldom recognized any enemies to the left. People of this persuasion saw themselves as Roosevelt's faithful followers and tended to accept Henry A. Wallace as his rightful heir.

FDR's Secretary of Agriculture (1933–40), Vice President (1941–45), then Secretary of Commerce (1945–46), Wallace had criticized Truman's foreign policy for opening a dangerous rift with the USSR. On September 12, 1946, before a pro-Soviet crowd in New York, Wallace challenged the administration's "get-tough" foreign policy. When he asserted that Truman had read and approved the speech himself, a crisis ensued. Vexed Republicans stated that Truman must decide between their cooperation on foreign policy or Wallace's. Secretary of State Byrnes also complained, and Truman was compelled to fire Wallace. As a leader in exile, Wallace had loyal followers. In 1948 the newly created Progressive Party, which included some stars of the New Deal era, nominated Wallace for President.

However, most liberals rejected the Popular Front orientation. Though they did not unreservedly support Truman's foreign policies, liberals who liked to think themselves more realistic than their Popular Front counterparts came to see the Soviets as a menace and Wallace as naive. Many of them, burned by experiences in the 1930s, concluded that cooperation with Communists was doomed. Even if Communists did not manipulate liberal groups to their own ends, their presence only opened such bodies to rightist attacks.

In 1947 anti-Communist liberals founded Americans for Democratic Action. The ADA embodied what one founder, Arthur M. Schlesinger, Jr., called Vital Center liberalism. This formula owed much to the ideas of theologian Reinhold Niebuhr, who posited the relevance to politics of the notion of "original sin." He warned of man's will to power, a menace which could never be eliminated, and of the fallacy of utopian thought, which failed to take human weakness into account. Communists, he argued, were the worst offenders.

Appropriately, Vital Center liberals were attacked from both sides.

The Left called them redbaiters, yet their anti-communism did not forestall charges by the Right that they consorted with Communists. Vital Centrists inhabited a political world of imperfection of the sort which Niebuhr warned about. Without a viable candidate more to their liking, the ADA grudgingly supported Truman for President in 1948.

The Communist issue embroiled other liberal entities. Vital Centrists and Popular Fronters battled to control the American Veterans Committee. Minnesota's Democratic Farmer-Labor Party, a merger of the radical Farmer-Labor Party and the Democrats, was similarly riven. Anti-Communists led by Hubert H. Humphrey, the young liberal mayor of Minneapolis, ultimately won out. In New York state, anti-Communists who lost control of the American Labor Party had founded the Liberal Party. Other groups had met the Communist issue even earlier. In 1941 A. Philip Randolph's March on Washington Movement cleansed its ranks of Communists. In 1940 the American Civil Liberties Union purged its national board of Communist directors. During the Cold War, the ACLU hedged on its defense of Communists, a trend its rightist critics missed.

The labor movement became a battlefield. Communists ruled some CIO unions; in others, pro- and anti-Communist factions jockeyed intensely. In the United Electrical Workers Union, the antis under James C. Carey lost control to a Communist-led group. In the United Auto Workers, a conflict that simmered during the war boiled up in 1946 when Walter Reuther, a staunch anti-Communist, was elected president. CIO President Philip Murray's tolerance of the Communists was wearing thin. At the 1946 convention, he engineered a resolution that deplored meddling by Communists or members of any other party in CIO affairs. The fate of the Communist-led CIO unions took three more years to resolve, but the tide was running against them.[6]

Thus, by early 1947 fission and realignment had reshaped the ranks of the American Left. Amid this choosing of sides, growing world tension, rising fears of Communist subversion, and Republican resurgence came a key moment in the second Red Scare: the decreeing of the federal employee loyalty program. This act helped fix the assumptions, language, and methods that fueled the assault on American liberalism mounted by McCarthy and other anti-Communist politicians. Truman's critics contend that with this blunderbuss he both wounded civil liberties and shot himself in the foot. His defenders argue that he acted out of political necessity: had he not moved first, Republicans in Congress, spoiling to act, might have concocted a program even more harmful.

The loyalty program was no sudden inspiration. Truman did not invent so much as codify, institutionalize, broaden, and tighten FDR's jury-rigged wartime program. Unloved by New Dealers, the earlier effort ran out of money and gas in 1945. Its standards varied from agency to agency and needed improvement. Throughout 1946 charges issued from Congress that the government teemed with subversives. Attorney General Tom Clark fueled the fire by calling for increased viligance. (Truman's Attorneys General had a habit of undercutting his efforts to balance security and liberty with their fright-laden oratory and calls for stern action.)

Buzzings from Congress pressed Truman to act. In 1946 a House subcommittee held a two-week inquiry into government employee loyalty. In July the two-man Democratic majority's report urged the selection of a commission to canvass and solve the problem. The lone Republican's minority report called more pointedly for "immediate and thorough housecleaning"—with Congress in charge. Truman dawdled. According to Congressman Jennings Randolph, chairman of the parent Civil Service Committee, Truman had agreed to name a commission; when he failed to act, Randolph jogged his memory.[7]

The Republican victory in the 1946 congressional elections resolved Truman's doubts about the political necessity of establishing such a commission. On November 25, 1946, he named a President's Temporary Commission on Employee Loyalty. Though a few PTCEL members sought to gauge the seriousness of the loyalty problem, the rest simply assumed it. The FBI gave scant help; its spokesman said only that the number of disloyal federal workers was "substantial." Calls for more detail or for testimony by Hoover were turned aside. Though conceding that the problem's gravity had lessened, Tom Clark termed even one faithless bureaucrat a threat. A. D. Vanech of the Justice Department, who chaired the PTCEL, followed his boss's hardnosed assumptions, as did delegates from military and naval intelligence. Their view won out over the more skeptical attitude of the members from the State and Treasury departments, but the disagreement prolonged discussion so that the PTCEL overshot its deadline by nearly three weeks. It submitted its report on February 20, 1947.

The PTCEL prescribed a loyalty program to meet the peril of subversion, despite the commission's inability to "state with any degree of certainty how far reaching that threat is." It posited that any disloyal employee was a menace and that "the inadequacy of existing loyalty procedures is demonstrated." It urged that all federal job applicants undergo loyalty tests, while all incumbents' names be checked against FBI files and vetted more fully if need be. Departments would have their own loyalty boards. A Loyalty Review Board would advise these boards and supervise the overall program.[8]

On March 22, by Executive Order 9835 Truman established the federal loyalty program. Each agency would make initial findings in cases involving its employees; a Loyalty Review Board would have appellate jurisdiction, disseminate information to the departments, and coordinate procedures. Accused employees had the right to a hearing, to which they could bring counsel and present evidence and favorable witnesses; they were to be told the specific charges against them (but not the identities of informants). If recommended for dismissal, they could appeal to the head of their agency and then to the Loyalty Review Board.

The standard for dismissal was the existence of "reasonable grounds . . . for belief that the person involved is disloyal to the Government of the United States." An employee would run afoul of the loyalty program for such offenses as sabotage, espionage, treason, advocacy of forceful or violent revolution, performance of duties "so as to serve the interests of another government," and affiliation with any group "designated by the Attorney General as totalitarian, fascist, communist, or subversive." Thus the executive order formalized the role of the Attorney General's list that had been improvised in 1942.

Coming barely a week after the unveiling of the Truman Doctrine, in which the President had asked Congress to help Greece and Turkey to resist Communist pressures, EO 9835 did not gestate in a vacuum. Historian Richard M. Freeland has argued that in issuing the order Truman "was only incidentally concerned with national security" and more interested in providing dramatic counterpoint to his anti-Communist crusade abroad. Without such a pledge to fight communism at home, the pennypinching, isolationist Republican Congress was unlikely to muster enthusiasm for fighting the Red menace abroad.

Yet the order's timing, while it had much to do with domestic politics, had little to do with foreign policy. Had members of the PTCEL not pointedly resisted Tom Clark's effort to rush them into approving a crude first draft, their report would have come out sooner, a good month before the Truman Doctrine speech, and would have been followed shortly by an executive order. The PTCEL's first assigned reporting date of February 1 suggests that Truman wanted the loyalty issue resolved quickly, before the Eightieth Congress, which convened in January, could make political hay with it. The refusal of some PTCEL members to treat their task perfunctorily resulted in a report submitted just as the Greek crisis was heating up. Truman seems not to have held up issuance of EO 9835 in order to tie it to foreign policy. When the PTCEL's chairman asked why the executive order had not yet been published, he was told that Truman "had several pressing things on his desk" to dispatch first; presumably the Greek emergency was among them.

Some people did connect foreign and domestic communism. A few administration foes drew this link in demanding tougher anti-communism at home. Conceding that Greece must have help, Congressman Charles Kersten insisted that "we should also immediately deal with Communism in America." Congressman John Taber, chairman of the Appropriations Committee, which would pass on any aid program, said that "before we do anything there [Greece and Turkey] there must be a 'clean-up' in the State Department." The linkage of communism at home and abroad may well have had adverse rather than supportive impact upon Truman's effort to implement his foreign policy.

If meant to stave off a Republican Red hunt, EO 9835 had only slight success. It did forestall legislation. Both J. Parnell Thomas and Edward Rees, Republican chairmen of HUAC and the House Civil Service Committee, intended to offer loyalty bills. Rees's measure even passed the House. In early March 1947, an administration official assured a House panel mulling over a bill to establish a loyalty program that the President would soon offer his own solution. When the solution came in the form of EO 9835, Democratic Congressman Adolph Sabath chortled that it "stole the Republican thunder." White House strategists had similar hopes.[9]

Ultimately, however, EO 9835 did not pacify anti-Communists. Several committees of Congress, HUAC in the lead, rushed joyously to probe communism—in government, Hollywood, unions, and elsewhere. Truman got an inkling of his limited leverage when he sought funds for the loyalty program. He wanted the Civil Service Commission to do most of the investigating and get most of the funds, but Congress thought otherwise. Truman grimly but correctly predicted that Hoover would "get this backward-looking Congress to give him what he wants." An aide noted that Truman was "afraid of [a] 'Gestapo.' " Congress drastically pruned the funding request and gave Hoover most of it.

Although Truman expressed determination to safeguard employee rights, his fine intentions often yielded to the very political forces that called the loyalty program into being. Moreover, the loyalty bureaucracy harbored opinions and generated a momentum that menaced individual rights. A finding of guilt usually entails commission of an overt act—but not under the loyalty program, which punished tendencies or potentials in employees' associations or thinking. The program's defenders found virtue in its ambition to detect "potential subversives" before they could commit treachery. This goal posed obvious problems. Who was to say which associations or thoughts proved potential disloyalty? In a field with few precedents, where the safeguards of a criminal proceeding were lacking, the accused was at the mercy of personal views and arbitrary interpretations of members of the loyalty boards.

Since 1942 the Attorney General had listed organizations adjudged to be subversive; membership in them might raise a question but not conclusively prove disloyalty. The list was first made public in 1948. One might have joined one of these groups because its expressed aim seemed laudable—civil rights, support for migrant workers, or opposition to Hitler. One thus risked unknowingly entering into subversive company. Communists might eventually take over a group, in which case the dates of one's membership became crucial (but not always conclusive) evidence of political views.

Ordinary acts of association brought hazards. In one sample of eighty-five loyalty cases, the commonest cause of suspicion was membership in the Washington Bookshop Association. The Bookshop offered literary and musical evenings and an intellectual ambiance. It also leaned left. (Because it shared its mailing list with Communist-front groups, many of its members appeared on other suspect lists.) Many names in its files were those simply of bargain-hunting book-lovers. Another group on the Attorney General's list was the International Workers Order, a CP umbrella organization. However, many members of its federated ethnic subdivisions had joined to find companionship; its main attraction was a superb insurance program.

Groups got on the Attorney General's list by fiat. During the war, the list grew to forty-seven organizations. By March 1948, it numbered seventy-eight. Additions continued until, at its longest, the list included twenty-two "totalitarian" groups (mostly pro-Japanese and long gone, like the Black Dragon Society); twenty-two "Fascist" organizations; 110 "Communist" groups (the CP, its defense committees, labor schools, the International Workers Order, and fourteen national subgroups, and numerous fronts); and other "subversive" groups that advocated force, violence, or unconstitutional forms of change.

Given the trouble that associations of whatever motivation or duration might bring, among government employees a tortoise-like caution in social relations often resulted. That keen observer Alexis de Tocqueville had discerned a national trait in the way Americans came together to form myriad societies to pursue mutual ends. A century later, this essential democratic attribute carried undreamed-of dangers. It was safest, one loyalty board member advised, to limit one's joining to the Methodist Church.

The loyalty program also penalized thoughts and mindsets. An employee's opinions, expressed to someone who wished him ill or deplored his views, could return to haunt him. One man aroused suspicion because, among other things, "he did all his buying at co-ops and didn't believe in small business," circulated petitions to keep the Office of Price Administration's price controls in operation and said "he was not a Communist but was left of left-wingers." One employee, said the head of a loyalty panel, was no Communist, but he upheld free speech so firmly that he would be overprotective of Communists' rights to propagandize during a crisis; hence, he was a loyalty risk.

Loyalty boards often grilled federal jobholders about their views of current or past foreign-policy issues. Their opinions of HUAC, labor, religion, marriage, the loyalty program, and (often) race relations were also canvassed. Dorothy Bailey, who challenged the program in court after being found a loyalty risk, was asked if she favored mixing the blood of blacks and whites in blood banks. A Navy employee was asked, "What do you think of female chastity?" One's reading became fair game. An employee was asked if he read the *New Republic*. Did he own any books "concerning the Government of the USSR?" Taste in music—the records of pro-Communist Paul Robeson or of Russian composers—might trigger concern. If one rented out one's home, it became accepted prudent behavior to remove books that might raise a renter's eyebrow. An employee questioned in the 1950s ruefully recalled reading Communist literature in the freer atmosphere of the 1930s. "Now I am afraid to read anything. I'm telling you. You never know what can happen 20 years from now."

The accusers' anonymity made it harder to refute charges. (The initial charges were often stated vaguely; more pointed assertions were saved for the hearing, perhaps to nonplus the employee.) Loyalty files often accumulated gossip, some of it malicious. A person outraged that a neighbor entertained people of another race might prattle to the FBI. Possibilities for malevolence were numerous—from a rival at work, a jilted lover. Then, too, the loyalty investigator might garble the testimony. In one case a charge of disloyalty was based on an agent's report of interviews with two co-workers; the employee later got affidavits from the same two people that directly contradicted the negative assessments attributed to them.

Confusion between the loyalty and security programs caused trouble too. Born in 1940, the security program authorized the Army and Navy to discharge anyone whose employment contravened national security. In 1946 this power was extended to the State Department and later to other agencies. A security risk might also be disloyal, but the label covered many other categories. One might be a blabbermouth, or a drunk, or prey to blackmail because of a moral blemish or because one's relatives lived behind the Iron Curtain. Employees who too flagrantly delighted in the opposite—or the same—sex might also qualify as security risks. In turn, those fired as security risks often suffered by being confused with those found to be disloyal. The State Department added to the confusion by having one panel, the Loyalty-Security Board, police both programs.[10]

The loyalty program decisively affected American politics. Truman's critics emphasized rightly how EO 9835 and similar actions pointed political discourse and maneuver down the road to McCarthyism. However, what also needs to be measured is the degree to which momentum carried Truman along. His loyalty program merely extended (albeit significantly) Roosevelt-era initiatives. Moreover, it is not clear whether, with the more absolutist civil-libertarian stand that some might have preferred, Truman could have blocked those Republicans determined to assert congressional authority in the field of loyalty—or resisted the concerns of Democrats feeling Republican pressure. From time to time Truman expressed the need for a balance between the imperatives of national security and those of individual rights. Nevertheless, that his loyalty program fell short of such a balance does not indicate that having no program was a likelier solution.

ANTI-COMMUNIST zeal ran high in the Eightieth Congress. Two lawmakers proposed to outlaw the Communist Party. One solon urged that federal employees be compelled to join either the Republicans or Democrats—"we do not need more than two parties." Congressman Karl Mundt offered a bill to make the CP and its fronts register with the Attorney General. Passed by the House in 1948, it died in the Senate. The 1947 Taft-Hartley Act included a provision requiring all labor-union officials to file a non-Communist affidavit every year. This measure gave management a new anti-labor weapon and CIO anti-Communists a lever to use against Communist or pro-Communist rivals.

However, Congress harried communism more with investigations and exposure than with legislation. While the Seventy-ninth Congress had launched four probes of communism, the Eightieth conducted twenty-two.[11] Three House panels inspected State Department loyalty files to gauge the effectiveness of the loyalty program. HUAC was soon to reach the pinnacle of its prominence. In 1947 it targeted Hollywood.

The film industry's appeal was also, so to speak, its soft underbelly. Traditionalists had long condemned the Gomorrah on the West Coast for offering sexual titillation and flaunting hedonistic lifestyles. Hollywood's origins, Jewish money from New York's garment district, and its talent, often foreign and Jewish, heightened its alien aura. In 1941 isolationists also complained about allegedly pro-interventionist movies. Martin Dies poked about the film capital in preliminary fashion and heard some testimony in executive session, but he never mounted a public inquiry. Later, such wartime pro-Soviet films as *Mission to Moscow* and *North Star* alarmed hardshelled anti-Communists.

In fact, Hollywood did serve as an oasis for the Communist Party, providing both the funds to grease Party causes and the glamor to grace them. The movie community backed the standard 1930s leftist crusades—civil rights and sharecroppers, anti-fascism and Spanish

Loyalists. Some actors flirted with communism, but the screenwriters, Hollywood's intelligentsia, were primarily the ones who joined the Party. Of some three hundred members of the Party's "talent branches" in Hollywood, almost half were screenwriters.[12]

In the 1930s, Hollywood writers were radicalized by both local circumstances and the Depression. The studios dispensed high salaries but low status. Producers ruled as if by divine right, and Hollywood's labor policies could be described as feudal. The Screen Writers Guild (SWG), one of several talent unions, became a focus of the activities and influence of Hollywood radicals. During the 1930s and the war, liberals and radicals in the Guild were loosely allied; afterwards, as the Cold War jelled, most liberals in the SWG, as elsewhere on the American Left, distanced themselves from the radicals.

Radical writers played conflicted roles. They might debate endlessly the Marxist aesthetic of their craft, but they lacked final control over their product. They fought to keep such unprogressive contents as demeaning portrayals of blacks off the screen, and they helped make some social-problem films of the late 1940s. Yet they seldom escaped routine fare—like Abbott and Costello films or musicals. Supposedly, Communist writers were urged by the Party to sneak five minutes of propaganda into every film. Communist actors were allegedly told to seize every opportunity to demean capitalism and advance the Communist cause. If cast as white-flanneled country-club layabouts, they should look especially "decadent." In one scene, waiting for an elevator, actor Lionel Stander whistled a bit of "The Internationale." "Even in Brazil," he boasted, "they'll know where I stand." However, fellow Communists criticized Stander for this indiscretion, and the scene eventually ended up on the cutting-room floor.

Indeed, films were such layered, collective enterprises that no group of writers could skew their contents politically. Authors Larry Ceplair and Steven Englund compare the Communist writers' plight to Penelope's in *The Odyssey*: at work "they unraveled the efforts of their evenings and weekends as political activists, for the movies they wrote reinforced the reigning cultural ethos and political-social order." Seekers of Red propaganda had to squint hard to find it. On a convoy run in *Action in the North Atlantic*, two U.S. sailors search for an airplane they hear; a close-up of a Soviet plane is flashed on the screen; actor Dane Clark exults, "It's one of ours all right!"[13]

Studio moguls did not relish the anti-communism of outside censors but cherished their own. Some labor leaders also found it handy. In battling to represent studio workers, Roy Brewer of the International Alliance of Theatrical Stage Employees (IATSE) effectively redbaited the rival Conference of Studio Unions (CSU). (Herbert Sorrell, head of the CSU, was no Communist, but he accepted Party help, and the CSU often mirrored the Party line.) Beginning in 1945, a series of strikes convulsed the film community. With Brewer's aid, the studios brought in scabs; firehoses and teargas were used; cars were overturned and heads bloodied. Radicals in the talent guilds, especially the SWG, sought to swing these groups behind the CSU but were outvoted.

Hollywood also had a Right, which nursed grievances against the Left and ascribed un-American views to it. In 1944 the Right's leaders founded the Motion Picture Alliance for the Preservation of American ideals to forward their views. (Sam Wood, MPAPAI's first president, even required in his will that every heir but his wife either file a non-Communist affidavit or be cut off without a dime.) These conservatives shared the management view of the recent labor troubles and would provide the principal testimony against Hollywood's Left. Hollywood's divisions would be mirrored before HUAC.

The hearings opened in October 1947 with testimony by the "friendly" witnesses. Several film magnates defended the Americanism of their industry and its product. Jack Warner of Warner Bros. exclaimed that he had never seen a Communist "and wouldn't know one if I saw one," yet earlier in an executive session he had boasted of ousting writers whom he suspected of communism. HUAC found few signs of Red-tinted films, but even fewer of *anti*-Communist ones. Asked if any were in the works, MGM's Louis B. Mayer got the hint: there was "the one we are going to start shooting promptly."

Studio heads denied ever screening pro-Communist material, but writer Ayn Rand disagreed, citing *Song of Russia*. The film enraged her by depicting "clean and prosperous-looking" streets and "happy kids," not homeless waifs. To show Russians smiling was a lie—in real life they did so only "privately and accidentally." Other witnesses testified that the Communists had manipulated various front groups, controlled the Screen Writers Guild, favored friends, and hindered enemies in the Hollywood steeplechase.

"Friendly" actors added a touch of glamor. Ronald Reagan, president of the Screen Actors Guild, recounted how Communists deviously exploited well-intentioned film folk. But the good guys were winning,

75

and Reagan, then still a liberal, hoped never to see Americans "by either fear or resentment . . . compromise with any of our democratic principles." Adolph Menjou expounded on communism at length, even offering the committee a list of suggested readings. Gary Cooper, as terse as on screen, tendered no scholarship but knew why he disliked communism—"because it isn't on the level."[14]

The "unfriendly" witnesses, soon known as the Hollywood Ten, met a less genial welcome. The group included screenwriters Lester Cole, Alvah Bessie, Ring Lardner, Jr., John Howard Lawson, Albert Maltz, Samuel Ornitz, Adrian Scott, and Dalton Trumbo; and directors Herbert Biberman and Edward Dmytryk.[15] Some, like Trumbo, made big money; others had passed their heydays. All of the Ten were or had been Party members, but they heatedly declined to discuss their political views or affiliations, invoking the protection of the First Amendment.

John Howard Lawson, widely regarded as dean of Hollywood Communists, led off. Did he belong to the Screen Writers Guild? He denied HUAC's authority to question him about affiliations or political views. "I am not on trial," he bellowed. "This committee is on trial here before the American people." Chairman J. Parnell Thomas gaveled him down. Lawson was then asked what came to be called the "$64 question": "Are you now, or have you ever been a member of the Communist Party of the United States?" It was shameful, Lawson retorted, "that I have to teach this committee the basic principles of American[ism]." Thomas had him removed. A staff member then displayed a purported copy of Lawson's 1944 CP registration card, and his other activities and affiliations were recited.

Testimony by other unfriendlies followed a similar pattern. They had much to say but little chance to say it. Dalton Trumbo called the hearings "the beginning . . . of an American concentration camp." Albert Maltz said he would rather die than grovel before Thomas and HUAC member John Rankin, both of whom "now carry out activities in America like those carried out in Germany by Goebbels and Himmler." Alvah Bessie, who fought in Spain, declared that HUAC aimed to denigrate that cause, "smear New Dealers," and spearhead the forces "preparing a Fascist America." Ring Lardner, Jr., said he could answer the $64 question, "but if I did I would hate myself in the morning."[16]

The Ten were cited for contempt of Congress. They had gambled by citing the First Amendment rather than the Fifth, the constitutional guarantee against self-incrimination that eventually gave ample protection to witnesses who chose not to answer congressional queries. Their lawyers and they believed that their refusal to divulge their political affiliations or beliefs was protected by the First Amendment's guarantee of free speech, that the courts (especially the strongly Rooseveltian Supreme Court) would uphold them, and that they could win the battle for favorable public opinion.

They erred all around. At first Hollywood seemed to stand with them. The Committee for the First Amendment, marshaling stars like Danny Kaye, Humphrey Bogart, and Lauren Bacall, took out ads, broadcast radio programs, and flew East to whip up indignation against HUAC. What next? Frank Sinatra asked. If you spoke "for a square deal for the underdog, will they call you a Commie?" But the absence of either a popular groundswell or support from the studio owners, as well as the Ten's raucous behavior, prompted a loss of enthusiasm. Attacking the Committee for the First Amendment, Congressman Rankin stressed that Danny Kaye's real name was Kamirsky, Melvyn Douglas's was Hesselberg, and so on. That group became a dead letter, its members apologetic for their indiscretion in questioning HUAC.

The Ten's legal strategy misfired too. In 1948 Lawson and Trumbo were found guilty of contempt in federal district court (in cases whose outcome governed those of the other eight). They banked on a reversal by the Supreme Court. However, two justices died in 1949, and with Truman's two replacements, it was a different court that declined to hear the appeals. It was also a different country. In 1950 the Ten went to jail—two for six months, the rest for a year. It was small solace that J. Parnell Thomas, convicted of accepting kickbacks, served time at Danbury prison along with Lester Cole and Ring Lardner, Jr. Working one day in the henhouse, Thomas cracked that Cole was "still spouting radical nonsense." And the ex-Congressman, Cole replied, was "still shoveling chicken shit."[17]

The resistance of Hollywood's leaders, who had first bridled at letting politicians dictate their hiring practices, collapsed soon after HUAC's hearings ended. On November 24–25, 1947, studio heads met at the Waldorf-Astoria Hotel in New York to frame a policy. The Ten had "impaired their usefulness to the industry" and were forthwith suspended or fired, not to be rehired until they had purged themselves of contempt, been acquitted, or sworn they were not Communists. Hollywood was on notice that no Communist would knowingly be employed. Thus the blacklist was born.

Fear of hostile public reaction prompted this step. The moguls were reminded that the American Legion was muttering; that in two towns boycotts were launched; that three nations might ban films by the Ten; and that one audience stoned a screen on which a Katharine Hepburn film was being shown (she belonged to the Committee for the First Amendment). Evidence of public wrath was spotty, but Hollywood faced several economic problems in the postwar years. Its leaders did not welcome new difficulties. By jettisoning the Ten, they hoped to appease the Right. Like the Ten, they had badly miscalculated. In subsequent years, Congress's hostile interest in Hollywood continued unabated.

In keeping with the Waldorf Statement, the studios began to question employees about their politics and affiliations. If the answers were unsatisfactory, work fell off or ceased. Film content was also affected. After the war, Hollywood (with the Ten in the vanguard) made several films about issues such as anti-Semitism and race. After 1947 the number of "message" films declined. "I now read scripts through the eyes of the DAR," a studio exec confessed. In the next few years, Hollywood made some forty anti-Communist films, none distinguished or profitable. Leaving nothing to waste, studios often used old gangster types in these movies, as in the climactic chase scene of *My Son John*. When the title character, a Commie, tries to redeem himself by confessing to the FBI, he is gunned down gangster style on the steps of the Lincoln Memorial.[18]

The blacklist would encompass other entertainment fields. In 1947 three ex-FBI men in New York launched *Counterattack*, a newsletter that listed a performer's Communist or front activities and liaisons, and citations of the subversiveness of these groups from the Attorney General's list and from the reports of HUAC and other sources. These authorities did not always get their facts straight and issued debatable judgments, yet reprinted in *Counterattack*, the charges took on a gloss of authenticity, and the burden of proof fell on the accused. Dependent on advertising revenues and ruled by sponsors' whims, radio and the emerging television industry were leery of threats of consumer boycotts. Though pressures for blacklisting in radio and TV began to grow in 1947, they had only a slight effect before 1950. As in Hollywood, the worst was yet to come.

These show business disturbances were one aspect of the cultural dimension of Cold War anti-communism. Celebrities of all sorts felt pressure to manifest their loyalty and condemn dissent from the orthodoxy. The great singer, actor, and spokesman for blacks Paul Robeson had long backed Soviet and Communist causes. In April 1949, at a Paris peace conference widely denounced as Communist-inspired, he declared it "unthinkable" that his race would go to war against the Soviet Union "in the interest of those who have oppressed us for generations." The utterance evoked outrage. Black spokesmen disavowed it in hearings before HUAC. Jackie Robinson took time out from the Brooklyn Dodgers' pennant quest to testify that Robeson's remark was "very silly." He added, however, that racial discrimination could not be dismissed by HUAC as merely "a creation of Communist imagination."

Sports generally—and baseball in particular—had long provided modes of identity for people and were deemed the embodiment of American virtues. The American Legion and the Veterans of Foreign Wars, influential forces for patriotism and anti-communism, made sponsorship of youth baseball a key part of their programs. "Boys and baseball are synonymous," the *VFW Magazine* expounded, but its support for youth leagues had a deeper motive. Donning a VFW baseball uniform was often a boy's first sense "of belonging to a 'team' " and having "to subordinate his own personal interests to those of the team as a whole." By accepting this "social obligation," a lad "takes an important step toward adulthood and good citizenship." As Herman Welker, a conservative Idaho Republican elected to the Senate in 1950 (and a sometime baseball scout), once proudly stated: "I never saw a ballplayer who was a Communist."

Other sports also carried symbolic burdens. Football, which expressed America's corporate side even more exactly than did baseball, grew similarly entwined with national identity. In 1951 an academic cheating scandal blew up at West Point; since it involved Army's mighty football team, it stimulated national debate. When Senator William Benton called on the service academies to drop football, Senator Welker (again) orated: "I shudder to think what America would do without intercollegiate football."

Popular sports stars were co-opted for political purposes as well. In 1946 heavyweight champ Joe Louis was guest of honor at a Los Angeles Americanism rally. Mayor Fletcher Bowron, his chief topic communism, lauded Louis for "above all, good Americanism." The "voices of good, quiet, forthright citizens like Joe Louis" were needed to offset preachments of "discord, disunion and strife."[19]

Thus, by the late 1940s, a growing preoccupation with anti-communism had come to be reflected in every niche of American culture.

FOR ALL OF HUAC's efforts against Hollywood and the entertainment business, the Committee's main hunt was for still bigger game. In February 1947, it summoned Gerhard Eisler, reputedly the chief Comintern agent in the United States. Eisler refused to testify, was convicted of contempt of Congress, and while his case was on appeal, fled the country. HUAC also took up the case of Eisler's brother, Hanns, a composer and radical; the committee was especially intrigued by Eleanor Roosevelt's interest in getting this refugee from Nazi Germany admitted to the country during the war. Throughout the Eightieth Congress, HUAC sought to discover the ties that it firmly suspected ran from Communist Party headquarters to the New Deal's inner sanctums.

The coming of the age of the atom also whetted fears of communism. When Truman chose New Dealer David E. Lilienthal to head the new Atomic Energy Commission (AEC), a few Senators insinuated that the nominee was pro-Communist. Soon foes accused the AEC of laxity regarding infiltration and spying. (In fact, most espionage occurred while the Army ran the Manhattan Project during the war.) Some of them had always opposed having civilians direct the nation's nuclear program. That scientists favored international control of the atom made conservatives even more mistrustful. J. Parnell Thomas rued the surrender of control to such "a group of milktoasts."

Edward U. Condon, head of the National Bureau of Standards, became a focus of attack for Thomas and HUAC. An advocate of civilian control of the atom, an ally and appointee of Henry A. Wallace, and a defender of cooperation with Russia, the scientist offered a choice target. A 1948 HUAC subcommittee report called him "one of the weakest links in our atomic security." Asserting that an FBI report in Condon's loyalty file impeached his loyalty, HUAC called on the Commerce Department to hand the report over. Truman then issued an executive order that this and any such demands were to be denied. He claimed a presidential power, anchored deep in precedent, to withhold confidential data—a doctrine later labeled "executive privilege." He also warned that loyalty files held such a mishmash of fact and gossip that their publication would harm innocent people.

Truman's order met loud objections. A House resolution demanded that the Executive Branch yield whatever information Congress needed to perform its duties. Congressman Nixon of HUAC, taking a line he might regret twenty-five years later in the Watergate furor, declared the President's stand unconstitutional and, if tolerated, a means to conceal all sorts of wrongdoing. The resolution died in the Senate, but conflict over the loyalty issue would continue to pit Congress against the Executive.[20]

HUAC struck gold at last in August 1948. First Elizabeth Bentley told a Senate panel that during the war she had passed on to the Soviet espionage apparatus data given to her by federal employees. Not to be outdone, HUAC heard her too. Among others, she implicated William Remington of the Commerce Department, Lauchlin Currie, an aide to FDR, and Harry Dexter White, a high Treasury official and then a director of the International Monetary Fund.

On August 3, Whittaker Chambers corroborated Bentley's story and told of dealings in the 1930s with fellow Communists employed by the federal government. Two days later, Alger Hiss, the most prominent of those whom Chambers named, refuted Chambers's charges before HUAC. However, the FBI, which had long watched Hiss, had fed tidbits about him to favored Congressmen on HUAC, including Richard Nixon; Karl Mundt was even secretly shown Hiss's dossier by a concerned friend in the State Department. Thus HUAC continued to pursue Hiss and to probe for the long-sought link between the New Deal and communism.

The Harry Dexter White episode was similarly tantalizing. On August 13, White, ill with a weak heart, avowed himself no Communist but simply a follower of FDR's ideals. A few days later, he died—a victim, said his friends, of HUAC's hazing. Enigmatic, brilliant, and upwardly mobile, White had advanced the careers of several people who moved in Communist circles. Chambers called him "a fellow traveler so far within the fold that his not being a Communist would be a mistake on both sides." He had helped draft the Morgenthau Plan to dismember and pastoralize Germany after the war—a scheme critics believed tailor-made to advance Soviet goals. Like Hiss, White had been under suspicion for some time.[21]

As the 1948 presidential campaign drew on, partisan vibrations from the hearings soon intensified. On August 5, President Truman accepted a reporter's characterization of the Hiss-Chambers flap as a Republican "red herring" dragged across the trail of the inept Eightieth Congress. This flippancy aside, the White House was worried. One aide termed the "spy" issue "the Administration's weakest link."

Yet the Communist issue, neutralized by several developments, proved less damaging to Truman's campaign than first feared. Wallace and the Progressives, the evident object of Communist ambitions, served as a "lightning rod" for charges that might otherwise have ionized Democrats. The President's campaign also benefited from the absence of a significant break in the Hiss case. The most devastating revelation—the pumpkin papers—came only after the election. Moreover, Tom Dewey and the Republicans exploited the Communist issue less than they might have—less than they had in 1944 against FDR. Dewey had since lost some gusto for the topic, resisting suggestions to pound it harder. More energetic redbaiting might not have changed the election's outcome, but its absence was an instance of Truman's luck.

Indeed, the GOP had no monopoly on the issue. The Democrats did their own redbaiting, chiefly of Wallace and his party. Truman's top adviser, Clark Clifford, proposed that liberals attack the "Communists and fellow-travelers" around Wallace and so achieve his "insulation"; Clifford also suggested that, on the Right, Republicans would be pinned down by Truman's loyalty program, which "adroitly stole their thunder," and by the Cold War's deepening "sense of crisis."

This scenario came true in part. Early in the campaign, Truman spurned any help from "Henry Wallace and his Communists." In speeches he lumped all his foes together—Communists, Progressives, and Republicans. The first, he argued, backed the second to elect the third; Communists "wanted a Republican victory" to trigger the isolationism and depression best suited to their aims. Americans for Democratic Action issued pamphlets identifying Communist influences around Wallace. The Democratic National Committee hired several veteran anti-Communist liberals to keep watch on the Wallace campaign. Yet as that campaign lost headway, the researchers turned to other tasks, and Truman to other challenges.

The issue still worried Democrats enough that they felt a need to underscore their anti-communism, however. Republicans only talked the game, said Attorney General Tom Clark, but because they failed to tighten immigration law as he had asked, J. Peters, a dangerous Soviet agent, "roams our streets and carries on his sinister Communistic activities." Happily, the FBI was "working day and night," the loyalty program functioned despite Republican footdragging, and the administration had deported Red aliens and won indictments of twelve Communist Party leaders under the Smith Act for allegedly conspiring to overthrow the government.[22]

Critics have speculated that the deportations and particularly the Smith Act indictments owed more to political calculation than to coincidental timing or real concern with the Red menace. Might the deportations themselves have served to cow left-wing and impress right-wing opponents of the administration's foreign policies?[23] Certainly, strategic considerations may have played some role in the decision to unsheath the Smith Act, but the chief impetus, as was often the case in the Truman years, came from outside the White House—that is, from the FBI and the Justice Department's Criminal Division. Both agencies were part of the administration, but they—the FBI especially—often acted as independent sovereignties whose zeal for internal-security steps frequently exceeded Truman's own goals. Truman aides who tried to make the agencies conform to administration policies often were treated as emissaries from a suspect rival power. The FBI had gained vast clout after Hoover spent years cultivating his and its image. His practice of keeping files on politicians—even Tom Clark, a Bureau ally—no doubt had some empowering effect on the Bureau. The political aims best served by the Smith Act prosecution thus appear mostly to have been those of Attorney General Clark, his department's Criminal Division (and its Internal Security Section), Hoover, and the FBI.

Clark first supposed that simply deporting radical aliens would suffice to contain both Communists and Republicans, but he would reconsider. Testifying before HUAC in February 1948, he was pressed on the question of why he had not yet used the Smith Act against the CP. He said the act was of little use, but once back at his desk, he acted. Earlier, the Criminal Division had begun sketching a case against the Communists, and by 1948 the FBI had amassed an 1,800-page brief. Clark asked U.S. Attorney John F. X. McGohey to assess the FBI brief and the prospects of obtaining Smith Act indictments from the New York grand jury that was then investigating Communist espionage.

Pushed by Congress and his own lower echelons, Clark wanted action. He pressed McGohey, "What are you going to do about commies?" Although McGohey's swift work actually nonplussed the White House and Clark, they saw no alternative but to let the case proceed. To avoid charges of political motivation, Clark did ask that the indictments be held up until after the Democratic Convention, which opened July 12. Served on July 20, the arrest warrants came in time for use in the fall campaign, and Truman, Clark, and others duly pointed to them.[24]

However motivated, the indictments yielded few political gains for Truman's campaign. Since the trial's beginning was delayed until 1949 by defense motions, the anticipated political benefit, if any, was largely dissipated. Truman's surprise victory in 1948 stemmed mostly from his identification with the party of FDR and the New Deal. He barely held together the Roosevelt coalition, but that nevertheless carried the day. Despite the crises of 1948 (the Czech coup, the Berlin airlift), the bite of the Communist issue in 1948 was rather gummy.

Language does have consequences. Yet the thesis of some historians that the Democrats' overripe anti-Communist oratory against Henry Wallace in the 1940s created a nurturant soil for McCarthy's bombast in the 1950s puts too heavy a burden on political rhetoric.[25] Its effect was marginal in 1948; that it could be crucial, let alone remembered, two years later is doubtful. Having already had ample practice, the Republicans needed no tutoring by Democrats in anti-communism. If the Truman Democrats merit blame for composing the litany of anti-subversion, one could as well criticize the New Dealers of the late 1930s and early 1940s.

Even if their oratorical excesses had no documentable effect on political discourse, however, the Democrats did help create an atmosphere amenable to McCarthyism. More important than speeches were *actions* that sited anti-communism at the center of American politics. The loyalty and security programs, deportations, and Smith Act prosecutions all planted the notion that Communists were indeed to be pried out of office, harried out of the land, or tried and jailed. One might argue that some of these measures—the loyalty and security programs in some form—were necessary. Events in Canada, Britain (subsequent evidence of espionage), and the United States showed that subversion was a problem. One might surmise, too, that the GOP Eightieth Congress would have enacted a more stringent loyalty system had Truman not moved first. But for the Smith Act trial, there is much less, if any, excuse. A response largely to domestic political considerations, the trial was far more dangerous to the republic it purported to protect than were those who were under indictment.

By 1949 several essential ingredients of a red scare were in place.

Public opinion, now soured on the USSR, was fast losing what little tolerance for domestic Communists it ever had. Opinion polls found large majorities in favor of outlawing CP membership or of the proposal that Communists be made to register with the government.[26] Influential interest groups also agitated for sterner measures. The American Legion and other veterans bodies pressed at local, state, and national levels for vigilance and action; picketed leftist gatherings; watched campuses for outbreaks of subversion; and scrutinized the Americanism of fellow citizens. The U.S. Chamber of Commerce raised the alarm against Communists in the media, in the unions, and in the government. Powerful segments of the press (especially the Hearst and McCormick papers) were beating the same drum.

Key strata of the federal government also spurred the rise of anti-communism, and simultaneously (or earlier) local and state politicians warmed to the topic. In Congress, conservatives in both parties fixed on the Red menace; Republicans frustrated by defeat in 1948 were eager to grasp its electoral potential. Though HUAC led the hunt for subversion, other committees scoured the landscape. The Executive Branch at minimum acceded to the need for tough anti-communism. Moreover, it had within it leaders (Hoover and several Attorneys General) and fiefs (the FBI, the Immigration and Naturalization Service) that fostered and exploited the anti-Communist drift of opinion. In February 1946, Hoover launched an "educational" campaign to inform Americans of the sinister nature of communism (broadly defined to include a number of left-liberal programs). He fed information from FBI files to favored allies in the media and politics. Soon his informal network of staunch anti-Communists encompassed reporters, columnists, publishers, Congressmen, conservatives in the entertainment field, the Chamber of Commerce, religious leaders, and anti-Communists in the labor movement.[27]

Such anti-communism often dovetailed closely with the aims of economic interest groups. In 1947, for example, a gathering devoted to the "preservation of our fundamental liberties" met in New York. Participants included one of Alger Hiss's nemeses, Father John Cronin of the National Conference on Catholic Welfare, and representatives of the American Legion and Chamber of Commerce, as well as a doctors' group fighting national health insurance and several rightist patriotic outfits. A second conference addressed the task of "uncovering and combatting the communistic and collectivist philosophies which have successfully infiltrated their ideas into every field of American life."

Redbaiting continued to serve as a weapon in disputes between management and labor and within labor's ranks. Though it is hard to separate spontaneous rank-and-file anti-communism from the externally manufactured sort, it is clear that in some cases the latter variety prevailed. Whatever the sins of Communists in the labor movement, the righteous anti-communism expressed by management often had a more than patriotic basis. Redbaiting by management proved a useful union-busting device in several 1948 strikes, such as those at the Bucyrus-Erie plant in Evansville, Indiana, and at American Zinc in Fairmont, Illinois.[28]

As the Right coalesced, the Left split. In politics, the issues dividing Popular Front from Vital Center liberals had led to their formal separation in 1947–48. In labor, the process took somewhat longer. CIO anti-Communists, as Phil Murray gravitated to their side, won control and in 1949–50 ousted from the CIO eleven unions declared to be Communist-dominated. Whatever its benefits, purification had its cost: a diminished spontaneity and militance in the CIO.

By the end of 1948, views charitable to American (or Soviet) Communists had grown scarce; dissent on foreign policy had declined; Communists and Popular Fronters were increasingly isolated. All that was lacking for a more thoroughgoing red scare was a sharper sense of crisis and a leader to focus and dramatize anti-communism. The year 1949 would bring the menacing events. In 1950 the nation would discover a person to harness anti-communism as a political weapon.

4

The Rise of
the Communist Issue

IT WAS IN 1949 that anti-communism planted itself squarely in the nation's political consciousness. Important groups like the CIO and influential educators closed ranks against Communists, politicians continued to hunt Reds, and front-page trials stamped judicial disapproval on communism. Reinforcing each other, public opinion and government policy together narrowed the range of tolerated politics. Advocates of peace, civil rights, and other causes had the growing burden of proving that they were not acting as "fronts" for or "dupes" of communism. Along with outright Communists, they encountered vigilante action and occasional low-level violence. To be leftist was to be suspect.

As its influence grew, anti-communism refracted perceptions of the most commonplace events. Thus it struck columnist Anne O'Hare McCormick that New York's Easter parade "would probably irritate Stalin" greatly, for many five-year plans would pass before Soviet women could afford the Easter outfits bought routinely by "any American working girl." Another New York parade, by Barnum's Circus, addressed the theme directly: as the girls marched in red, white, and blue halter tops and short shorts, the Big Top's performers dedicated themselves to "the struggle to maintain our way of life against the menacing horde of aggressors."

Opinion polls graphed the new mood, though revealing that people's everyday problems—jobs, in-laws, cost of living—usually elbowed aside remoter national issues. (One man-on-the-street said foreign affairs were "for people who don't have to work for a living.") A 1949 poll listed strikes and labor as America's chief worry (18 percent), followed by "preventing war" (14 percent), and then the high cost of living, government spending, taxes, "handling Russia," unemployment, "controlling [the] atom bomb," housing and rent control, foreign affairs (all in the 4-to-9 percent range). Just 3 percent cited "Communism," but several other answers, with a combined 50 percent frequency level, may also have embodied some fear of communism. Even if it did not leap off every tongue, anti-communism was evident. Another 1949 poll found that 68 percent would outlaw Communist Party membership; 83 percent would make Communists register with the government; 73 percent would ban them from college teaching.[1]

The fragile political balance that kept anti-communism in check in 1948 crumbled in the next two years as remote events bumped aside bosses and in-laws as concerns of the average Joe. The year 1949 should have yielded the first political harvest of Truman's containment policy abroad. The crises of 1948 had ebbed. With time would come agreement that in Europe communism had been checked. But elsewhere events seemed to offer more menace than promise; revealed that America's capacity to "contain" had limits; and, by calling into question the Democrats' record against communism, made way for McCarthyism.

In 1949 Jiang Jieshi and his Nationalist Army were defeated. In January Mao's forces took Beijing without a fight. In April they crossed the Yangtze. Nanjing, then Shanghai fell. The Nationalist commander in Changsha went over to the Communists and surrendered the city; in two weeks, his successor defected. In October the Red Army surged through Guangzhou as supporters danced the *yangko*, Jiang fled to the island of Taiwan, from where he maintained the fiction that he still ruled and would soon "liberate" mainland China. Domestic political pressures and later the Korean War left the United States handcuffed to Jiang and unwilling to recognize the Communist regime. For a generation, Red China would remain a *terra incognita* to Americans.

China throbbed as an open wound in American politics. The Republican Party, Pacific-oriented since William McKinley's day, had always regarded China with special tenderness. Protestant mission activities tightened the linkage. The influential publisher of *Time* magazine, Henry Luce, came from missionary stock. Congressman Walter Judd, a

GOP spokesman on China policy, served there as a medical missionary, and Congressman John Vorys took part in the Yale-in-China program. "With God's help," exclaimed Republican Senator Kenneth Wherry, "we will lift Shanghai up and up, ever up, until it is just like Kansas City." Visions of trade and investment also colored American hopes. All these dreams were dashed by the Communists' takeover.

Some American diplomats in wartime China had reported Jiang's slippage and the Communists' inroads. For such bad news and unwanted counsel, they would suffer as scapegoats for the Right. In 1945, resigning as Ambassador to China, Republican conservative Patrick J. Hurley charged officials in his embassy and in Washington with sabotaging American policy in China. From 1946 on, Republicans (and a few Democrats) singled out the so-called China Hands for attack.

In its August 1949 White Paper, the State Department blamed Jiang's defeat not on niggardly U.S. aid but on the decay of the Nationalist regime itself. Jiang's armies "did not have to be defeated; they disintegrated." But critics would have none of it. "China asked for a sword," declared Senator Styles Bridges, "and we gave her a dull paring knife." Jiang's partisans (including Henry Luce, columnist George Sokolsky, businessman Alfred Kohlberg, and politicians like Judd, Bridges, Nixon, William Knowland, and Pat McCarran) persistently harried the State Department. Though less cohesive and influential than its enemies feared, this loose coalition, labeled the "China Lobby," leaped to McCarthy's aid in 1950; its charges made up much of his stock in trade.[2]

On September 23, 1949, President Truman announced more trouble: the Russians had exploded a nuclear device. Forever ending the age of sure, ocean-bound safety, "Joe 1" jarred America's sense of security and produced a heavy political fallout. Some Congressmen urged that federal agencies be dispersed from the District of Columbia. Realtors soon advertised properties "a safe 58 miles" from the capital or "out of the radiation zone." In January 1950, Truman gave the go-ahead to build the hydrogen bomb. Government and media generally downplayed the enormity of the new weapons. *Look* soothingly described the H-bomb, "one of the cheapest forms of destruction known to man," as the size of a living room.

In 1950 the Office of Civil Defense was established, making nuclear survival a national goal. This modestly funded program was manifest more in culture than in structures. Asked one manual: "Can Junior fall instantly, face down, elbow out, forehead on elbow, eyes shut? Have him try it tonight as he gets into bed." New York City experts, fearing that an attack would rupture communications, pondered using trained pigeons as a back-up. They also expected to use Good Humor trucks to deliver blood to hospitals. (It is unclear how the pigeons, let alone the Good Humor men, were to survive.)[3]

The Soviet A-bomb sharpened fears of espionage. Viewing the bomb as a product of Yankee "know-how," some politicos surmised that "Asiatic" and primitive Russians could not have built a bomb unless they had stolen "the secret." (Indeed, spies had penetrated the Manhattan Project during the war: their plottings helped the Soviets but were not essential.) The AEC under Chairman David Lilienthal had just endured more charges of lax security at its facilities. Then the news came out that one AEC fellowship holder was a Communist. Bowing to political realities, the AEC phased in loyalty oaths for all fellowship recipients and FBI clearances for those engaged in secret work. Soon Congress mandated FBI investigations of every scholarship recipient.

Sniffing for atom spies, HUAC summoned several Manhattan Project veterans who had had Communist affiliations. It subpoenaed the brother of J. Robert Oppenheimer, the "father" of the A-bomb. Frank Oppenheimer, also a physicist, had belonged to the CP until 1941, quitting before he joined the Manhattan Project. Before testifying, he resigned his post at the University of Minnesota.[4]

In December 1949, George Racey Jordan gave sensational testimony before HUAC. During the war, Jordan expedited Lend-Lease shipments to Russia at a Montana airbase. He claimed that at the base he spotted cargoes of uranium and blueprints of the Oak Ridge nuclear plant; attached to the latter was a note to a Soviet commissar from FDR's right-hand man, Harry Hopkins, who wrote that he "had a hell of a time getting these" from General Leslie Groves, chief of the Manhattan Project. Hopkins "gave Russia the A-bomb on a platter," Jordan argued. However, Groves refuted the story, saying he had only filled Soviet requests for uranium lest a refusal pique their interest. Jordan's concoction went flat like day-old beer, but the issue of atomic espionage was far from dead.[5]

SEVERAL TRIALS in 1949, often competing with each other for headlines, spotlighted the threat of subversion. The trial of eleven out of the twelve Communist leaders originally indicted under the Smith Act consumed much of the year. An employee in the Justice Department, Judith Coplon, was convicted, the first of two times, for what amounted to espionage. In addition, the Hiss-Chambers controversy moved from Capitol Hill to the courtroom. Besides serving to adjudicate charges, trials, like other political acts, have an educational (or theatrical) function. Those of 1949 clearly fulfilled that role.

Coplon's case was the first to implicate an American spying for the Soviets. Her job in the Justice Department gave her access to secret FBI reports, some pertaining to Soviet espionage. She apparently shared her gleanings with Soviet intelligence. Its suspicions alerted, the FBI tapped her phone, bugged her office, and trailed her to a rendezvous with Valentin Gubitchev, a Soviet employed by the U.N. A trap was baited with phony reports. When Gubitchev and she were arrested in March 1949, her handbag contained classified data.

Two trials offered steamy melodrama. Coplon argued that she had taken documents only to help write a novel (entitled *Government Girl*) and that she and Gubitchev met not as spies but lovers. To refute the latter claim, the government produced evidence of a love life quite independent of Comrade Gubitchev. In the first trial, which ended on June 30, 1949, Coplon was found guilty of stealing classified documents. After the verdict, an angry crowd milled about the courthouse, one onlooker exclaiming that "the hussy" deserved "a rope around her neck." On March 7, 1950, she was convicted again, this time of conspiring to deliver the documents to a foreign agent.

However, illegal acts by the FBI destroyed the cases. In the first trial, the defense demanded to see the contents of Coplon's purse. These embarrassed the FBI, showing it had investigated such menaces as Henry A. Wallace supporters, Hollywood leftists, even the author of a thesis on the New Deal in New Zealand. It later emerged that FBI agents had wiretapped illegally, lied about it at the first trial, and destroyed some records. Because Coplon had been arrested and tapped without a warrant, the second verdict was overturned on appeal, and a new hearing was ordered on the first conviction. When the Supreme Court let both appellate rulings stand, the government declined to retry Coplon. The case fell into a legal limbo. The indictment stood and Coplon's guilt seemed obvious, but she was set free by the demands of due process. Gubitchev, in the interests of diplomacy, was sent back to the USSR.

This close call did not curb Hoover's imperial reach or ideological agenda; it did make him more cautious. To prevent future embarrassment, he ordered reports based on "highly confidential" sources (like wiretaps) to be kept in a separate file system—called "June mail." So as not to compromise the FBI, as in the first Coplon trial, agents who were to testify in future cases would be kept insulated from details of illegal surveillance. (Another of Hoover's ploys was engagingly labeled the Do Not File file.)

The FBI also shadowed its critics. The leftist National Lawyers Guild (NLG), already a target, earned further enmity by protesting FBI misdeeds in the Coplon case. In the 1950s, the FBI would spy on the NLG, sabotage it, try to put it on the Attorney General's list, and abet right-wing attacks on it. Perhaps the Guild's decline was inevitable, given its unpopular orientation, but FBI harassment hastened it. The FBI survived this scrape with its image unscathed. "In other hands," *Time* magazine chirped in 1949, "the FBI was a potential danger to every free citizen," but not in Hoover's.[6]

Upstaging the Coplon case were Alger Hiss's two trials. All too well Hiss symbolized the New Deal, whose colors he flaunted. Hiss claimed that HUAC meant to "discredit recent great achievements . . . in which I was privileged to participate"—the New Deal, Yalta, and the founding of the United Nations. His role at Yalta had been minor, but to critics it explained the rapid march of Soviet power. Just before the case exploded, Chairman J. Parnell Thomas credited HUAC with "unearthing your New Dealers for two years, and for eight years before that." The Hiss case was HUAC's jackpot.

The battle raged over style as well as policy. Whittaker Chambers contrasted poorly with Hiss's tailored good looks and "Eastern" sophistication, but demeanor like Hiss's had long graveled the sensibilities of anti–New Deal Congressmen. Karl Mundt noted that Hiss "looks so smooth and intelligent and speaks such an effective Harvard accent." A member of "the lush Washington social set who traveled in the top hierocracy [sic] of that nose-tilted group," Hiss had plenty of defenders, Mundt marveled sadly. Mundt was a conservative Republican, yet even Senator Paul Douglas, a liberal Democrat, resented State Department types who "modelled themselves upon the British Foreign Service in the days of Edward VII" and who disdained "the common hardworking people of this nation."

Since Hiss's foes loathed the New Deal, many liberals initially gave him the benefit of the doubt. Most, but by no means all, liberals conceded his guilt, taking it as proof that the domestic Communist threat was small but real. To some Cold War liberals, those who questioned Hiss's guilty verdict were dangerously naive in the era of Stalinism. Until Hiss's guilt was fully acknowledged, wrote Leslie Fiedler, "we cannot move from a liberalism of innocence to a liberalism of understanding." Some even suggested that Hiss and his defenders paved the way for McCarthy. For years to come, the Hiss case divided "tough-minded" Vital Center liberals from those who still inhaled the Popular Front spirit of the 1930s.

The Hiss case offered a fulcrum on which tilted the political balance of the McCarthy era. For Republicans it confirmed two decades of suspicion of Democratic rule. After the guilty verdict on January 21, 1950, they unleashed a chorus of I-told-you-so's. When Secretary of State Dean Acheson told reporters that he for one would not turn his back on Hiss, there were yowls of outrage. The case threw Democrats on the defensive. Many thought Acheson's resignation would relieve them of a burden. By confirming a Communist threat, the Hiss case also made it harder for them to resist the logic of the hunt. Questioned about "McCarthyism," Paul Douglas later felt compelled to state, "We have had some Alger Hisses in government."[7]

The Truman administration showed off its own anti-communism in *Dennis v. United States*, the Smith Act case of the top Communist Party leaders—including Eugene Dennis, the Party's national secretary—which began in January 1949. Under the gavel of flamboyant Harold Medina, the courtroom reverberated with caustic exchanges between judge and accused. At the trial's end, Medina found the defense attorneys and several defendants guilty of contempt of court. This marked an early instance of what would become a general attack on lawyers who assisted Communist defendants. Reds soon found it hard to hire counsel.

Even under Medina's tight leash, the trial lasted until October. The defendants did not pound the law or the facts—an approach which offered promise, given the government's weak case. Instead, pursuing a "labor defense," they tried to make the trial "a mighty tribunal of the people so that the accused become the accusers." On the streets around New York's Foley Square, the Party mounted a protest. Hundreds chanted, "Hey judge, we won't budge until the twelve are free." (In fact, the case of William Z. Foster, the twelfth defendant, was severed because he was ill.) Little girls carried placards with the message, "My

Daddy Fights for Peace. Fight Now for his Release." (None actually had a father on trial.) Mass opposition to the trial did not materialize, however; the demonstrations only enraged conservatives.

The government's case reduced to the proposition that the defendants had conspired to organize for the purpose of teaching and advocating forcible overthrow of the American system. The 1945 decision to fold the Communist Political Association, which had only been formed in 1944, and to reestablish the CPUSA was cited as proof. The law of conspiracy enabled the prosecution to sidestep the usual need to implicate each defendant in an overt act.

To prove a commitment to Leninist revolution, federal attorneys recited excerpts from sacred Communist texts. This premise the Eleven vehemently denied. They sought only peaceful change: blood would run only if organized capital violently resisted the people's march. The state called Louis Budenz as an expert witness. Once an editor of the *Daily Worker*, Budenz had quit the CP in 1945, returned to the Catholic Church, and begun a long career of testifying in legislative and judicial hearings. His main contribution to the trial was to dismiss Communist disavowals of violence as "Aesopian language" meant to hide their real aims. The state contradictorily implied that Communists took Marxist-Leninist classics literally—but not those which clashed with the prosecution's case.

The government also marshaled testimony from thirteen undercover informants—another hallmark of the times. High drama unfolded when Herbert Philbrick, an FBI informant since 1940 and Party member since 1944, took the stand. After the trial, Philbrick wrote a book about his years as a Communist and FBI plant. It inspired "I Led Three Lives," a TV series redolent of dark streets, clandestine meetings, and deception.

The case served justice badly. The government sought less to convict the Eleven than to proscribe their Party: as late as May 1948, lawyers drafting the case had not known whom precisely they were trying to indict. Nor was a single defendant shown to have advocated a violent action. Medina's charge to the jury answered a question that jury itself should have decided: did Communist statements amount to a clear and present danger or just "abstract doctrine"? The Eleven were found guilty; ten received the maximum five-year jail term. Eventually they were released on bail, pending appeals (which would last until 1951). Communism, for top Party officials at least, was now apparently illegal.

To CP leaders, the trial confirmed a fear that fascism loomed ahead. Key comrades were ordered underground. Some were regrouped into an atomized "system of threes" to prevent wholesale round-up when night descended. Party cards were destroyed, dues records no longer kept. After *Dennis*, the sense of crisis deepened. A foundation was laid in Mexico for an underground-in-exile; three Party members sent there were trained to use code and invisible ink. The fear was exaggerated, and these moves, most of them known to the FBI, only confirmed suspicions that conspiracy was afoot.

Since 1945 the CP had pursued a militant, exclusionist line. It burned its bridges to the CIO and other leftist groups. Nor was its defense of civil liberties universal. With Communist prompting, a 1949 Bill of Rights Conference condemned the Dennis trial—but not the wartime Smith Act convictions of the Trotskyites. Paul Robeson dismissed them as "enemies of the working class." This orientation as well as deepening Cold War pressures helped reduce Party membership and influence. Further repression led to more self-isolation, which meant increased vulnerability and apparent evidence of conspiracy—prompting further repression. The Party's excessive fearfulness thus advanced its demise. Yet the curbstone wisdom—that if they're really after you, it's not paranoia—may also apply.[8]

These trials may well have signaled to the public that Communists, never beloved, had lost what scraps of legitimacy they ever had. Vigilantism against the Left mounted. In 1947 veterans groups and pols in several cities forced cancellation of Paul Robeson concerts. Communists in New Jersey were denied use of a public hall; a meeting in Trenton was disrupted. In March 1948, a crowd in Columbus drove off Communist leafleters; days later a mob wrecked a Communist leader's home in the Ohio capital. Communists meeting in Rochester, New York, were forced to disperse, their literature burned in the street. In September an unknown assailant stabbed and beat Smith Act indictee Robert Thompson near his home in Queens. The atmosphere made FBI informant Angela Calomiris fear for her safety—as a Communist—before her court appearance in the Dennis trial.

In 1948 Henry Wallace and his supporters had also been targets of mob action. In Binghamton, New York, a judge stated he would deny child custody to Wallaceite parents.[9] Violence also flared in the workplace, exacerbated by the conflict between pro- and anti-Communist forces in the CIO, which culminated in the ouster of eleven Communist-run

95

unions in 1949–50. In 1949 three workers circulating the Communist-backed Stockholm Peace Petition at Milwaukee's Seaman body plant were forced to leave. When one of them later reported to work, fellow workers flung him down the stairs and out of the factory. In February 1949, organizers seeking to woo members of the Farm Equipment Workers Union over to the United Auto Workers passed out leaflets at International Harvester in East Moline, Illinois. FE'ers sallied out with crowbars and hinges; shouting "Go back to Moscow," the Auto Workers fought back with fists and brass knuckles. The following May in Birmingham, Alabama, the Steelworkers tried to raid a local of the pro-Communist Mine, Mill and Smelter Workers, savagely beating a group of leaders, one of whom lost an eye.

Evansville, Indiana, witnessed what could serve as a model of labor strife complicated by the Communist issue. An anti-union company, Bucyrus-Erie, battled a resentful workforce represented by the United Electrical Workers. A strike in 1948 sparked violence on the picket lines. The UE expressed rank-and-file militance, but its Communist leadership gave management a pretext for union-busting, government a rationale for intervening, and some UE members second thoughts. Claiming it could not deal with a union whose leaders refused to sign the Taft-Hartley anti-Communist affidavit, Bucyrus-Erie broke off bargaining. In barged an AFL union to call for a National Labor Relations Board election (which the UE, under Taft-Hartley, could not contest). A House Education and Labor subcommittee arrived to air charges of Red influence. In this angry climate, the strike collapsed, the UE lost its grip at Bucyrus-Erie, and unions at other plants were shaken. Anti-communism welled up in several factories, where unionists named in the congressional hearings were physically threatened by colleagues, who halted work until the unionists left the plant.

Evansville exemplified anti-communism's sources and impact on the labor movement at the local level. There was real rank-and-file hostility to Communist UE leaders—fisticuffs broke out at some union meetings—but much anti-communism was externally orchestrated. Management, government officials (Congressmen, judges, and state police), segments of labor, and Catholic and veterans groups all stirred the cauldron. One historian of the strike argues that hostility to the accused Communists was far from spontaneous: supervisors and foremen agitated until co-workers took action against the alleged Reds.[10]

The Rise of the Communist Issue

The worst outbreak of strong-arm tactics in 1949 occurred at Peekskill, forty miles from New York City. In August Paul Robeson was to sing at a benefit for the Civil Rights Congress, a group on the Attorney General's list. Local patriots led by the American Legion vowed to prevent it. Their roadblocks and a rock-throwing mob turned back the concert-goers. The resolute sponsors held the event a week later, now aided by 1,000 police and 3,000 "security guards" from leftist unions who carried ball bats and tire irons. But as the audience left the grounds, rioters set upon and stoned their vehicles, chasing some as far as twenty miles from the site. About 150 were injured. Public officials blamed the victims; Judge Medina even said Communists engineered the riot to end the Smith Act trial.

Was the political climate soured by independent "public opinion" or by the actions of government and anti-Communist interest groups? Historians who blame the Cold War and the accompanying hysteria primarily on the Truman Admnistration claim that government policy, operating on malleable public opinion, was the chief causal agent. The Executive Branch, in an often uneasy alliance with conservatives in Congress, did play a mighty role in fomenting anti-communism. But the government was also helped by the U.S. Chamber of Commerce and other business groups; by Catholic organizations ranging from local societies to the Knights of Columbus and from parish priests to princes of the church; by elements of the labor movement; and by other influential groups. (Much of this "help," it should be noted, consisted of criticism of the government's lack of vigor in meeting the Red menace.)

Some influential anti-Communists, fretful about public apathy, hoped to kindle new vigilance. Thus, when a recent poll revealed a low level of anti-Communist feeling, Congressman Richard Vail of HUAC called for raising public consciousness of the Red menace. In 1946 J. Edgar Hoover launched his "educational" campaign to build public awareness of the threat posed by the "basically Russian" CPUSA. Amid the Chambers–Bentley "spy" revelations of August 1948, the Hearst newspapers lamented that after many years of sounding the tocsin over communism, they had failed to dissuade most Americans from believing that the danger was "greatly exaggerated" and the price of fighting it too costly to civil liberties.[11]

The subject of American liberties and the dangers to them were the focal point of numerous exercises in civic education from the late 1940s on. In 1947 the administration, led by Attorney General Tom Clark, helped launch a cross-country tour of the Freedom Train, a streamliner that carried the Constitution, the Declaration, and other historic documents for public viewing. Americans were summoned to board the train and to relearn and implement the blessings of liberty, but the tour also had the Cold War task of spreading the administration's world view. The Freedom Train and the many local activities tied in with it were not value-free. Celebrating the virtues of "free enterprise" was one aim. Another, of special concern to Clark, was to call back American youth from "crime and juvenile delinquency" and from the postwar "unrest" he discerned.

The Freedom Train's impact exceeded its sponsors' fondest hopes, but it may have represented more than a recruitment of public opinion by an elite. In fifteen months, over four million people visited the train in 350 cities, some braving bitter weather. Bostonians lined up four abreast for over a mile; 500,000 trooped through the train in Chicago. Engines of mass persuasion—the media, the Advertising Council, churches, schools, local governments—were all revved up to promote the train, but the outpouring of interest seems to have outstripped the effort invested. That people, who often evade exhaustively preached civic duties, chose to participate in this pageant may tell more about public opinion than about efforts to manipulate it.[12]

Local communities also conducted civic exercises ranging from sober appreciations of American freedoms to dramatic Cold War spectacles. In September 1948, the Junior Chamber of Commerce of Kansas City, Missouri, sponsored "Democracy Beats Communism Week." The Jaycees organized an elaborate series of lectures, speeches, and banquets and staged a play and a parade that observers found inspirationally anti-Communist. The program was replicated elsewhere. Honolulu's Elks held a "Wake Up America Week" rally. Since speakers nearly outnumbered the audience, however, the event was called off.

More dramatically, American Legionnaires staged a mock Communist coup in Mosinee, Wisconsin, on May Day 1950. Striking the tiny papermill town at dawn, they seized strategic facilities, set up roadblocks, arrested local leaders and clergy, purged the library, and provided a grim, if playful, picture of life behind the Iron Curtain, complete with identity checks, propaganda speeches, and a diet of black bread and potato soup. Mosinee garnered vast publicity—on radio, TV, newsreels, and the pages of *Life*. The ex-Communist warhorse Ben Gitlow, who helped mount the coup, termed it "one of the first effective steps taken" in the psychological war against communism and toward capturing May Day for "Americanism." Some towns offered imitations. Hartley, Iowa's effort in June 1950 elicited a less enthusiastic response (some townspeople especially feared having their homes searched). Rushville, Indiana, had itself conquered by Commies in December 1951. In the 1950s, civil-defense drills—pageants in their own way— became common.[13]

The meaning of all this activity is ambiguous. Americans lined up in crowds to see the Freedom Train, but the turnout may have been a tribute more to a reverence for (and curiosity about) the hallowed charters of American liberties and other historic documents than to any adherence to the more conservative agenda of the train's sponsors. Citizens participated, for the most part good-naturedly, in the anti-Communist programs conducted in Kansas City and Mosinee and spoke positively of them; but it would appear that the initiators of such endeavors, not surprisingly, felt greater enthusiasm than did those at whom the programs were aimed. The ho-hum—and sometimes hostile—responses to attempts to imitate some of these programs elsewhere may confirm the fears held by mid- and top-level leaders that the public was rather apathetic about the Red menace. Everyone was against communism, but there were limits to the exertions the average citizen was willing to invest in that sentiment.

BY THE LATE 1940s, anti-communism had become standard policy in most American institutions. The CIO offered a case in point. Communist power in the CIO had declined gradually. Anti-Communist Walter Reuther's capture of the presidency of the United Auto Workers in 1946 was one milepost. For "Red Mike" Quill, the once pro-Communist leader of the Transport Workers, the break from the Party came in 1948. (One factor was Communist opposition to a New York subway fare increase, which Quill needed to fund a wage hike for his union.) Once tolerant of Communists, CIO chief Phil Murray hardened after the war. The issue of whether to back Wallace or Truman in 1948 was the last straw and Truman's victory the clincher. At the 1948 CIO convention, Murray ripped Communists for betraying "every decent movement into which they have infiltrated themselves," and he pushed through anti-Communist resolutions. The CIO ordered the pro-Communist Farm Equipment Workers to merge with the United

Auto Workers; when they refused, their locals were raided. At the 1949 convention, the FE and the United Electrical Workers were expelled; nine more Communist-led unions left or were thrown out after perfunctory hearings.

The purge of the Communists resulted from several motives: factional rivalries, deeply felt distrust, and a sense that to survive in a hostile and conservative climate labor must put its house in order. So it did, but not without cost. The CIO's early militance vanished, replaced by a tamed bureaucracy, still powerful but no longer very dynamic. Communist-led unions took with them many of the sins their foes ascribed to them, but also much of the CIO's vigor.[14]

Educators also felt the winnowing hand of anti-communism in the late 1940s. In 1949, egged on by the Sons of the American Revolution, HUAC asked for reading lists from over seventy universities and colleges in order to uncover Communist textbooks. Some schools complied; others resisted. If the lawmakers were curious, Cornell's chancellor said, they should enroll in courses at his university. The inquiry sputtered out ingloriously. National politicians did not launch a sustained investigation of the schools until 1952–53.

However, other critics of education took up the slack. The Right had long warned that subversive educators in the "little Red schoolhouse" were poisoning young minds. The Cold War's chill gave bite to such charges. They came from such rightist entities as the Conference of American Small Business Organizations, whose publication sounded alarms about left-wing texts; the National Committee for American Education; and the American Legion, whose magazine carried such articles as "Your Child is Their Target." Save for the Legion, such groups were small, but their strength multiplied in locales where anti-subversion crusades meshed with less frenzied yet deep worry about the cost of progressive education's "fads and frills" and about the rise of "life-adjustment" courses at the expense of the "three R's."

Such an alliance emerged in Pasadena, California. In 1950 a self-styled School Development Council (SDC) launched an attack on school superintendent Willard Goslin. A dreaded "progressive," Goslin was accused by the SDC of betraying the three R's and raising taxes. Often meeting at the American Legion hall and using the literature of Allen Zoll's right-wing National Committee for American Education, the SDC defeated a bond referendum and a redistricting plan that would have integrated the schools. It next urged "an ideological investigation of curriculum, methods, and personnel." To pacify critics, the school board asked Goslin to resign. Similar groups using materials by Zoll and other rightist pamphleteers sprang up in such cities as Los Angeles, Denver, Port Washington, New York, and Englewood, New Jersey.

Universities had long been pilloried as nurseries of radicalism. In 1935 drugstore magnate Charles R. Walgreen pulled his niece from the University of Chicago to save her from Communist indoctrination; a State Senate inquiry ensued. After their son died in Spain's civil war, a Kansas couple demanded a probe of the University of Kansas's role in radicalizing this formerly pious, patriotic, "normal" Boy Scout. A 1935 tract exposed radicalism's inroads at the University of Wisconsin, including faculty who advocated "free love," syllabi that listed Communist readings, and even a bad football team, which lost seven out of eight games for the year. Posed photographs pictured a Wisconsin student telling his horrified mother that belief in God was "just bunk." "In how many Wisconsin homes—perhaps in your own," asked the caption, had such influences "shaken the family circle?" Fourteen states adopted teacher loyalty oaths in the 1930s.[15]

In the late 1940s, political attacks on the universities mounted. In 1948, after an inquest by the state legislature's Canwell Committee, the University of Washington lodged charges against six professors. Three of them who had refused to testify before the Canwell Committee were accused of concealing Party membership and of dishonesty and professional incompetence evidenced in following the Party line. Two of the men conceded to the faculty tenure committee, which heard the cases, that they were Communists; the third denied ever being one. The tenure committee's majority found Party membership to be insufficient grounds for dismissing their two colleagues, but they held that the third man's evasiveness and other behavior justified loss of tenure.

However, university President Raymond B. Allen took a sterner view and proposed that all three be fired. Allen was convinced that to retain Communist instructors was political folly. Elaborating a view that soon became writ in academe, he argued that Communists lacked the independence of thought needed for the scholar's calling and so had no place in education. Since the classroom was often termed the "chapel of democracy," teachers as "priests of the temple of education" must cleanse their ranks of Communists. In January 1949, Washington's Regents concurred, and the three professors were dismissed.[16]

The next great Cold War controversy embroiled the University of California. In 1949, partly to head off intrusions by the state legislature, the Regents prescribed a loyalty oath for university employees. Most professors did not dispute the bedrock position, framed in 1940, that no Communist could teach at California, but an oath, they argued, would weed out only non-Communists of firm conscience, not Reds. The dispute lasted several years. Committees formed, deliberated, dissolved. Compromises and alternatives were considered, but negotiations failed and both sides grew embittered. At length the Regents insisted: sign the oath or be fired. Concerned for their jobs, the damage to the university, and a political climate roiled by the Korean War, many faculty gave in. While hundreds had protested the oath, ultimately only thirty-one refused to sign it. In August 1950, they lost their jobs.

The plot thickened when the California legislature enacted an oath for all state employees, obviating the complaint that the original test singled out teachers. In 1952 the voters grafted the oath into the state constitution. Meanwhile, after twenty nonsigners sued, the state's Supreme Court invalidated the Regents' oath because the legislature had preempted the field. Since most had now signed the new state oath, the resisters' victory was muddled. They had made a profound moral point—and regained their jobs.[17]

In contrast, the three men fired from University of Washington never again held academic jobs. Their cases sparked national debate over the proper response of the educational profession to communism. Earl McGrath, U.S. Commissioner of Education, saw "no justification" for hiring teachers "whose commitments are contrary to . . . freedom itself." Philosopher Sidney Hook supported President Allen's view and reiterated that those who bowed to Party discipline did not have the independence of thought that was the essence of academic freedom. Some disputed this position. Harold Taylor, president of Sarah Lawrence College, found students impervious to doctrines from any quarter. Senator Robert A. Taft, an exception among politicians, did not think "a man should be dismissed simply because of his thoughts." Others sought middle ground. Might not a Communist teach math without polluting the subject or the students' minds? A government class, on the other hand, was different. Some would tolerate honest Marxists or those who avowed past Party membership, but not those who concealed their true colors. Anti-Communists, including Hook, thought it essential to oust Communists but wanted academics, not meddling politicians, to do it.

In 1949 much of the academic establishment lined up with Hook. The National Education Association voted to bar Communists as members or teachers. It also sponsored a report by a blue-ribbon panel—whose members included Dwight Eisenhower, then president of Columbia, and James B. Conant of Harvard—which declared Communists "unfit" to teach. This anti-Communist chest-thumping, it was hoped, might "take the stinger out of some of the attacks" on educators. The American Federation of Teachers espoused a similar position. Only the American Association of University Professors argued that Party membership per se did not warrant dismissal, but the AAUP also stated that "lying and subterfuge" about one's affiliations evidenced unfitness to teach.

Universities often followed tortuous paths to defend their turf. Harvard's Conant adamantly opposed an "inquiry" into his faculty's political views, but neither would he hire Communists. If one were already on campus, he said, that would be a "difficult" question to resolve, but "no such problem exists at Harvard." Yet how could he know without "inquiry"? According to sociologist Sigmund Diamond, by 1950 Harvard and the FBI had an "arrangement" to exchange information. Other schools had similarly unadvertised relationships with the FBI. These links permitted quiet preventative action, which universities preferred over messy open battles with legislators, but they were not without cost. What the schools gave up in autonomy and academic freedom, they yielded knowingly, if not wisely.

Still, one was safer at Harvard and other prestigious, privately endowed universities than at state schools or smaller private colleges. In addition, senior faculty whose politics became a public issue were more secure than instructors or graduate students who might well—even at Harvard—find contracts and fellowships not renewed. As universities grew increasingly reliant upon federal research funds, they became more vulnerable to government definitions of loyalty and proper political behavior. The problem was most acute for scientists, but no scholar was entirely insulated from the demands of national security.[18]

Nightmare in Red

AS THESE BATTLES in the schools and universities indicated, anti-communism was no monopoly of the federal government. The Communist issue also engaged the energies of state and local politicians, thus revealing the layered multiplicity of anti-Communist politics and the deep roots of the anti-radical impulse. From 1919 into the 1930s, many states had enacted statutes against criminal syndicalism and anarchy, red flag laws, teacher oaths, and other devices. Later, in the second Red Scare, state and local anti-subversive efforts often resonated to stimuli from Washington, but sometimes the initiative was local and more or less independent.

New York, heavily denizened by native and foreign-born radicals, had the longest tradition of anti-radicalism. The state legislature's Lusk Committee had confronted the radical threat in the fevered days of 1919. It invaded left-wing meeting halls and seized files and literature. Concerned that schoolchildren were vulnerable to subversion, the Lusk Committee suggested that teacher certification be based on loyalty and good character and that schools be licensed. Enacted in 1921, these proposals were repealed two years later at the urging of Governor Al Smith.

But New York's conservatives continued to fret over the schools. In 1934 legislators adopted a teachers' loyalty oath. One suggested that schoolroom subversion be stemmed with loyalty oaths to be taken by *students* (at the secondary level); another prescribed red, white, and blue school buses as a remedy. In 1939 the issue heated up when City College of New York offered a post to the noted British philosopher Bertrand Russell, whose freethinker's views on such topics as religion and marriage horrified Catholic leaders.

This flap, persisting fears of classroom subversion, and the issue of state aid to education combined to bring about the Rapp-Coudert investigation. In 1940–41 State Senator Frederic R. Coudert and Assemblyman Herbert Rapp led a committee that hunted for subversives among the faculties of New York's city colleges. One ex-Communist witness named over fifty colleagues as Party members. Pressured by the legislature, the Board of Higher Education validated the charges in all but one case and fired twenty instructors (eleven more resigned). Although there were in the city colleges a number of Communists (many of whom lied to Coudert about their affiliation), CP membership was not illegal, their unfitness to teach had not been proven (no classroom propagandizing was ever adduced), and the evidence in some cases was flimsy.

The Rapp-Coudert inquiry set important precedents. A Senate committee investigating Gotham's schools in the 1950s used many of the same informants, staff experts, and hostile witnesses. With a total number of dismissals that exceeded the output of other states, New York's legislative probers and the educational authorities who executed their will provided a model of zeal.[19]

Led by Jack Tenney, California wrestled with communism more flamboyantly than did New York. A musician and songwriter (he wrote "Mexicali Rose"), then a lawyer and politician, Tenney ran a Los Angeles musicians' union local and after 1936 was a state legislator. In the 1930s, he grazed with the Left, even urging abolition of the Dies Committee (before which one witness had called Tenney a Communist). In 1938, however, his union leadership was challenged. Denied reelection as local president, he blamed this and broader social ills on Communist intrigues. He used his seat in the Assembly and, after 1942, the State Senate to launch a career as the country's leading state-level foe of the Red menace.

In 1940 Tenney and Assemblyman Sam Yorty eagerly pursued charges of Communist infestation of the state relief agency. This attack on Governor Culbert Olson wrote *finis* to the state's exotic Depression politics, which had witnessed such strife as the 1934 dock strike and efforts to organize farm workers and many radical movements. Though Olson was a liberal, conservative forces dominated the legislature. Tenney and Yorty were both Democrats (until Tenney became a Republican in 1944). Their shift rightward and seizure of the Communist issue aptly reflected the political trend.

In 1941 Tenney headed the Joint Fact-Finding Committee on Un-American Activities, charged with unearthing subversion that might "affect the preparation of the State for National defense, the functioning of any State agency," the administration of public aid, and the management of state educational institutions. With this sweeping mandate, he eyed union activities, investigated schools, and kept tabs on Hollywood's Left. In 1946 he heard testimony that two Los Angeles high-school teachers were insinuating Red propaganda into their classes; when the board of education dismissed the charges, Tenney cried "whitewash." In 1947 the committee considered whether a high-school sex-education program in Chino was Red-inspired. "Tenney Fears Sex May Be Un-American," spoofed one headline.

Tenney's extravagances went far to discredit his legislative aims. The many bills he sponsored gained considerable legislative support but also earned the hostility of potent interest groups. His bill to regulate loyalty in the professions angered lawyers. His attacks on textbooks and teachers also sparked opposition. A proposal to have the legislature ensure the loyalty of University of California employees displeased the Board of Regents, but in March 1949, to forestall further incursions, the Regents mandated their own loyalty oath, thus igniting the roaring controversy of 1950 that led to the dismissal of thirty-one professors.

By then Tenney himself was out of the picture. Having alienated so many political interests and colleagues, he had to quit the California Un-American Activities Committee in 1949 as the price of its continued existence. Still, he left probably the broadest legacy of any state anti-subversionist. Other Red-hunters often cited his panel's voluminous, if unbalanced, findings as proof that some group (such as the ACLU) or individual had fronted for or given aid to the Communists.[20]

Illinois' campaign against subversion was briefer than California's but more tumultuous. Prompted by the state's powerful American Legion, in 1947 the legislature appointed a special commission chaired by Republican State Senator Paul Broyles to study the problem of subversion and to prescribe remedies. Known as the Seditious Activities Investigating Commission, this panel heard friendly anti-Communists testify behind closed doors. One witness claimed that public libraries befriended communism: "The Marx books are too numerous." But the panelists paid primary heed to subversion in the universities. They assumed that Red teachers treated "foreign isms" preferentially in the classroom, even though their investigator found no proof of such practices.

In 1949, without holding public hearings, Broyles sponsored several bills, including one to punish Communists or those who subscribed to their programs. The bills sparked protests by college students, which in turn scandalized the legislators. When a Springfield eatery refused to serve black students, some white students held a sit-in. One solon declared he had never seen "such a dirty, greasy bunch of kids." Indignantly, the Seditious Activities Investigating Commission held public hearings to assess the loyalty of the faculties of the University of Chicago and Roosevelt College.

In President Robert M. Hutchins of the University of Chicago, the commission met its match. Hutchins managed both to defend his faculty's loyalty and to ensnare the bumbling inquisitors with his wit. His professors, he said, were not Communists; those who had joined "so-called 'Communist front' organizations" ought not to be assumed guilty by association. The nation's instititions faced danger "not from the tiny minority who do not believe in them" but from the growing "miasma of thought-control" abroad in the land.

To interrogate Hutchins the commission specially imported J. B. Matthews, a busy expert on communism who had worked for the Dies Committee and the Hearst papers. For Broyles he itemized the "front" memberships of Hutchins's faculty. He singled out one retired professor who had worked with mice in cancer research. From her position of prestige, Matthews wondered, might she not have been capable of "indoctrination by example?" "Of mice?" Hutchins riposted, amid laughter from the audience.

Not all educators defended their turf so ably. Southern Illinois University's president concluded that academics "may have to admit that now it is time for indoctrination in the American way of life." The president of Western Illinois State College asserted that his faculty numbered only two "liberalists [*sic*]." One, having been "reported," angrily resigned; as for the other, "we are not employing this man next year."

These hearings may have raised pressures for censorship, but they also discredited the Broyles Commission. The legislature neither renewed the panel nor enacted its program. (Governors Adlai Stevenson and William Stratton would veto subsequent measures sponsored by Broyles.) The commission's ineptness rather than any general public outrage with its performance probably explained its failure to have a more lasting impact on Illinois political life. [21]

Washington's state legislature more enduringly forwarded the second Red Scare. The state had both a long tradition of redbaiting and an active leftist community. In the 1930s, Communists figured importantly in such groups as the Washington Commonwealth Federation and Pension Union, and many University of Washington faculty took part in these and various United Front causes. Redbaiting flavored the 1946 election in Washington as Republicans—and some Democrats— charged that the Democratic Party had fallen under Communist sway. A committee on un-American activities was created and chaired by Republican Assemblyman Albert F. Canwell. In July 1948 the Canwell Committee focused on the Communist affiliations of ten University of Washington professors; five conceded past CP membership; two denied it; and three men who refused to testify were later dismissed by the university after lengthy proceedings. These firings of professors accused of being Communists, the first formally acknowledged as such in the Cold War years, set an important precedent.

Despite the scalps it could claim, the Canwell Committee had a brief life. Canwell and two other members lost bids for either higher office or reelection in 1948. The committee's legislative proposals, which included a loyalty oath for welfare recipients, were rejected, and the inquiry was not renewed in 1949. Later developments in the case of Professor Melvin Rader stigmatized the inquiry. A philosophy professor, Rader was falsely accused of communism and of attending a Party training school. Although he managed to refute the charges and the testimony of the professional ex-Communist witnesses who named him, it was later revealed that the Canwell Committee had concealed evidence which would have exonerated him sooner.[22]

Oklahoma had tussled sporadically with the Red menace since the late 1930s. In 1940 two "sixth columns"—the Sooner state's answer to the fifth columm—were founded to rout un-Americanism and subversion, and several politicians speculated that the state's colleges harbored Communists. In 1941 a State Senate committee investigated Communist activities, chiefly at the universities. The probers left little to subtlety. One witness was asked how he had voted in 1940; another, if he attended church. The panel's report lambasted past efforts by Communists and "unamerican liberal minded crackpots" at the University of Oklahoma but gave the latter and the state colleges a generally clean bill of health. The committee espied "a large amount of communistic influence" in some of Oklahoma's "laboring organizations."

In 1949, stirred by a radical guest editorial in the Oklahoma University newspaper, the legislature's lower house enacted a loyalty oath for both teachers and students. Angered by opposition on campus, it next voted to sniff out communism in higher education. The proceedings were enlivened by such questions as: "Where was you borned at?" Under criticism from colleagues, the investigators cut off the hearings quickly and wrote an innocuous report. However, with strong American Legion support, the legislature in 1951 replaced an earlier loyalty oath with a more stringent one, which applied to every public employee in the state. In 1952 the U.S. Supreme Court struck it down, reasoning that its sanctions against those who joined groups on the Attorney General's list without knowing the groups' aims violated due process. An oath that mended this flaw was passed in 1953.[23]

Michigan's hunt for subversion went through several phases. In 1947 the State Senate established a committee that for two years chiefly probed leftism on university campuses. Legislators passed the Callahan Act to control actions of foreign agents in the Wolverine State. Some wry observers wondered if this law might not catch such entities as the Catholic Church or Boy Scouts in its meshes. The Attorney General declined to enforce it, so it remained a dead letter. In 1950 Republican State Senators established a Senate Loyalty Commission to assay the loyalty of state employees. [24]

Maryland added in legislative vigor what it lacked in investigative zeal. After attorney Frank B. Ober decried the loose rein granted Maryland Communists, he was asked to chair a commission to solve the problem in 1948. The resultant Ober Law borrowed freely from the Smith Act, the federal loyalty program, and Karl Mundt's and Richard Nixon's bill to register the members of "Communist" organizations. It outlawed seeking the forcible overthrow of government, advocacy of that end which posed a "clear and present danger," and participation in subversive organizations. Each public employee or political candidate had to certify that he or she had abided by these requirements; a state loyalty program was created. Admiringly Karl Mundt termed the law "as full of teeth as an alligator's jaw." All but one lawmaker voted for it. He lost his bid for reelection, and over three of every four voters endorsed the law in a referendum.

Other states copied Maryland—Mississippi in 1950, New Hampshire and Washington in 1951. Elsewhere, new wrinkles were added. In 1949 Ohio made recipients of unemployment compensation take a loyalty oath. Pennsylvania ruled all subversives, except those who were blind, to be ineligible for public aid. Michigan's 1952 Trucks Act swept Communists from the ballot and public employment, made them and their organizatons register, and declared a public employee's use of the Fifth Amendment to be tantamount to admitting disloyalty. Texas lawmakers enacted an oath for college faculty and students in 1949 and formally recognized a "Communist Threat to the United States" as exceeding that posed by our enemies in World War II. In 1951 Texas enacted a Communist registration law. [25]

Cities also leaped to arms. In 1947 Los Angeles County required employees to avow that they belonged to no subversive groups; the City of Los Angeles followed suit in 1948. Detroit amended its charter in 1949 to create an elaborate loyalty program. The process began when a city official charged that 150 municipal employees were Reds and warned that cities were "far more important in the Communist take-over plan than the Federal government." Other local pols and the *Detroit News* took up the cry; voters approved the program by over three to one. In 1949 Saginaw, Michigan, and Columbus, Ohio, enacted loyalty oaths. In 1948 New York City's mayor purged some 150 adherents of the left-wing American Labor Party from the city payroll. Most municipal loyalty programs had scant effect, but New York's, by one estimate, sacked over half the total number of city employees fired nationwide for disloyalty in the next decade.

Redbaiting tinted city politics. It had figured in Detroit campaigns since the 1930s; in 1945 the GOP mayoral aspirant warned that his Communist-backed foe would make Detroit a "guinea pig" for radical experiments. Russell Root, Chicago's 1947 Republican mayoral candidate, called the election a vote "for or against Communism." (Root lost.) In Cincinnati, Republicans opposed the city's charter form of government, arguing that its complicated proportional representation system would permit Communists to win seats on the city council as they had in New York.[26]

In both their causes and their consequences, these state and local anti-subversion campaigns constituted a mixed bag. The presence of a strong Left or of a radical tradition sometimes accounted for the existence of a resurgent Right, as in Michigan, California, Washington, and New York. Local business organizations, Catholic groups (especially in New York and Maryland), and veterans groups cried out for action against communism. The American Legion played an important role, especially in Oklahoma and Illinois. Conservative newspapers (as in Seattle, Detroit, and Los Angeles) did much to stir up concern about communism.

Similarly, areas with a history of militant unionism bred political antibodies; in the proper time and circumstances, labor's opponents could ply the Communist issue effectively, as in Michigan. Conservative forces also arose within labor's ranks. Dave Beck, the Seattle Teamsters leader, happily fostered local anti-communism to help in his struggle with his enemies, Harry Bridges and the ILWU. The United Public Workers of America (UPWA), eventually booted from the CIO on charges of pro-communism, had adversaries in the labor movement that included the AFL's American Federation of State, County, and Municipal Employees. In Michigan, the AFCSME advocated a loyalty program for government employees, knowing the advantages that might accrue in its rivalry with the UPWA. The UPWA also served as a prominent target for political leaders in New York, Detroit, and Chicago.

Yet these generalizations do not always fit the events. A strong political Right could coexist with—and explain the plight of—weak unions. Mississippi passed a stringent anti-Communist law, but had no labor movement and, according to J. Edgar Hoover, only one CP member inside its borders. Despite a tradition of political ferment, Wisconsin (except for a brief flurry in the 1930s) avoided a state-level red scare. Milwaukee elected Socialist Frank Zeidler as mayor in 1948 and kept him until 1960. The University of Wisconsin enjoyed a freedom from political interference denied to most other Midwestern universities.

Some likely locations for anti-Communist exertions proved remarkably unproductive. Indiana had conservative political leaders and a powerful American Legion (whose national headquarters were in Indianapolis). From 1949 on, the Indiana Legion drafted bills to initiate an anti-Communist investigation and even offered to subsidize it. Only belatedly, in 1957, did the legislature authorize such a panel but gave it no subpoena power or funds. Among Hoosier lawmakers, fiscal may have outweighed ideological conservatism. In 1951 the Iowa legislature rejected a shotgun loyalty measure.[27]

Political ambition had much to do with state and local redbaiting. The brass ring glimmered with special brightness to Albert Canwell and Jack Tenney. Yet bush-league anti-Communists seldom enjoyed dramatic political advancement. Tenney went to the State Senate in 1942, but seven years later he lost control of California's Un-American Activities Committee; his subsequent political ventures all failed. Sam Yorty, once Tenney's comrade-in-arms, later distanced himself but abandoned neither anti-communism nor ambition. He went to Congress and became mayor of Los Angeles. Canwell lost a race for the Washington State Senate in 1948; two members of his committee were not reelected. Moreover, State Senator Matthew Callahan, sponsor of Michigan's foreign-agent law, was not renominated in 1948. Some states produced skimpy legislative results: the wilder the investigation, it seemed, the smaller the legal end-product. The Broyles Commission in Illinois illustrates this inverse correlation, the Ober Law in Maryland its converse.

Did such local activity flow spontaneously from the grassroots, or was it a response to actions in Washington, D.C.? Sometimes national events played a role. The Dies Committee inspired Tenney; Canwell and Broyles consulted congenially with HUAC. Federal laws and regulations offered models for states and cities; the Attorney General's list rang with authority to local politicians establishing loyalty criteria. Perhaps most important, state probers used expert witnesses whose national credentials gave the proceedings the proper gloss. The Canwell Committee heard J. B. Matthews, Howard Rushmore, Manning Johnson, and George Hewitt, all busy as witnesses before congressional committees and executive agencies. (Rushmore even made charges against Alger Hiss—two weeks before Whittaker Chambers's testimony to HUAC.) The Broyles Commission used Rushmore, Matthews, and Ben Gitlow. As Walter Gellhorn has noted in his study *The States and Subversion*, these professional witnesses rushed about like lecturers on the Chautauqua circuit.

Yet more striking than the derivative nature of state-level anti-communism was its strong local flavor. The year 1947 was pivotal for federal government commitments to anti-communism at home and abroad, but major investigations in California and New York predated them. States did not rely solely on the national model; they learned much from each other. The motion to create Canwell's committee drew on Tenney's California precursor. Maryland's Ober Law was much copied. At Jack Tenney's invitation, ten states sent conferees to the Interstate Legislative Conference on Un-American Activities held in Los Angeles in September 1948. The delegates focused more upon seeking uniform procedures in all the states than upon a federal solution.

On balance, these state exertions show a broad-based concern with communism around the country. They reveal emphases somewhat different from national anti-Communist politics. Most notably, state politicos worried more—or at least sooner—about communism in the schools than did their national counterparts, but that was understandable since education lay in their realm.

These state activities also show that anti-communism was not simply the concoction of the Truman Administration, although local politicos often did take cues from Washington. For example, in Hawaii, whose territorial governor the President appointed, the roots of the anti-Communist campaign that began in 1947 correlated closely with events in the nation's capital. (There was plenty of local motivation, however: conservatve economic interests confronted a radical threat from the Longshoremen's Union, some of whose leaders were Communists.) Yet while state and local political leaders did respond to Washington's initiatives, they were themselves quite capable of reaching an active, anti-Communist perspective on national and world events without the intermediation of national leaders.[28]

By 1949 signals of the salience of anti-communism were transmitted from active constituents and from local and state leaders as well as from the nation's capital. Average citizens might hear the message of anti-communism in their school or union, church or civic organization, and pervasively in popular culture. They would increasingly find it in the national political headlines.

THE OUTBREAK of fighting in Korea on June 25, 1950, gave staying power to the Communist issue. The war began grimly as hastily sent troops were soon driven into a small enclave, but in September General Douglas MacArthur led a risky landing at Inchon, flanked the North Korean invaders, and nutcrackered them northward. As U.N. forces galloped well past the 38th parallel dividing North from South Korea and neared the Yalu River on the Chinese border, the Chinese became alarmed. They gave notice that they would resist further encroachment on their border. In October they aimed a warning punch, but Mac-Arthur and Washington discounted it. In November the Chinese attacked en masse. The U.N. troops were isolated, overwhelmed, and chased south under the gathering mantle of winter.

The retreat lasted until 1951; a new front held below South Korea's capital and inched painfully north to roughly the original parallel. For two more years, the "police action" went on—bloody meatgrinder battles to capture a hill, often only to lose it to a "human wave" attack. At home patience ebbed. Though Communist aggression had been repelled and a military form of containment had worked, Truman's policy did not allay growing discontent. Americans thought they were destined to win wars quick and clean, not to bleed and die in nameless skirmishes on a stalemated front.

The Korean War drastically narrowed the nation's limited tolerance of political dissent. As Congress stampeded to enact repressive law, the President called the atmosphere of repression "the worst it had been since the Alien and Sedition laws of 1798." Yet federal officials themselves played a leading role in snuffing dissent. They took such actions as requesting the lifting of Paul Robeson's passport and the revocation of bail for union leader Harry Bridges and the *Dennis* defendants.

113

These steps only fed the growing public distemper and sense of danger in the grim first months of the Korean War.

States rushed to act. Michigan Governor G. Mennen Williams had opposed right-wing proposals, but Korea sapped his resistance. The legislature passed several bills and created a state red squad. A 1951 measure nullified any will making a bequest to a subversive cause. A 1952 law ordered Communists to register with the state of Michigan, but the courts struck it down. Ohio's legislature established a little Un-American Activities Committee, which in 1952 accused one witness of being insane. A judge sent him to a mental hospital, but two weeks later the order was reversed. Indiana's Executive Branch mandated "voluntary" loyalty oaths for its employees. In 1951 subversives were barred from state jobs. The Hoosier state, vowed one legislator, would be no "sanctuary for Communists." Massachusetts' search for subversion did not gain momentum until 1953. In that year, New Hampshire eschewed a committee but charged its Attorney General with investigative functions.

Cities adopted loyalty programs and erected novel defenses. In July the Birmingham, Alabama, city council gave Communists and their associates forty-eight hours to leave town. Macon, Georgia, followed suit. The Lafayette, Indiana, council banned advocacy of "the political ideology known as communism." Evansville's forbade Communists or adherents of their ideology to enter, live, or work in that city. (The mayor vetoed the measure.) New Rochelle, New York, McKeesport, Pennsylvania, and other embattled burgs acted to make resident Communists register with the authorities. In many towns, Communist leafleters or circulators of the Stockholm Peace Petition were often hassled by the police or fellow citizens.[29]

Courts took judicial notice of the Korean crisis. On August 1, 1950, the U.S. Court of Appeals, Second District, upheld the *Dennis* convictions, the decision written by civil libertarian Learned Hand. Invoking Justice Oliver Wendell Holmes's "clear and present danger" doctrine of 1919, Hand cited the events of the Cold War leading up to the trial in 1949. In June 1951, the Supreme Court accepted Hand's formula, alluding to the "inflammable nature" of current world conditions. Citing the fevered state of public opinion in his dissent, Justice Hugo Black hoped that "in calmer times, when present pressures, passions and fears subside, this or some later Court will restore the First Amendment liberties to the high preferred place where they belong in a free society."

In 1952 Felix Frankfurter advised fellow Justice Robert Jackson to soften the language of an opinion on some deportation cases. "A bit of blue can color a whole tub of water; a bit of anti-Communist harangue . . . will be put to uses far from your own wisdom of action by people who have none of your scrupulosity."

Korea expanded use of the legal system against the Left. After Hand's *Dennis* ruling, the Justice Department got the defendants' bail revoked, arguing that they should not be free "in this hour of national crisis." Harry Bridges's bail also was lifted. A Brooklyn jurist meted out lengthy jail terms to five people who painted "peace" signs in Prospect Park. After the Supreme Court decided *Dennis*, the Justice Department prosecuted the Party's "second string" under the Smith Act. Thus, in June 1951, the FBI bagged seventeen Communists in New York City. In July, fifteen were indicted in California; in August, six in Maryland; then six in Pennsylvania; and seven in Hawaii. Another round-up occurred during the 1952 presidential campaign. The defendants found attorneys hard to hire. Communist leader Steve Nelson had some seventy-five lawyers turn down his request for legal representation.

The trial most deeply shadowed by Korea was that of Julius and Ethel Rosenberg, who were charged with conspiracy to steal and pass atomic secrets to the Soviets. Many writers insist that the two were framed as Cold War scapegoats. Yet as authors Ronald Radosh and Joyce Milton have cogently argued, Julius was no hapless "progressive" entrapped by government scheming and by the perjured testimony of his brother-in-law, David Greenglass. A Party activist until entering "secret work," he was deeply involved in a spy ring. His wife knew what he did and may have been an accomplice. Pursuing a trail leading from Klaus Fuchs, the German-born physicist who in February 1950 confessed to spying for the Russians, the FBI arrested Julius the following July. On weaker evidence, Ethel was picked up in August. Her arrest, prosecution, and death sentence were designed to pry a confession from Julius. This bloody gambit failed. Despite worldwide protest and after various appeals and stays, the Rosenbergs were electrocuted on June 19, 1953.

The Rosenbergs were indeed scapegoats, but not innocent ones. At the same time, the FBI, Justice Department, and Judge Irving Kaufman were guilty of misconduct that beclouded the trial. The Korean War quickened the rush to capital punishment. Kaufman termed the crime "worse than murder," for, he argued (wrongly), "Years before our best scientists predicted Russia would perfect the bomb," the couple gave it to them. This act "has already caused . . . the Communist aggression in Korea . . . and who knows but what that millions more innocent people may pay the price of your treason."[30]

Korea made passage of a federal anti-Communist law inevitable. That 1950 summer's "tragic days" compelled even Senator Wayne Morse, often a civil libertarian, to espouse a "drastic" anti-Communist law. The measure likeliest to pass was a toughened version of the 1948 Mundt-Nixon bill. Now known as the Mundt–Ferguson–Johnston bill, it would make Communist and Communist-front groups register with the Attorney General. Emanuel Celler of the House Judiciary Committee tried to stall but expected "terrible pressure." Senate Majority Leader Scott Lucas also dawdled, but Korea and his own reelection fight in Illinois tested him sorely. Gleefully Karl Mundt told Lucas's Republican foe Everett Dirksen of reports from Illinois suggesting "that if you can keep the feet of Brother Lucas on the hot fires of Communism . . . you should be able to walk in standing up."

Truman felt heat too. He had long opposed extremist measures, but the reflexive anti-communism of members of his administration complicated his task. At times Truman's emissaries stated his opposition to a bill only to learn that the Justice Department had endorsed it. The war wiped out Truman's scant leverage over internal-security policy. His staff decided that, to block the Mundt–Ferguson–Johnston bill, they needed an alternative. It was hard, said one aide, "to beat something with nothing." On August 8, Truman submitted to Congress a measure to mandate stiffer treatment of espionage and deportable aliens.[31]

Two days later, Democratic Senator Pat McCarran trumped the White House by introducing S. 4037, which combined his own shotgun bill against alien Communists with the Mundt–Ferguson–Johnston bill and several other proposals. The House version breezed to passage. The White House bill was such weak tea next to these strong spirits that seven liberal Democratic Senators offered a more potent measure to authorize, in a national emergency, interning those deemed likely to engage in sabotage or espionage. It was swiftly labeled the "concentration camp bill."

Next ensued one of the era's most pathetic charades, as liberals sought to dose the Right with its own anti-Communist medicine. Lucas tried first to amend McCarran's S. 4037 by substituting the liberal Senators' detention bill for the registration provision. When that maneuver was defeated, he attempted simply to add the detention bill to the unmodified S. 4037; again he failed. Then Senator Harley Kilgore, a cosponsor of the detention bill, tried to substitute it for McCarran's measure. Both sides indulged in bizarre posturing. Vaunting the toughness of the detention bill, Hubert Humphrey derided S. 4037 as a "cream-puff special." McCarran retorted that the liberals' bill was "not workable under any of the accepted standards of Americanism" and violated the Fifth and Sixth Amendments—if not others. However, after Lucas rounded up more votes and safeguards were written into the measure, the Senate passed the McCarran bill—with emergency detention—by a 70-to-7 vote.

Though allies in Congress urged Truman to sign the bill, it violated his libertarian sensitivities, and he vetoed it. It would, he said, only help the Communists, not hurt them; it mocked the Bill of Rights; and it put government in the "business of thought control." The House briskly overrode the veto, 248 to 48. In the Senate, a few critics filibustered. William Langer, a Republican maverick from North Dakota, orated until he fainted from exhaustion. The Senate voted 57 to 10 to override. Many legislators knew of the bill's perils but declined to risk leaving an impression of lukewarm anti-communism. Whatever fault may be found with other aspects of Truman's defense of civil liberties against reckless anti-communism, his forthright veto of the McCarran bill was a proud moment.

Having lost the battle, Truman now had to enforce the Internal Security Act, as the McCarran Act was formally known. Title I of the law determined that the U.S. "Communist organization" was a "clear and present danger" to national security, but that Party membership per se was not a crime. The officers—or failing that, members—of Communist-action and front groups were required to register with the Attorney General. A Subversive Activities Control Board (SACB) would decide which groups would be covered under these strictures. The law also barred covered individuals from government or defense jobs or from holding passports; tightened espionage laws; denied entrance to aliens who had ever belonged to Communist or totalitarian parties or advocated the violent overthrow of government; banned obstructive picketing of federal courts (as at the Dennis trial); and more. Title II mandated detention of likely spies and saboteurs during an internal-security emergency declared by the President. Detainees could make appeals to a review board, however.

The McCarran Act soon got tangled in the politics of anti-communism. Conservatives blocked two Truman appointees to the Subversive Activities Control Board, including chairman-designate Seth Richardson, a rock-ribbed Republican. As head of the Loyalty Review Board, Richardson had displeased the flintier conservatives. Unconfirmed, he resigned from the board in 1951.

In November 1950, the SACB began proceedings to show that the Communist Party must register. The Party won delays; the hearings took over a year; finally, in 1953, the SACB ruled that the CP did have to register. Then came years of appeals and rearguments. The Supreme Court upheld the constitutionality of registration in 1961. When the CP did not comply, ten leaders were indicted. However, in 1963 a U.S. Court of Appeals determined that the government had found no Party official who could register without thereby laying himself open to prosecution under the Smith Act. In 1964 the Supreme Court declined to review the case. Thus no group ever registered under the McCarran Act. If the aim was to harass the CPUSA with legal proceedings, the law was a success, but probably its authors were not so Machiavellian.

Title II of the McCarran Act also rang hollowly. No internal-security emergency was ever invoked, but when the Bureau of Prisons readied six detention sites (old POW and military camps) just in case, some people were frightened. Senator Morse reassured them that "standby facilities are being prepared only as a precautionary measure." The Internal Security Act produced several ironies, and one of them involved the American Legion. The Legion led the cry for anti-Communist legislation, but a Legion post in California protested the Tule Lake camp because it was too close to an elementary school. Although after 1957 appropriations ended and five of the sites were sold or leased, the persistence of a law mandating detention without arraignment, bail, or jury trial troubled civil libertarians, and the law remained a monument to the fear-ridden atmosphere of the early months of the Korean War.[32]

The period 1949–54 marked the nadir of civil liberties during the Cold War. Not coincidentally, these years bracketed the Korean War, which produced a military stalemate that chafed steadily at the American temper. The era witnessed bitter, scarring political conflict. American politics is often bruising, but political comity was particularly lacking in those times. They were ripe for a quintessential demagogue to carry the Communist issue to its ultimate extremity. That man, Joseph R. Mc-

Carthy, gave his name to the era. However, it is important to note that the anxieties of the Cold War, culminating in the Korean crisis, and the pressures building at all levels of politics and in the life of the nation's major public institutions would guarantee that this period—with or without McCarthy—would be a grim one.

5

The Age Finds Its Name

FEBRUARY 1950 was Joseph R. McCarthy's moment. On the heels of 1949's jolts, news stories datelined London, February 3, revealed that the German-born physicist Klaus Fuchs had confessed to spying for the Soviets while working on the Manhattan Project. Early accounts suggested (incorrectly) that thanks to Fuchs the Soviets had passed the United States in the race for the hydrogen bomb; one story even claimed he had betrayed the secret of a "hormone ray" that had the potential to "feminize" enemy troops. On February 6, Republican leaders issued a campaign tract scoring the Democrats for tolerating disloyalty in government and the theft of vital secrets. Now all that was needed to put the anti-Red crusade into high gear was a politician ready to commit himself with reckless, career-dominating totality to the Communist issue. The junior Senator from Wisconsin would fill this role.

Like much of his life, McCarthy's discovery of communism is enshrouded in legend. Story has it that three fellow Catholics took the irresponsible young Senator in hand at dinner on January 7, 1950. They canvassed issues he might use politically, communism came up, and Joe eagerly grabbed it. His February 9 speech at a Lincoln Day celebration in Wheeling, West Virginia, allegedly marked his first speculation in anti-communism. This tale intrigued McCarthy's foes. It spotlighted his boundless opportunism and belated awareness of the

120

Communist threat; it even hinted that his crusade had been germinated by the Catholic Church's obsessive anti-communism—by a bargain-basement Popish Plot.

Yet this dinner did not introduce McCarthy to communism. He had redbaited casually as early as 1946. Late in 1949, he attacked a critical home-state newspaper as a Communist "mouthpiece." In the weeks before Wheeling, McCarthy jabbed at those who had "lost" China, sabotaged American foreign policy, and winked at the presence of subversives like Alger Hiss. Still, some such dinner did occur, and it may have helped Joe make the cognitive leap toward realizing more fully that communism was a viable national issue.[1]

McCarthy's capture of the Communist issue contained elements of both chance and choice. He had not just to use but to seize it; other Republicans had to accept his claim; and the Democrats had, in effect, to ratify his ownership by singling him out for attack. None of these was preordained, however. If McCarthy were factored out of the equation, the features of the age named for him would have looked much the same. Even so, the might-have-beens surrounding the beginning of McCarthy's crusade are worth some attention.

When he left on his Lincoln Day speaking tour, McCarthy did not go to Wheeling committed to a campaign, let alone a career, of decrying communism. Angling for any issues in early 1950 that would promote his political career, he toyed briefly with crime and with pensions for the elderly. Advance publicity touted him as an expert on pensions; about Reds it said nothing. He arrived with two speeches—one on housing, one on communism. His host advised him to use the latter. Before dinner, McCarthy reworked that speech, which had been assembled for him by a Washington newsman out of snippets from recent anti-Communist speeches and articles. Thus was history bent.

Despite his previous dabbling, McCarthy came late to the Red menace. Asked when he had discovered it, he allegedly said (perhaps in April 1950): "about two-and-a-half months ago." After February 9, he was briefed by experts, including Richard Nixon, Styles Bridges, J. Edgar Hoover, congressional staffers, and journalists. He once dumbfounded his mentors by professing ignorance of Earl Browder, former head of the CP. One tutor recalled that Joe "didn't know a Communist from a street cleaner." He absorbed the lore quickly, but his hasty preparation often betrayed him, disturbed those whose tips he abused, and encouraged foes to see in him an easy target.[2]

Critics soon uncovered many ethical shortcuts in McCarthy's past. Once a gung-ho Democrat, he coolly switched parties. He first won office as a Wisconsin circuit court judge after lying about his rival's age. Contrary to the state constitution, he twice ran for Senator without resigning his judgeship; he improperly campaigned in 1944 while still a Marine—with funds from stockmarket profits on which he did not pay taxes. As a Senator he caddied for such interests as Pepsi bottlers (he opposed sugar price controls), realtors (he battled public housing), and pro-Nazi constituents (he assailed the Army's harsh handling of the German killers of some eighty American soldiers in the 1944 Malmédy massacre during the Battle of the Bulge).

McCarthy's early career had ugly features, but it was less grotesque than the mythical version his enemies perpetuated. His youth did not, as such accounts suggest, reveal a brute in the making. He came from a close, loving family, firm in its Catholicism, committed to the work ethic. "Nobody starves in America," his mother used to say. His career embodied her belief in the American dream. After his brief success as a teenaged chicken farmer ended in disaster, McCarthy ran a grocery store in Manawa, Wisconsin. Helped by a friendly principal and teachers, sustained by relentless energy and ambition, he mastered high school in one year. At Marquette University, he earned a degree in law and practiced for several years.

Smitten by politics, Joe toiled for the Democrats, lost a race for district attorney, and edged calculatingly toward the Republican Party. His tireless campaign won him a circuit judgeship in 1939. The lie about his opponent's age augured things to come but had modest immediate effect. The sitting judge, though not ancient, was old, stubborn, and unpopular with attorneys in his circuit, who applauded McCarthy's victory.

When war came, Joe joined the Marines as a first lieutenant (not, as he later boasted, as a private); earned promotion to captain; flew several times as a tailgunner (as a lark, not a duty); and embroidered his service record—apparently even forging a letter of commendation. Home on leave in 1944, he unsuccessfully sought the GOP nomination for U.S. Senator in an irregular, mysteriously financed campaign. Resigning his commission in late 1944, he returned to the bench to seek the 1946 GOP senatorial nomination.

This time, despite resistance from party leaders, he won, edging Senator Robert M. La Follette, Jr., in the primary. Though a renowned statesman, "Young Bob" was vulnerable. He hardly campaigned. Democrats and conservative Republicans alike resented his return to the GOP, which he had quit in 1934. He even angered Communists by criticizing Soviet expansion. (Nursing the irony, foes later charged that McCarthy owed his election to the Reds. It is clear the Communists desired La Follette's defeat, but less so that they achieved it.) After the primary, McCarthy's campaign revealed his vast energy and engaging personality; the platitudes he mouthed left his ideology less certain. In November he creamed his Democratic opponent.

McCarthy's first years in the Senate, if less scandalous than critics imagined, did not burnish his reputation. By flouting Senate customs—the florid courtesies, the deference to seniority—he irritated powerful colleagues and earned their mistrust. By 1950 he had dismal committee posts, no record to impress constituents, and enemies and rivals whetting knives back in Wisconsin. He took up anti-communism in the nick of time.[3]

Joe's exact words in Wheeling are lost. Critics claimed he said: "I have here in my hand a list of 205 . . . a list of names that were made known to the Secretary of State and who nevertheless are still working and shaping the policy of the State Department." Never sure what he said, McCarthy denied saying *that*. Flying west, he scratched "205" from his speech, wrote in "57," and used that figure in later talks. The State Department acquired several documents tending to confirm the "205" version, but its evidence relied heavily on Joe's rough draft, not the delivered version of the speech. A local editor heard mention of "over fifty persons of known Communistic affiliations." Others recalled two numbers—one (smaller) referring to actual Reds, the other to security risks. McCarthy got the number 205 from a 1946 letter of then Secretary of State Jame F. Byrnes, who said that 79 of 285 security risks in his agency had been "separated." Simple but faulty math led Mc-Carthy to 205. In fact, he had no list at all—and was far out on a limb.

The State Department and the Democrats, long under fire on the Communist issue, saw a chance—or need—to make an object lesson of McCarthy. Perhaps that was why, from the torrents of Lincoln Day anti-Communist rhetoric, they singled out his. The State Department issued three denials of McCarthy's claims and demanded his "list," and on February 16, Truman asserted there was "not a word of truth" in the charges.

From the start, McCarthy was a media demagogue, thriving on an ability to seize and hold headlines. Mostly it was the artillery of the press, not swelling legions of followers, that sustained his campaign. What if the Democrats had ignored him—never danced the two-step of charge and denial? Unfortunately, that scenario would require the unlikely premise that the media also ignore McCarthy. Press coverage constricted the Democrats' choices. It was a United Press effort to get a response to a story by the Associated Press that first brought McCarthy's charges to the State Department's attention, and Truman was asked about them at his next news conference.

McCarthy sensed in mid-junket that the initiative was his. In every city on his tour, he tantalized reporters. They turned out in Denver and Los Angeles, even though he gave no speech at either city. His use of large and exact numbers may have stirred the interest of the press and the administration and prodded events along. In Milwaukee he boasted that he had "a sockful of shit"—and knew how to use it. Facing a narrow range of choices, and given the newspaper publicity and Joe's intention to seek more, it is not certain that the Democrats erred in paying him so much attention. They had no choice but to attack him in an effort to call his bluff.[4]

On February 20, McCarthy recited to the Senate what he claimed was his Wheeling speech. He fudged on which number he had used there. He also read excerpts from summaries of State Department loyalty files sampled by a House committee three years earlier, before Truman's order that these dossiers be kept secret. These summaries, which disclosed no names, constituted the so-called "Lee list" (after the chief investigator, Robert E. Lee). While there were 108 case summaries in the list, McCarthy purported to discuss only eighty-one (actually fewer, given omissions and repetitions). He changed the wording to make the cases sound more sinister and implied that they were hot new data slipped to him by "good loyal Americans." (A few Republican colleagues were aware of McCarthy's source—and hence of the shell game he was playing.) The ensuing debate signified that the Communist issue had become hopelessly mired in partisan politics. This simple, inescapable fact governed the political dynamic of the "McCarthy years."

Both parties called for an investigation. Republicans demanded that the probers gain access to the loyalty files, by subpoena if need be. They thus hoped to crack Truman's 1948 order denying such files to Congress. A subcommittee of the Foreign Relations Committee took up the inquiry under the chairmanship of Democrat Millard Tydings, a Senate veteran who had survived Roosevelt's effort to "purge" him in 1938. Brien McMahon and Theodore F. Green, both Democrats of stature, and Republicans Bourke Hickenlooper, an Iowa conservative as well as McCarthy ally, and Henry Cabot Lodge, Jr., a Massachusetts internationalist and moderate, filled out the panel.

At the first subcommittee hearing on March 8, the Democrats went for a knockout, attacking a contradiction in Joe's charges. Tempers flared. Thus was set a tone of partisan rancor that lasted throughout the hearings. McCarthy's leaps from one filmsy "case" to the next understandably exasperated the Democrats, but their gunslinging approach hurt their cause and lent at least surface plausibility to charges that they sought a "whitewash." No matter how baseless McCarthy's charges or endless his evasions were, the Tydings probe never escaped that damaging label.

McCarthy ducked the eighty-one cases—he still had no names. He made new charges instead. Those he named—Dorothy Kenyon, Esther and Stephen Brunauer, Haldore Hanson, Gustavo Duran, Owen Lattimore, Harlow Shapley, Frederick Schuman, John Stewart Service, and Philip Jessup—were a mixed bag. Not all currently worked at the State Department; some, like academicians Shapley and Schuman, never had; Kenyon's connection was tenuous; Ambassador Jessup was a major figure.

All had been butts of past Republican charges. Duran's troubles stemmed from the Spanish Civil War; because he fought for the Republic, Franco's intelligence service falsely labeled him a Communist. He was not a State Department employee in 1950. Nor was Kenyon (who had been a delegate to a U.N. commission). McCarthy said she had joined twenty-eight suspect organizations, but only four were on the Attorney General's list, just one of them while she was a member. That several of his targets had been in Asia revealed that McCarthy had joined in the ongoing wake for the loss of China. He had early, crucial help from members of the so-called China Lobby.

McCarthy's early charges made little headway and stirred skepticism in the press and among colleagues. He alarmed many Republican moderates, but conservatives foresaw political dividends and lent support. Senator Styles Bridges gravely warned that a nameless "master spy" who had given Hiss orders was still in government. Bob Taft, though highly dubious of McCarthy, reportedly told Joe to "keep talking and if one case doesn't work he should proceed with another." The delicate interlock—balanced like a Calder mobile—between Republican and Democratic partisan interests, and between GOP rightists and moderates, saved McCarthy from early defeat. But the loyalty of even the conservatives was contingent: success would bring cheers and rewards; if Joe flopped, he could be disowned.[5]

Ever the gambler, McCarthy took a huge risk to regain momentum. He said he would "stand or fall" on the single case of a "top Russian spy." After a series of teasing news leaks, he identified the figure as Owen Lattimore. On March 30, though conceding that he had overplayed the espionage charge, McCarthy called Lattimore the " 'architect' of our far eastern policy."

A journalist and academic expert on China and Central Asia, Lattimore had had only intermittent ties with the State Department: service on the Japanese reparations commission, one State Department lecture and one seminar. He had also gone with Henry Wallace to China in 1944, had briefly been an adviser to Jiang Jieshi, and had worked in the Office of War Information. Earlier he had edited the journal of the Institute of Pacific Relations. The China Lobby believed IPR to be riddled with Communists who had invented the blasphemy that Mao's forces were mere agrarian reformers. Lattimore returned blow for blow. He charged McCarthy with lying and serving as a conduit for the China Lobby. The fiction of espionage could scarcely have come from even a "perverted mind." When Lattimore finished testifying, he was informed that a summary of his FBI file, which had been made available to the committee, put him in the clear.

McCarthy rebounded by producing Louis Budenz, who said he had heard CP leaders refer to Lattimore as a Communist and seen "onionskin documents" in which the Asian expert was listed in code. Though to call Lattimore a spy was "not technically accurate," he had had the key job of charting the Party line that China's Reds were agrarian reformers. Budenz, a founder of the troubling new profession of ex-Communist witnesses, was not very convincing. Neither his onionskins nor his hearsay evidence could be confirmed. The FBI had debriefed him for thousands of hours, but oddly he did not mention Lattimore until just a few days prior to testifying before the committee.

Yet Budenz's story prompted new doubts about Lattimore. It shook even the State Department's chief anti-McCarthy spokesman, John Peurifoy. "My guess," he confided, "is that Lattimore is guilty, but

McCarthy can't prove it, anymore than we can." Lattimore again defended himself briskly, but he did not escape unscathed. No policy "architect" or spy, he was no mere academic innocent either. As a scholar and gadfly, he had followed the "progressive" line on China and Russia, and some foolish utterances (including an effort to justify the Soviet purges in 1938) returned to haunt him. As an editor and wartime official, he engaged in maneuvers that, while hardly evidence of a Red plot, dimmed his reputation for scholarly dispassion.

The prospect of exposing another "Hiss" and of renewing the China inquest intrigued Republicans. The rest of the Tydings Committee's hearings dealt mostly with Lattimore and with collateral charges that the China Hands had betrayed U.S. interests in Asia. Tydings was also pressured into reexamining the 1945 *Amerasia* episode.[6] Although the Democrats on the Tydings Committee eventually exonerated Lattimore, suspicions about him and about the China Hands lingered. In 1951–52 the Senate Internal Security Subcommittee would give them closer scrutiny and thus impart a certain rebound velocity to McCarthy's flimsy accusations.

Though McCarthy could not confirm his charges against Lattimore, the Democrats had a hard time proving the negative—Lattimore's innocence. On balance, the Lattimore episode raised McCarthy's standing among newsmen, GOP colleagues, and apparently the public. Polls in April 1950 showed that those who had followed his charges (about 70 percent) sided with McCarthy by a 4-to-3 margin—not overwhelming, but substantial support. Money, usually in small donations but totaling thousands of dollars, poured into his office.

McCarthy's appeal worried Democrats and made urgent Tydings's pleas that the President let his committee see the loyalty dossiers of McCarthy's eighty-one cases. Publicly Truman upheld his two-year-old policy of refusal, but he told his legislative leaders that he would reserve judgment. For the record, Tydings issued subpoenas and Truman ignored them, but as political seepage continued, Tydings and the State Department convinced Truman to reconsider. In May he yielded, allowing the subcommittee to examine the eighty-one files.[7]

This tedious work did not bring rescue. Hickenlooper and Lodge complained about the terms of access—the files had to be read at the White House—and soon bailed out. Only McMahon and Tydings read every file. Sensing that they could get loose of the tarbaby only by assigning the loyalty issue to a body less entangled in partisanship than

127

their panel, they urged Truman to name a blue-ribbon committee to examine the eighty-one cases. Facing reelection, Tydings was feeling heat from his constituents.

Variations of this scheme had won growing support—first from moderate Republicans, then anxious Democrats. Even before McCarthy's advent, some Truman aides had lobbied for such a program. Truman chafed at the idea, which struck him as irregular and extreme, but the hemorrhaging Communist issue gave him pause. On June 22, he convened a meeting to consider creating a Commission on Internal Security and Individual Rights. Tydings and McMahon again warned that their investigation could not escape the trap of partisanship. Opinions about the efficacy of the commission were divided, however, and the project was deferred. Indeed, the plan might never have worked to uncouple the loyalty issue from the express train of party politics, but June 1950 was probably the last chance to find out for sure. By the end of the month, the Korean War brought a press of other worries, and the 1950 congressional campaign, new bitterness.[8]

To cut their losses, the Democrats on the Tydings panel ended the inquiry and, over Republican protests, ordered that a report be drafted. The outbreak of war in Korea on June 25 seemed at first to offer a chance to close out the episode. Issued July 17, the Tydings Committee's majority report savagely indicted McCarthy. His charges were "a fraud and a hoax" and represented America's first experience with "the totalitarian technique of the 'big lie' employed on a sustained basis." "The result has been to confuse and divide the American people," while American blood was being shed in Korea, "to a degree far beyond the hopes of the Communists themselves. . . ."

On July 20, Tydings formally submitted the report to the Senate with an uncommonly bitter speech. He itemized McCarthy's lies and lack of evidence, defended the committee's inquiry and rebuked its critics. Republicans replied in kind. McCarthy said the report gave "a green light to the Red fifth column." His ally William Jenner called Tydings a "trained seal" guilty of "the most scandalous and brazen whitewash of treasonable conspiracy in our history." And so on. Three votes were taken on whether to accept the report, and on each, 100 percent party-line voting prevailed.

McCarthy had not been without critics in his own party, however, and among them was Maine's Senator Margaret Chase Smith, who assailed unnamed fellow Republicans for playing politics by "selfish exploitation of fear, bigotry, ignorance, and intolerance." Her "Declaration of Conscience," co-signed by six other Republicans, inspirited McCarthy's critics but led nowhere. Several signers soon waffled. Instead of widening intraparty rifts, the Tydings investigation cast partisan divisions over the Communist issue into concrete.

That the Democrats had workable alternatives is not self-evident. The proposal for a blue-ribbon loyalty commission guaranteed no solution. Tydings subsequently mused about another road not taken: before starting an inquiry, the full Foreign Relations Committee should first have called McCarthy in to see if he "had the facts to justify investigation of his charges." A day after passage of the resolution to pursue the allegations, two journalists wrote that the charges had originated with the Eightieth Congress in 1947, not with underground patriots in the State Department—the so-called "good loyal Americans." White House staffers, puzzling over McCarthy's first claims, had suspected the same thing. But the bottle had been uncorked. McCarthy had received a formal hearing, a rostrum from which to make his warmed-over charges an everyday news topic, and thereafter he managed to stay a step ahead of his critics. [9]

AS LONG AS it lasted, the Korean War ensured the persistence of the politics of disloyalty on which McCarthy thrived. The passage of the Internal Security Act attested to the fevers the war had induced. McCarthy had no role in the enactment of this measure, but the same forces that maintained his presence in public life prompted his colleagues to rush the bill to passage.

The 1950 congressional elections also revealed how Korea amplified the politics of anti-communism. Even before the war, redbaiting tinted several Democratic primary races. Senators Claude Pepper of Florida and Frank P. Graham of North Carolina both were labeled pro-Red. (White-supremacy rhetoric also flourished.) Pepper's foe termed him "an apologist for Stalin." Senator Glen Taylor, Henry Wallace's ex-runningmate, lost the Idaho Democratic primary to a man who called him a Communist "dupe." In California's senatorial primary, liberal Congresswoman Helen Gahagan Douglas survived similar aspersions by conservative Democrats, but they continued to dog her in the general election, which she lost to Richard Nixon. The Nixon forces put out "pink sheets" detailing Douglas's leftist votes in Congress.

At first Democrats fancied that the war might protect them from redbaiting. Liberal commentator Elmer Davis observed hopefully that McCarthy's "campaign against imaginary Communists looks sillier than ever when the very people he has attacked most bitterly are trying to stop the real Communists." By November, however, the growing casualty lists, the vexations of fighting an undeclared war of uncertain scope, and China's crushing intervention made Korea a Republican, not a Democratic, asset.

In state after state, Republican candidates leveled lances at the Stalinist dragon. Anti-Communist rhetoric resounded in Senate races in California, Utah, Illinois, Connecticut, Idaho, and Maryland and less boistrously in nine other states. McCarthy spoke in several places, notably Connecticut, Maryland, and Illinois, where critics of his sought reelection. Most stunning was the failure of his chief adversary, Millard Tydings, to retain his seat in the Senate. One observer likened the Communist issue's impact to "political polio."

Still, while redbaiting did contribute to the campaign's uniquely gamy flavor, most observers exaggerated its potency. The Democrats' loss of five Senate and twenty-eight House seats actually fell below the norm for midterm elections. McCarthy received excessive credit for the defeat of Tydings, Scott Lucas, and other Democrats. The Korean undertow weakened all Democrats, and the candidacies of Tydings and Lucas were damaged by local issues. But columnist Marquis Childs expressed a prevalent, if overheated, view of the time when he wrote that "in every contest where it was a major factor, McCarthyism won." Such expansive assessments of McCarthy's political muscle undergirded the fear in which his colleagues held him and consequently his staying power as a demagogue.[10]

McCARTHY WAS now a long-term factor and indeed a byword in American politics. He could make charges against Democrats, sometimes do damage, and reap headlines. With a heavy speaking schedule, he regaled numerous prayer breakfasts and banquets with visions of conspiracy. Yet his power resided mostly in his continuing potential as an election-year threat. He would not control a committee until 1953. He remained more terrier than bulldog, more Swamp Fox than Napoleon.

By the spring of 1951, Korea was a festering wound for the Democrats. Chafing under the "limited war" he was compelled to fight, MacArthur criticized his superiors once too often. In April Truman fired him. On his return home, millions acclaimed him as a hero. Gleefully pouncing on the administration's unpopularity, Republicans raked Truman and his foreign policies. His Gallup poll approval rating would bottom out at 23 percent.

The Korean War put both a floor under McCarthy's influence and a ceiling above it. Certainly the war confirmed rightist suspicions of conspiracy. "If our far eastern policy was not betrayed," asked columnist and China Lobbyman George Sokolsky, "why are we fighting in Korea?" The momentum of the loyalty and security programs also kept McCarthy in the news. As new charges arose, once-settled loyalty cases were reopened. In 1951 the Loyalty Review Board tightened its dismissal standard from "reasonable grounds" for suspecting an employee's disloyalty to "reasonable doubt" of his loyalty. Meant to appease critics, the new formula provided more human sacrifices but no end to trouble. The revised standard and multiplying charges gave further torque to the axles of the loyalty-security machinery and more headlines for McCarthy.

Yet if Korea enhanced McCarthy's longevity, it marginalized him too. He entered the Truman-MacArthur fray like an upstaged vaudevillian. First, he announced that Truman decided to fire the General under the influence of "bourbon and benedictine." Then, on June 14, he delivered a long harangue against General George C. Marshall, the former Chief of Staff and Secretary of State and current Secretary of Defense, who had recommended MacArthur's dismissal. Most of McCarthy's colleagues shunned this hatchet job.

Paradoxically McCarthy's strenuous efforts to grab headlines led some observers to suggest in the summer of 1951 that he had actually slipped out of the spotlight. Communism was being investigated, but not by him. A State Department strategist ventured that "the initial wave of public hysteria caused by McCarthyism has considerably subsided." Yet fellow Republicans still thought McCarthy was a political asset. With their blessings, he operated as a freelancer in the 1952 campaign, and his *apparent* success would maintain his reputation for political influence—the ultimate source of his power. Thanks to his own and his critics' efforts, "McCarthyism" had become synonymous with the extremist anti-communism that characterized the era. Reelected to the Senate in the Eisenhower landslide, McCarthy was ready to seize political center stage.[11]

EISENHOWER'S election as President meant that McCarthy's days were numbered, but at the time that outcome was not self-evident. In its early stages, the Eisenhower Administration seemed unlikely to plug the dike against rampaging anti-Communist excess. Even its Inaugural Concert felt the flood. After Fred Busbey complained, composer Aaron Copland's "A Lincoln Portrait" was scissored from the program. There were, said the Illinois solon, "many patriotic composers available without the long record of questionable affiliations of Copland." As McCarthy ran roughshod, journalist Walter Lippmann delicately suggested that after two months in office Ike's figure as a leader had "grown a little dim."

Eisenhower and many other Republican leaders well knew that McCarthy's capacity for mischief was bipartisan, but generally they tried to contain the menace by subtle indirection, sometimes cajoling the Wisconsin Senator, sometimes diverting him, and sometimes trying to steal his thunder by appropriating the Communist issue for themselves. Eisenhower never had anything but a profound distaste for McCarthy. However, his sense of political proprieties and tactics prevented him from publicly confronting the Senator. He knew that many Republicans respected McCarthy and his anti-Communist zeal. With the Republicans holding control of Congress by only a thin margin (forty-eight to forty-seven in the Senate, with Wayne Morse having declared himself an Independent), Ike sought to avoid alienating any member of his party.

Even at the peak of his influence in 1953–54, McCarthy did not lack critics. Indeed, he became a national fixation. The press was obsessed. Hostile newspapers suffered from what one McCarthy foe called "phobofilia"—being in love with their enemy. They criticized but also publicized him. Columnist Dorothy Thompson lamented that "the press, almost unanimously, hates McCarthy, but obliges him with the front page, and condemns him in an editorial." His leapfrogging charges and round-the-clock newsworthiness gave squeamish journalists an arduous life. The miseries of two years spent covering him—acting as a "recording device for Joe"—caused one wire-service man to lose eighteen pounds.

McCarthy's grand coup was to identify himself with anti-communism, but his critics' constant references to "McCarthyism" helped copperplate that link. Entreated to speak out against Mc-Carthy, Minnesota's liberal Democratic Senator Hubert Humphrey replied that "we are approaching a national neurosis on this subject." If liberals spent all their time attacking McCarthy, he would only thrive on the publicity, and social-welfare concerns central to liberalism would be neglected. Minority Leader Lyndon B. Johnson strove to keep the Democrats out of verbal jousts with McCarthy. Johnson had no relish for a "high school debate on the subject 'Resolved that Communism is good for the United States,' with my party taking the affirmative."[12]

Though much maligned for not squelching McCarthy, liberals had no attractive options. Verbal licks achieved little, and most other means of resistance were foreclosed. Republicans, after all, controlled the Presidency, Congress, and its committees; they set the political agenda; they had to act if McCarthy were to be unhorsed. But so long as he was counted as a political asset—until 1954—they tolerated his offenses. Also, since the GOP ratified the primacy of the anti-communism for which its right wing had long clamored, few of McCarthy's premises were questioned.

The Eisenhower Administration set out to prove its mettle by launching into vigorous anti-communism. In April 1953, Executive Order 10450 replaced Truman's loyalty and security decrees with one program under which an employee's retention or hiring must be "clearly consistent with the interests of national security." It meshed past loyalty-security rules with standards for employee "suitability" and extended security criteria to all departments. EO 10450 broadened administrative discretion and vested authority in each agency head. It provided fewer avenues of appeal than had the old loyalty program. Even Hiram Bingham, the hardly tender-hearted chairman of the Loyalty Review Board, termed this feature "just not the American way of doing things" and predicted a "Pandora's box of troubles."

The administration hoped its sleeves-rolled attack would capture the loyalty issue from McCarthy. It also argued that since employees dismissed under the new program were not *labeled* loyalty or security risks, they would be less stigmatized than before. Such faith was misguided. Republicans all too readily trumpeted their vigor in firing Reds, and GOP leaders happily toted up the numbers of people they claimed were dismissed as loyalty or security risks. In October they boasted that the new program had removed 1,456 employees. The number became a mantra for GOP orators—some spoke of 1,456 "subversives." Early in 1954 the figure rose to 2,200. Angry Democrats protested this "numbers game," and eventually it came out that few of those fired were actually disloyal. Some were told they had lost jobs because of reductions in the workforce but were listed without their knowledge as security dismissals. The new program was such a travesty that it inspired political cartoonist Herblock to picture a just-deceased bureaucrat whose supervisor said, "Heart attack, poor chap—send flowers and list him as a security risk."[13]

In January 1953 Republican leaders hoped to sidetrack McCarthy by having him chair the Government Operations Committee (GOC), a panel given to humdrum chores. More reliable hands would steer committees that normally delved into communism. Senator William Jenner of Indiana, for example, would lead the Internal Security Subcommittee. "We've got McCarthy where he can't do any harm," Majority Leader Bob Taft crowed.

Such gossamer threads would never bind McCarthy. He soon seized headlines and momentum once again. He took command of the Permanent Subcommittee on Investigations, a subcommittee of the GOC that usually sifted government waste and abuse, but whose loose mandate let McCarthy lead it almost anywhere. He named Roy M. Cohn as chief subcommittee counsel. A law-school graduate at nineteen, young Cohn had won anti-Communist spurs by helping to convict William Remington of the Commerce Department (who had been charged with perjury concerning his Communist affiliations), the *Dennis* defendants, and the Rosenbergs. Cohn would pilot McCarthy toward his targets—and eventually into the rapids that capsized him.

Soon Joe was gleefully hurling rocks at the makers of American foreign policy. He held up approval of Ike's choice for Ambassador to the USSR. A "loyal American underground" of disgruntled federal employees fed him secret information. Adlai Stevenson heard that McCarthy spies so haunted the State Department that one high official went to the CIA when he wished to communicate with an embassy "and not have it reported to McCarthy."[14] A McCarthy ally ran the State Department security program. When Joe took credit for negotiations in which Greek shipowners agreed to halt trade with Red China, he appeared to usurp powers of the Secretary of State. Critics feared he had hamstrung the Executive Branch and upset the delicate balance constructed by the Founding Fathers.

Eisenhower enhanced this impression by avoiding public duels with Joe. When implored to do battle, he argued that to do so only gave McCarthy the initiative and the headlines, divided the Republican Party, and demeaned the dignity of the Presidency. He vowed, "I will not get down in the gutter with that guy." He resented the media's sermons that he should challenge McCarthy. They had built McCarthy up; now they sought "someone to knock off the creature of their own making." One author has argued that while Ike ducked fruitless public feuding, he directed the fight shrewdly, through proxies, by "hidden-hand leadership." This strategy presupposed that, given "enough rope," McCarthy would hang himself. Eisenhower deduced that "nothing will be so effective in combatting his particular kind of trouble-making as to ignore him. This he cannot stand."

Ike had deft political instincts, but his strategy had its costs. The laisser-faire approach left McCarthy with the initiative. Giving him "enough rope" enabled him to hang others first before hanging himself. "Eisenhower revisionism" understates the desperate tone of the eighteen months McCarthy ran wild, overlooks the limits of the eventual victory over McCarthyism, and ignores the degree to which the Eisenhower regime tolerated erosions of freedom. Even as it eventually disposed of McCarthy, the administration paid civil liberties only modest heed. Rhetoric about battling communism "the American way" abounded, but policy still rasped away at people's lives. Many government small fry were served up as *hors d'oeuvres* to McCarthy. These debits may have been balanced on the credit side of the ledger by the destruction of McCarthy's influence in less than two years, but this rendering of accounts is subject to dispute.

On the occasions that Ike did confront McCarthy verbally, he did so obliquely and never by name. In June 1953, after McCarthy had attacked the overseas library program, Ike adlibbed a plea that his audience not "join the book burners." Yet asked if he had meant McCarthy, he refused (as ever) to "talk personalities." He confined himself to generalities. Thus his greeting to the American Library Association scored censorship efforts by unnamed "zealots." He shunned fighting rhetoric. From a draft letter hailing a civil-liberties conference, he red-penciled the sentence: "Seldom in our history has the preservation of civil liberties been more clearly important."[15]

Meanwhile, McCarthy ran amok. Early in 1953, he maimed two programs of the State Department's International Information Agency (IIA): its overseas libraries and the Voice of America (VOA). Witnesses before his panel faulted the intellectual thrust of VOA programming, said that broadcasting in some languages had been sabotaged to Communist advantage, claimed that a transmitter had been mislocated, and called the head of the religion desk a nonbeliever. The charges were mostly baseless. Distraught at the direction the hearings had taken, one Voice engineer threw himself under a speeding truck.

McCarthy also combed the shelves of the IIA's overseas libraries. Some books stocked for foreign readers and some authors violated conservative tastes. Many doubted that tax dollars should go to buy books that derogated the U.S., but the panicky State Department raced beyond prudence to terror. It issued a directive vetoing use of "material by any controversial persons, Communists, fellows travelers, etc." Diplomats asked tartly what "etc." meant. Noting an order that writers who predated the Bolshevik Revolution would be spared political scrutiny, Senator Thomas C. Hennings of Missouri sardonically cheered the news that his home state's Mark Twain had been "cleared." Even Whittaker Chambers's books were swept from some libraries. Some books were actually burned.

McCarthy drew further attention in April 1953, when Roy Cohn and his friend G. David Schine, an unpaid subcommittee consultant, dashed to Europe, where they rummaged through card catalogs, pontificated to newsmen, and, said onlookers, rendered America ridiculous in their hunt for the Red influence at the overseas libraries. One editorial termed them the "Rover Boys Abroad." With other McCarthy antics, the Cohn-Schine junket raised deep misgivings. A U.S. propagandist in Rome called McCarthy "the chink in our shining armor, the embodied refutation of everything I am saying." He—and others—found Europeans fearful that McCarthy was leading the nation "down the all-too-familiar road to Fascism."[16]

Riding high in July 1953, Joe began to overreach. He twanged raw nerves by naming J. B. Matthews to his subcommittee staff. The former HUAC staffer had just written an article calling Protestant clerics "the largest single group supporting the Communist apparatus in the United States today." Irked Protestant leaders and Washington insiders who itched to combat McCarthy now mobilized. On July 7, the subcommittee's Democrats and Charles Potter, a Republican, called for Matthews's ouster. Sniping from the White House, other McCarthy foes invited a protest from leaders of the National Conference of Christians and Jews and drafted a presidential reply deploring attacks on the clergy's loyalty. While Vice President Nixon stalled McCarthy, they got to the press before Joe could announce Matthews's resignation and cut his losses.

McCarthy careened next into the clash that would destroy him. The roots of his war with the Army were tangled and trivial. A key *mise-en-scène* was that Cold War fixture, the draft. Cohn's pal Schine had not yet served; now, said his draft board, he would. Cohn and, less fervidly, McCarthy tried to convince the Pentagon that anti-communism could not spare Schine; if serve he must, then give him a job mated to his skills—a commission or a berth in intelligence. Once Schine was inducted, Cohn pestered the Army to free him for committee work. Schine set a record for excused absences from basic training, but Cohn, enraged that the Army refused to allow Schine more leeway, once allegedly threatened to "wreck" it. McCarthy and Cohn would claim that the Army was infested with Reds, that higher-ups tried to hide that fact, and that Schine was used as a hostage to avert inquiry.

In October McCarthy targeted the Army Signal Corps lab at Fort Monmouth. Many scientists there were alumni of New York's city colleges and its radical subculture. Joe hinted at a radar spy network crafted by Julius Rosenberg (who had worked for the Signal Corps and knew some of the scientists). As hearings began, forty-two employees were suspended pending fresh checks under the new security program. They had been examined before. Only McCarthy's embellishments were new. After closed sessions, he gave out distorted versions of the testimony, which led to lurid headlines. There was no spy ring. All but two of those suspended were later reinstated.

McCarthy next discovered Irving Peress, a dentist drafted into the Army and, as befitted his training, promoted to Major. On loyalty forms, Peress invoked the Fifth Amendment. The Army moved ponderously to discharge Peress, but once McCarthy had grilled the dentist, Peress was given an early release. McCarthy demanded to know who let him escape. When Peress's CO, General Ralph W. Zwicker, would not elaborate on the case, citing Truman's executive order, McCarthy blasted the much-decorated veteran as "not fit to wear that uniform." In coming months, McCarthy loyalists would flood the mails with thousands of postcards asking, "Who Promoted Peress?"

The abuse of Zwicker angered the Army, the President, and Senators of both parties. But when Army Secretary Robert Stevens, a political naif who had long appeased Joe, tried haltingly to protect his officers, the Republicans on McCarthy's subcommittee cajoled him into signing a humiliating capitulation. In Pentagon hallways, officers waved hankies at each other, mocking Stevens's surrender.

Stevens and John G. Adams, the Army's General Counsel, had borne the brunt of the pressure from McCarthy and Cohn. In January 1954, a gathering of key Eisenhower advisers urged the distressed Adams to make a record of McCarthy and Cohn's entreaties and threats. When Adams's chronology reached the press in March, it led inexorably, with McCarthy's countercharges, to the Army-McCarthy hearings, in which McCarthy's subcommittee (Joe having relinquished the chair for this set of hearings to avoid sitting in judgment of himself and staff) glumly tried to sort out the tangled recriminations. Simply put, the issue was: who had coerced whom?

For thirty-six days, from April into June, the Army-McCarthy hearings offered the nation an unparalleled spectacle. In their grip on the media, in their circus atmosphere, and in the emotions they churned up, they resembled the 1925 Scopes "monkey" trial. Neither side bathed itself in glory. Evidence of the Army's slavish appeasement of McCarthy undercut its charges of cruel pressures. The McCarthy camp's efforts on Schine's behalf, counterpointed by threats and investigations, were a squalid performance. The hearings proved little, but they helped to destroy McCarthy.

Chiefly, they exposed his uglier traits on TV. In January a Gallup poll found 50 percent of the public favorable to McCarthy; by June, the number fell to 34 percent; those negatively disposed increased from 29 to 45 percent. From the hearings emerged not ordered sequence but scattered vignettes. For instance, McCarthy displayed a "cropped photo" of Schine and Robert Stevens; a third person and part of a fourth had been sliced from the picture. Joe came over as boorish, disruptive (with incessant "points of order"), and anarchic (calling on federal employees illegally to give him confidential data). It was brute soap opera, not a civics lesson. Poll data showed few viewers reaching civil-libertarian conclusions; rather, they saw McCarthy as a bad guy, a bully, and a loner.

Joseph Welch, the Army's attorney during the hearings, was a lawyer's lawyer from Boston—and a consummate actor at ease amid the televised political theatrics. (He would later appear on TV and in the movie *Anatomy of a Murder*.) When McCarthy made his great blunder, Welch pounced. As the attorney teased Cohn about his eagerness to smite the Red menace, McCarthy burst in to attack Welch's concern as "phony" in view of his effort to "foist" on the committee Fred Fisher, a young associate who once belonged to the National Lawyers Guild, named "years and years ago, as the legal bulwark of the Communist Party." Before the hearings, Fisher had told Welch of this compromising tie and was sent home. Berating McCarthy for his "reckless cruelty," Welch orated: "Let us not assassinate this lad further. . . . Have you no sense of decency, sir, at long last?"[17]

After this dramatic peak, the rest of the hearings and the subcommittee's efforts to draft a report were an anticlimax. Cohn was eased out of his job soon after the hearings ended; John Adams left the Army in 1955, after a decent interval. Meanwhile, events had rushed beyond McCarthy's or the subcommittee's control.

Senator Ralph Flanders now summoned the Senate to judgment. Joe's antics and the alarm they caused abroad troubled the Vermont Republican. Twice in 1954 he had criticized McCarthy, once comparing the division he stirred to that which attended Hitler's rise. On June 11, Flanders proposed to curb McCarthy by stripping him of his committee chairmanships. Such a sanction breached precedent and had little support, so on July 30 Flanders proposed instead that McCarthy's conduct be censured as "contrary to senatorial traditions."

Opposition to McCarthy proliferated. On March 9, Edward R. Murrow assailed McCarthy on his television show "See It Now." "On what meat does this our Caesar feed?" asked the famed war correspondent. Not the first media figure to challenge McCarthy, Murrow was nevertheless the most esteemed. His show was hailed, perhaps excessively, as a turning point in the McCarthy uproar. It may have revealed as much as guided the drift of opinion. Another straw in the wind was Chicago Bishop Bernard Sheil's speech in April, excoriating his fellow Catholic. In Wisconsin, a small-town Republican newspaper editor launched the startling, but ultimately futile, "Joe Must Go" movement to recall McCarthy from the Senate. The Senate Republican Policy Committee revealed its own concerns about McCarthy by studying rules of procedure for investigating committees.

Many Republican professionals had come to see McCarthy as a liability to the GOP, and this shift in opinion was crucial. A Republican Congressman from Ohio advised the White House he was willing to "take an active role in opposing McCarthy. . . . It would be a very popular thing in my district." In March 1954, George N. Craig, the Republican Governor of Indiana, urged Eisenhower to "discipline the recalcitrants" so as to "leave no doubt in the minds of the people that you will not tolerate cheap headline hunting, self-aggrandizement and bad manners to imperil" the GOP program. In May Congressman George H. Bender, the Republican nominee for Ohio's vacant Senate seat, warned the President that " 'McCarthyism' has become a synonym for witch-hunting, star-chamber methods and the denial of . . . civil liberties. . . ." Once the GOP's most sought-after speaker, McCarthy was persona non grata in the 1954 congressional campaign.[18]

But the Senate still grudgingly lumbered to a showdown on the McCarthy issue. Few Senators wished to face it before the election in November, and most thought Flanders's resolution needed to be fleshed out with specific grounds for censure and heard by a proper committee. In response, Flanders and two colleagues offered forty-six specifications. These and Flanders's motion were referred to a select committee led by Arthur V. Watkins of Utah. The panel comprised three former judges, two ex-Governors, and a veteran of the House. They were solid, not flashy; had not been firebrands on McCarthy-related issues; and tended to be conservative, judicial, and fairly secure from McCarthy's onslaughts. At the first hearing, Watkins showed how the wind had turned: he barred TV cameras and gaveled McCarthy to silence after his first outburst.

In September the Watkins Committee recommended censuring McCarthy on two narrow grounds: for abusing General Zwicker and for behaving contemptuously toward members of the Privileges and Elections Subcommittee, which had weighed Senator William Benton's charges against McCarthy in the previous Congress. Most notably, McCarthy had termed committee member Senator Robert Hendrickson "a living miracle" for having "lived so long with neither brains nor guts."

Taking up censure after the election, the Senate defined the issue as disruptive behavior and violations of decorum, not "McCarthyism" in the broad sense. The key participants in the debate were not the liberals who might have waged a fight on such grounds but instead members of the Senate inner circle who emphasized how McCarthy had damaged the Upper Chamber's dignity. Indeed, the Zwicker count was dropped as a ground for censure: Generals could be mistreated, but not Senators. It was further proposed that McCarthy be censured for his contempt of the Watkins Committee, which he had described as the Communist Party's "unwitting handmaiden."

With this thin stick, the dog of McCarthyism was beaten. Efforts to divert judgment and to get McCarthy off with an apology failed, thanks to the care of the pro-censure forces and to Joe's stubbornness. On December 2, 1954, by a 67-to-22 vote McCarthy was censured. All forty-four Democrats present voted for censure, as did twenty-two Republicans and the Independent Wayne Morse. All twenty-two nay votes were Republican. Senate Republicans were split down the middle. The significance of the Senate's act was at first murky. Joe's allies chortled that the final resolution did not even speak of "censure"—the operative verb was "condemn." Senator Watkins himself wrote a McCarthy partisan that the vote was a "formal slap on the wrist, a pointed reminder" of unacceptable conduct; if McCarthy befittingly adjusted his behavior, "I feel that he can do an even more effective job of coping with Communists than he did before."[19]

Yet the censure wrote *finis* to McCarthy's five years as a figure of moment. Though it condemned him only for violating Senate "club" rules, it marked a point of no return. He still churned out statements decrying this or that Communist effrontery, but to the press he was yesterday's news. Politicians avoided and pitied but no longer dreaded him. Ike told his Cabinet a new joke: McCarthyism was now "McCarthywasm." When McCarthy challenged Democratic presidential hopefuls in 1956 to make public their views on the federal security program, by then a subject of criticism, they could ignore him.

Two days after his censure, McCarthy attacked the President. Enraged that Ike had privately complimented Senator Watkins on his handling of the controversy, McCarthy castigated the President's timid anti-communism and apologized for backing him in 1952. Other Republicans repudiated the outburst, confirming Joe's isolation on the GOP's conservative fringe. Further proof came in the summer of 1955, as Ike prepared to go to the Geneva summit conference with his British, French, and Soviet counterparts. McCarthy's resolution challenging Ike to raise the issue of the captive nations behind the Iron Curtain was rejected by a vote of 77 to 4. Even Majority Leader William Knowland, a McCarthy ally, deserted him. In 1955 the White House let it be known that McCarthy, alone of all his colleagues, was unwelcome at social functions.

Physical factors hastened McCarthy's swift collapse. Friends had noticed his growing dependency on alcohol as early as 1952. It deepened in 1954 and worsened after censure. With other physical ailments, it brought his death, ascribed primarily to a liver condition, on May 2, 1957.

His physical decline was accelerated by an emotional one, closely linked to his political fall. He felt betrayed by former friends like Richard Nixon. The Vice President had always played a game of close maneuver, at times supporting those trying to placate McCarthy to keep him on the administration's side, at other times helping to fend off his incursions. A pathetic indication of McCarthy's pariah status came during a Nixon visit to Milwaukee for the 1956 campaign. As the festivities began, Joe sidled into a seat near Nixon; an aide asked him to leave; a reporter found him weeping at curbside.

McCarthy was also sideswiped by a changed political context. Hard data to prove the connection are lacking, but it is reasonable to assume that some easing of Cold War tensions contributed to his decline. As the Korean War both fixed and maintained his national stature, so its end in July 1953 seemed more than just to coincide with the beginning of his descent. A measure of poison had been leached from the political atmosphere. Stalin's death earlier in 1953 and the two powers' groping quest for less tense relations also had some effect. McCarthy raged against the tendencies toward a more relaxed anti-communism, which set in during the mid-1950s, but his efforts were futile.

McCarthy's political demise, however, did not immediately end those manifestations of the broader "ism" to which he gave his name. He was but one of numerous political figures who manipulated the Communist issue. All of them (except Senator McCarran, who died in 1954) survived him. Laws such as the Smith and McCarran Acts, the vast panoply of loyalty and security programs, and institutions such as the FBI continued to stand guard over the thoughts and behavior of Americans. McCarthy had not, after all, been censured for anti-communism.

Yet the punishment of censure and the extremes of behavior that had brought it on did subtly and gradually bring a shift: the tide of all-pervasive anti-communism had crested and was moving out. McCarthy and his partisans, who sensed this shift, fulminated against the liberals and the Eisenhower Republicans. A shrewder observer was Whittaker Chambers, the chief icon of mid-century anti-communism. Early in 1954, Chambers wrote presciently that those of his persuasion lived "in terror that Senator McCarthy will one day make some irreparable blunder which will . . . discredit the whole anti-Communist effort for a long while to come."[20]

6

"Bitter Days"
The Heyday of Anti-Communism

EVEN independent of McCarthy, the years 1950–1954 marked the climax of anti-communism in American life. The Korean stalemate generated both a bruising debate over containment and a sourness in national politics. Korea's sapping effect and a series of minor scandals heightened the Democratic Party's anemia. In addition, the 1950 congressional campaign, revealing McCarthyism's apparent sway over the voters and encouraging the GOP's right wing, signaled that anti-communism occupied the core of American political culture. "These," said liberal commentator Elmer Davis in January 1951, "are bitter days—full of envy, hatred, malice, and all uncharitableness."[1]

Critics of these trends in American politics had scant power or spirit. Outside government, foes of anti-Communist excesses moved cautiously lest they be redbaited and rarely took effective countermeasures. Liberals seldom strayed from the safety of the anti-Communist consensus. Radicals met the hostility of the dominant political forces in Cold War America and fared poorly. In government, anti-communism ruled. Senate resistance to McCarthy was scattered and weak. In the House, HUAC did much as it pleased. Truman upheld civil liberties with occasional eloquence, but he remained on the defensive, and his Justice Department often seemed locked in near-alliance with the Right

"Bitter Days": The Heyday of Anti-Communism

in Congress. Eisenhower, when not appeasing the McCarthyites, appeared at times no more able to curb them than had Truman.

Even at his peak, McCarthy was not the sole anti-Communist paladin, though he cultivated that impression. As McCarthyism in its broader sense outlived the personal defeat of McCarthy himself, so, in its prime, it exceeded his reach. Its strength owed much to the wide acceptance, even by McCarthy's critics, of the era's anti-Communist premises. Along with McCarthy, they made the first half of the 1950s the acme of noisy anti-communism and of the ills to which it gave birth.

Soon after the 1950 campaign, skirmishing over the Communist issue renewed in earnest. In December Senator Pat McCarran joined the hunt for subversives by creating the Senate Internal Security Subcommittee (SISS). As chairman of that panel (and the parent Judiciary Committee), the crusty Nevada Democrat packed it with such like-minded colleagues as Democrats James Eastland and Willis Smith and Republicans Homer Ferguson and William Jenner. While McCarthy darted about unpredictably, McCarran moved glacially but steadily to his objective, crushing opposition.

McCarran's panel spotlighted themes that McCarthy had raised giving them a more sympathetic hearing than had the Tydings Committee. In February 1951, federal agents swooped down on a barn in Lee, Massachusetts, seized the dead files of the Institute of Pacific Relations (IPR) and trucked them under guard to Washington. After sifting this haul, a SISS subcommittee opened an extended probe of the IPR, which led to a new inquest on "who lost China" and resulted in renewed loyalty and security proceedings, dismissals from the State Department and prosecution—all to McCarthy's greater, reflected glory.

The subcommittee acquired a reputation—more cultivated than deserved—for honoring due process. SISS was punctilious on some points: evidence was formally introduced (when an excerpt was read, the full text was put in the record); hearings were exhaustive (over 5,000 pages); witnesses were heard in executive session before they named names in public; their credentials and the relevance of their testimony were set forth; and some outward courtesies were extended.

The fairness was only skin-deep, however. Witnesses were badgered about obscure events from years back and about nuances of aging reports. Diplomat John Carter Vincent was even asked if he had plans to move to Sarasota, Florida. When he termed it a most "curious" question, counsel could only suggest that perhaps the Florida Chamber of Commerce had taken an interest. The subcommittee strove to ensnare witnesses in perjury. One China Hand called the sessions "generally Dostoyevskian attacks not only on a man's mind but also his memory." To have predicted Jiang's decline or Mao's rise was interpreted as both premeditating and helping to cause that outcome.[2]

A product of the internationalist do-goodery of YMCA leaders in the 1920s, the IPR sought to promote peace and understanding in the Pacific. It had both national branches in countries interested in the Pacific and an international secretariat. Well funded by corporations and foundations in its palmier days, the IPR had more pedigree than power. McCarran's subcommittee insisted that IPR's publications pushed the Communist line on China. Louis Budenz testified that the Kremlin had assigned Owen Lattimore the job of giving the IPR journal, *Pacific Affairs*, a Party-line tilt. Budenz claimed that when he was in the Party, he received "official communications" describing Lattimore (and several China Hands) as Communists.

McCarran's panel spent a year grilling Lattimore, other IPR officials, and various China experts and diplomats as it tried to knit a fabric of conspiracy out of its evidence and presuppositions. McCarran claimed that, but for the machinations of the coterie that ran IPR, "China today would be free and a bulwark against the further advance of the Red hordes into the Far East." He charged that the IPR-USSR connection had led to infiltration of the government by persons aligned with the Soviets, of faculties by Red professors, and of textbooks by pro-Communist ideas. He called Lattimore "a conscious and articulate instrument of the Soviet conspiracy."

The hearings revealed naiveté about communism, showed that IPR principals had access to important officials during the war, and turned up levels of maneuvering that sullied IPR's reputation for scholarly detachment. Proven or accused Reds did associate with the IPR and may well have sought leverage through it. There were tendentious claims in IPR publications, as in one author's simplistic dichotomy of Mao's "democratic China" and Jiang's "feudal China." Lattimore was a more partisan editor of *Pacific Affairs* than he conceded. However, in political scientist Earl Latham's measured assessment, the hearings "show something less than subversive conspiracy in the making of foreign policy, and something more than quiet routine." Nor was it proven that IPR had much influence over policy. Perhaps the China Hands had been naive to think that a reoriented policy might prevent China's Communists from falling "by default" under Soviet control and thus might maintain American leverage. Yet those who argued that unblinking support of Jiang could have prevented China's "loss" were more naive still.

Unable to prove, in scholarly terms, its thesis of a successful pro-Communist conspiracy against China, SISS could still carry it politically. The loyalty-security program helped enforce it. New charges, however stale, motivated the State Department Loyalty-Security Board to reexamine old cases of suspected employees, even if they had been previously cleared. Moreover, nudged by the Right, Truman toughened the loyalty standard in April 1951, putting a heavier burden of proof on the accused. Thus under Hiram Bingham, a Republican conservative, the Loyalty Review Board ordered new inquiries in cases decided under the old standard.

Amid the growing acrimony, the careers of the China Hands withered. John Stewart Service was a case in point. He had been swept up in the 1945 *Amerasia* arrests. (The episode reminded a colleague of *Heaven's My Destination,* Thornton Wilder's 1930s version of *Candide:* "Jack Service went into a bawdy house thinking it was still a girls' boarding school.") In fact, Service had known of the magazine's radical orientation and was using it to disseminate materials that discredited Jiang Jieshi's regime. Though cleared of any crime, Service was a marked man, subject to recurrent loyalty and security probes. By 1950 his career seemed back on track. He was slated to be consul-general in Calcutta, but the China Lobby's ongoing attack prompted a downgrading to consul (to avoid Senate confirmation). Even this looked provocative, so he was switched to a job in the embassy at New Delhi.

On ship for India when McCarthy accused him, Service was ordered home. The Tydings Committee cleared him, but the Loyalty-Security Board took another look. George Kennan, intellectual father of containment, declared Service's China reports free of pro-communism. The Board heard new evidence, probably routed by the Chinese Nationalists through the FBI, but cleared Service in October. The Indian assignment was by now long gone. In 1951 the Loyalty Review Board called Service for a post-audit of his latest (eighth!) clearance. After the hearing, the Board added a new charge based on the *Amerasia* case: "intentional, unauthorized disclosure" of confidential documents "under circumstances which may indicate disloyalty." In December Service was deemed a security risk, and Secretary of State Dean Acheson fired him.

John Carter Vincent was another casualty. He once headed the State Department's Far Eastern Division, but his China connection led his superiors to ease him from the spotlight, sending him first as minister to Switzerland, then as consul-general to Tangier. In 1951 the Loyalty-Security Board called him to answer charges, including one that he had held "pro-Communist . . . views and sympathies" from 1940 to 1947. SISS quizzed him too. By convoluted reasoning, the Loyalty Review Board found him to be a loyalty risk. Acheson named·a select panel to review the decision, but his successor, John Foster Dulles, bypassed the panel and gave Vincent a choice: quit or be fired. He quit.

The McCarran panel also grilled John Paton Davies, Jr., another China Hand, and pressed the Justice Department to indict him for perjury. He was not prosecuted, but in 1954 he was summoned from his post in Peru for a security hearing. John Foster Dulles implemented a recommendation for Davies's dismissal on the basis of "lack of judgment, discretion, and reliability."

By late 1954, the chief China Hands had been cashiered from service, and others were scattered in a sort of diplomatic diaspora. Vincent retired to tend his garden and lecture occasionally. In Lima, Davies entered the furniture business. Service worked for a firm that made and sold steam traps, eventually patenting a lucrative improvement. But while the China Hands, their loyalty slurred, were exiled from their chosen field, the China Lobby rode high. At a fete thrown by Nationalist China's ambassador after the 1952 election, Senators Knowland, McCarran, McCarthy, and other allies of the Nationalists raised glasses in a triumphal if unrealistic toast: "Back to the mainland."[3]

By that point, the fate of Owen Lattimore had also been determined by SISS. In fact, the high point of McCarran's IPR inquiry was Lattimore's testimony in 1952. The committee questioned him for twelve days (on nine of which McCarthy attended), so peppering him with questions that his opening statement consumed three days. It pitted his memory against the massive IPR files and his word against those of ex-Communists like Budenz, whose testimony about Lattimore even the FBI doubted, and Harvey Matusow, who later confessed to perjury.

Often Lattimore's memory was hazy. The questions meandered over many years, he complained, "and it is getting increasingly difficult for me to remember what I remembered when." He denied knowing that one contributor to the journal he edited was a Communist or Marxist—only to be confronted with his 1937 statement that the author was reputedly at least a Marxist. Similarly, he dismissed the claim that he once answered mail for an absent aide to FDR, but his own correspondence contradicted him.

SISS also found it odd that, while claiming vindication from the Tydings inquiry and disclaiming any impact on policy, Lattimore had never told that panel of his meeting with Truman in 1945 to discuss China policy. "He visited the President once and forgot it," McCarran commented acidly. Another senator thought the fact that Lattimore had not mentioned giving Truman a memo after their meeting smacked of concealment. Lattimore was once asked to prove a negative: "can you say that the IPR and you had no influence upon the far-eastern experts of the State Department?" McCarran used post-hoc argument to rebut Lattimore's denial of any leverage. What else would explain the fact that, soon after his talk with Truman, State Department hardliners had been ousted and China Hands appointed, or that Marshall's policy while in China was "substantially the same" as Lattimore's memorandum had recommended? Exonerated by the Tydings Committee in 1950, Lattimore was not so fortunate in 1952. McCarran gave him a tongue-lashing. The witness was "so flagrantly defiant," so discourteous, and "so persistent in his efforts to confuse and obscure the facts, that the committee feels constrained to take due notice of his conduct." "That he has uttered untruths stands clear in the record."[4]

The aftermath of the Lattimore inquiry showed McCarran's power and malice. The committee's report charged that Lattimore had lied a number of times. Subsequently, McCarran's ragging of James McGranery, whose confirmation as Truman's Attorney General he held hostage, had the right effect: Lattimore was indicted for perjury in December 1952. Most of the seven perjury counts dealt with Lattimore's denials that he had known certain people were Reds or that he had published articles by authors he knew to be Communists. One count charged that he falsely denied being "sympathetic" to communism. When Herbert Brownell, Ike's Attorney General, took office, McCarran made sure that he put a zealous prosecutor on the case.

Federal Judge Luther Youngdahl heard the case and saw its flimsiness. He threw out as hopelessly vague the charge that Lattimore lied in denying pro-communism. The judge also weeded out three more counts and expressed doubt about the rest. The Appeals Court reinstated two counts, and in 1954 a grand jury added two new ones. Youngdahl struck down the two new counts, and the Appeals Court upheld him. The case was further dented when one witness, Harvey Matusow, confessed to perjury in *his* SISS testimony. The Justice Department dropped the case in 1955.

Critics, including some liberals, warned that Lattimore did not merit martyr status. He had defended the Soviet purges of the 1930s and romanticized the Chinese Communists and Soviet influence on Asia. Still, faulty or debatable views are rarely a crime. This nicety did not faze McCarran, whose power enabled him to define new crimes. Indeed, creation of new categories of illicit behavior was a salient feature of the era. Lattimore had a close call. Unlucky as he was to attract the enmity of the potent McCarran, he was fortunate to benefit from the "rule of law"—or the luck of the draw in having Judge Youngdahl preside over the case. It was not the last time the judiciary saved the country from McCarthyism's worst ravages.[5]

The purge of the China Hands had long-term impact. American attitudes toward China remained frozen for two decades. Battered by McCarthyite attacks, the State Department's Far Eastern Division assumed a conservative bunkerlike mentality. Selected by President John F. Kennedy to shake the division up, Assistant Secretary of State Averell Harriman found it "a disaster area filled with human wreckage." Personnel who did not bear wounds from previous battles were chosen to handle Asian problems. Vincent's successor on the China desk was an impeccably conservative diplomat whose experience lay in Europe. JFK named an ambassador to South Vietnam whose prior work had been with NATO. In the 1950s, the field of Asian studies felt the blindfold of conformity as the momentum of U.S. foreign policy carried the country toward the vortex of Vietnam.[6]

THE IPR INVESTIGATION was but one of many inquiries during the early 1950s that delved into Communist activities. The Eighty-first Congress spawned 24 probes of communism; the Eighty-second, 34; and the Eighty-third, 51. HUAC busily sought new triumphs. In 1953, 185 of the 221 Republican Congressmen asked to serve on it. But HUAC faced the problem all monopolies meet when competitors pour into the market. Besides McCarran and McCarthy, a Senate labor subcommittee probed Red influences in labor unions, two committees combed the U.N. Secretariat for Communists, and others dipped an oar in when the occasion arose.

In part HUAC met the competition with strenuous travel. Hearings often bore titles like "Communist Activities in the Chicago Area"—or Los Angeles, Detroit, or Hawaii. The Detroit hearings got a musician fired, a college student expelled, and UAW Local 600 taken over by the national union. In 1956 two Fisher Body employees were called before a HUAC hearing in St. Louis. When angry fellow workers chalked such slogans as "Russia has no Fifth amendment" on auto bodies and staged a work stoppage, the two men were suspended. The impact of junketing congressional probers was often felt in such local fallout rather than in federal punishments (though many witnesses were cited for contempt of Congress). That indeed was the point. A witness might use the Fifth Amendment to avoid perjury charges, but appearing before a committee of Congress left him open to local sanctions.

Lawmakers fretted over communism in the labor movement. The presence of left-wing unionists in a defense plant offered a frequent pretext for congressional excursions. HUAC addressed the issue often; McCarthy, occasionally; House and Senate labor subcommittees paid close heed. The liberal anti-Communist Hubert Humphrey held an inquiry designed both to meet the problem and to protect clean unions from scattershot redbaiting. Lest unions be handled too softly, in 1952 Pat McCarran, Herman Welker, and John Marshall Butler conceived the formidably labeled "Task Force Investigating Communist Domination of Certain Labor Organizations."

Attacks on radical union leadership from both within and without the labor movement proliferated in the early 1950s. During 1952 hearings in Chicago, HUAC jousted with negotiators for the Communist-led United Electrical Workers just as they mounted a strike against International Harvester. In 1953 McCarthy's subcommittee also bedeviled UE locals in New York and Massachusetts. Such hearings often led to firings and encouraged or counterpointed raids by rival unions. They hastened the decline of the left wing of the labor movement.

The UE was beset on all sides. When the anti-communist International United Electrical Workers Union (IUE), led by James Carey, was founded, Truman Administration officials intoned blessings. The Atomic Energy Commission pressured employers like General Electric to freeze out the UE; IUE literature warned that plants represented by the UE would lose defense contracts. The CIO lavishly funded Carey's war with the UE. Three days before a 1950 election to decide control of a Pittsburgh area local, the vocal anti-Communist Judge Michael Musmanno arrived at a plant gate to campaign for the IUE. Bedecked in naval uniform, he was convoyed by a detachment of National Guardsmen, bayonets fixed and flags unfurled. Many local Catholic clergy urged their flocks to vote for the IUE on the basis of anti-communism. Carey's union won a narrow victory.[7]

These labor wars sometimes produced odd bedfellows. Carey criticized McCarthy, but the latter's 1953 Boston hearings helped the IUE keep control of key GE plants in the area. GE management declared before the hearings that it would fire workers who admitted they were Reds; it would suspend those who declined to testify and, if they did not subsequently answer the charges, would dismiss them. Thus besieged, the UE often settled labor disputes on a take-what-it-could basis.

Where left-wing unions maintained reputations for effective bargaining, anti-communism had limited effect. The UE's tactical surrender of its youthful militancy probably eroded its rank-and-file support more than did any redbaiting. Yet the Longshoremen's Union, despite Smith Act prosecutions against its leaders in Hawaii and the effort to deport Harry Bridges, kept control of West Coast docks. (Indeed, having come to tolerate Bridges by the 1950s, business leaders had lost enthusiasm for persecuting him.) Similarly, the Mine, Mill and Smelter Workers Union held onto some strongholds despite recurrent redbaiting. Weaker leftist unions like the United Public Workers or the Fur and Leather Workers succumbed to raiding and harassment.

In an era when mainline labor was cautious, organizing initiatives often did originate with more radical unions and so fell prey to anti-Communist attack. In 1953 a CIO retail workers' union, some of whose organizers were Communists, struck stores in Port Arthur, Texas. A commission of inquiry named by Governor Allen Shivers (then seeking reelection) found "clear and present danger" of Communist sway over Texas labor. Shivers claimed he had foiled a Communist-led union's "well-laid plans to spread its tentacles all along the Gulf Coast and eventually into *your* community." Other Southern organizing drives succumbed to redbaiting too.

By the 1950s, labor's assertiveness had waned; where it persisted, it met defeat; and new organizing drives were few. Internal dissent—indeed, debate—was virtually stilled. Its momentum sapped and its membership reduced by over a third, the CIO merged with the AFL in a 1955 "shotgun wedding." Having won a place within the American consensus, labor paid a dear price to keep it.[8]

Conservatives feared Communist influence in the nation's schools as well as in its factories. The influence of the "Reducators" and of subversive ideas that ranged, in various investigators' minds, from outright communism to "progressive education" perennially intrigued legislators at the state and national levels.

The Communists' long-running control of the New York Teachers Union alarmed the Senate Internal Security Subcommittee. Previously, the 1940–41 Rapp-Coudert inquiry had led to the dismissal of a number of New York City teachers. In 1949 the Board of Education began a new purge. From 1950 to early 1953, twenty-four teachers were fired and thirty-four resigned under investigation. By one estimate, over three hundred New York City teachers lost their jobs in the 1950s. SISS thus served to reinforce local activities with its 1952–53 hearings in New York City. The refusal by Teachers Union leaders to testify about their affiliations established grounds for their dismissal under Section 903 of the city charter.

Ultimately, the probers failed in their aim to expose Marxist-Leninist propagandizing in Gotham's classrooms. Bella Dodd, a former Communist and Teachers Union leader, claimed that Communist teachers who knew Party dogma "cannot help but slant their teaching in that direction." A Queens College professor said he knew a score of students whom the Communists had "ruined" and turned into "misfits." Yet aside from a few parents' complaints and "one case where I think we could prove it," the city's school superintendent had no evidence of indoctrination. Though Communists had obviously acquired great leverage in the Teachers Union, SISS located its best case of university subversion in a book about *China*.[9]

HUAC quizzed educators too, but its scrutiny of the movie industry earned higher returns when it resumed its inquiry into Hollywood in 1951. By then the Hollywood Ten were in prison, the film industry's opposition to HUAC was shattered. and the blacklist was growing. Fear washed through the movie lots. The economic distress visited on Hollywood by the growth of television further frazzled nerves. Said one witness, the renewed assault was "like taking a pot shot at a wounded animal." When subpoenaed, actress Gale Sondergaard asked the

Screen Actors Guild for help, its board rebuffed her, likening her criticism of HUAC to the Communist line. The Screen Directors Guild made its members take a loyalty oath.

Yet few secrets were left to ferret out: the identity of Hollywood's Communists had long ceased to be a mystery. Early in the 1951 hearings, Congressman Francis Walter even asked why it was "material . . . to have the names of people when we already know them?" For HUAC, getting new information had become secondary to conducting ceremonies of exposure and penitence. Would the witness "name names" or not?

Of 110 witnesses subpoenaed in 1951, 58 admitted having had Party involvements. Some cogently explained why they had since disowned communism. Budd Schulberg recalled that while he was writing *What Makes Sammy Run*, the Party told him to submit an outline, confer with its literary authorities, and heed its artistic canons. The *Daily Worker* received his book favorably, but after being updated on Party aesthetics, the reviewer wrote a second piece thrashing the novel. One screenwriter recalled how the Party line on a studio painters' strike shifted perplexingly in 1945: we "could walk through the picket lines in February, and not in June."

Witnesses seeking to steer between punishment and fingering co-workers faced tearing ethical choices. Naming known Reds or those previously named might stave off harm, but this ploy was tinged with moral bankruptcy. Some soured ex-Communists did resist giving names, not wanting, in actor Larry Parks's phrase, to "crawl through the mud to be an informer." Some named each other; some said little, ducking quickly behind the Fifth Amendment. Others told all. The 155 names that writer Martin Berkeley gave set a record. Others gabbed freely. Parrying with humor the oft-asked question—would he defend America against the Soviets?—actor Will Geer, already middle-aged, cheerfully agreed to fight in his way: growing vegetables and entertaining the wounded. The idea of people his vintage shouldering arms amused him; wars "would be negotiated immediately."

In this as in all inquiries, witnesses trod a path set with snares. The courts disallowed the Hollywood Ten's use of the First Amendment to avoid testifying, so a witness's only protection was the Fifth Amendment guarantee against self-incrimination. Even this route crossed minefields. *Blau v. U.S.* (1950) ruled that one might plead the Fifth legitimately to the question of Party membership. However, the 1950 case of *Rogers v. U.S.* dictated caution: one had to invoke the Fifth at the outset, not in the middle, of a line of questions inching toward incrimination. Having testified that she herself held a Party office, the court ruled, Jane Rogers had waived her Fifth Amendment privilege and could not then refuse to testify about others.

HUAC tried to quick-march Fifth-takers into pitfalls. One gambit was a logical fork: if answering would incriminate him, a witness might use the Fifth; but if innocent, he could not honestly do so. Thus, the committee held, the witness was either guilty or lying—even though the courts did not accept this presumption of guilt. However, a new odious category, the "Fifth-Amendment Communist," was born. Such witnesses, whether teachers, actors, or others, rarely hung onto their jobs.

Legal precedent also demanded care in testifying about associations. One witness pled the Fifth in response to the question of whether he was a member of the American Automobile Association. HUAC members enjoyed asking if witnesses belonged to the Ku Klux Klan, hoping to nettle them into breaking a string of refusals to answer. On their part, witnesses devised novel defenses like the so-called "diminished Fifth." A witness resorting to the "slightly diminished Fifth" would deny present CP membership but refuse to open up his past or that of others; those using the "fully diminished Fifth," on the other hand, testified about their own pasts but no one else's. (The "augmented Fifth"was like the slightly diminished Fifth, but the witness also disclaimed any sympathy for communism.)[10]

The question of whether to testify freely or take the Fifth convulsed the higher precincts of American arts and letters. Writer Lillian Hellman, subpoenaed in 1952, took the bold step of writing HUAC's chairman that she would take the Fifth only if asked to talk about others. She realized that by answering questions about herself, she waived her privilege and was subject to a contempt citation, but better that than to "bring bad trouble" to innocent people. She simply would not cut her conscience "to fit this year's fashions." When she testified, she did invoke the Fifth but scored a coup with her eloquent letter and managed to avoid a contempt citation. In 1956 the playwright Arthur Miller also refused to discuss other people but, unlike Hellman, did not take the Fifth. (His contempt citation was later overturned.)

Art came to mirror politics. Miller had previously written *The Crucible*, whose hero welcomed death rather than implicate others in the seventeenth-century Salem witch trials. Admirers stressed the play's relevance to modern witch-hunts. In contrast, Elia Kazan, who had named names, directed the smash movie *On the Waterfront*, whose hero (Marlon Brando), implored by a fighting priest (Karl Malden) to speak out, agreed to inform against criminals in a longshoremen's union. None of these works dealt with communism, but their pertinence to current political issues was not lost. Among the arbiters of American culture, these moral choices prompted heated debate, which still reverberated in the 1980s.

The issues were not only philosophical. The sanctions were real. Noncooperative witnesses were blacklisted, their careers in Hollywood shattered. Many drifted into other lines of work. Many became exiles, moving to Europe, Mexico, or New York. Some suffered writer's block. Some families endured steady FBI surveillance and such vexations as sharply increased life insurance premiums (for an assertedly dangerous occupation). Being blacklisted so dispirited several actors that their health was impaired, and premature death resulted. Comedian Philip Loeb, blacklisted and unemployable, his family destroyed, committed suicide in 1955.

Even though several hundred members of the entertainment industry forfeited their livelihoods after HUAC appearances, the studios, networks, producers, and the committee itself did not admit publicly that a blacklist existed. (Privately, some were candid. "Pal, you're dead," a soused producer told writer Millard Lampell. "They told me that I couldn't touch you with a barge pole.") In this shadow world, performers and writers wondered if their talents had indeed eroded. Had one's voice sharpened, one's humor dulled?

For blacklisting to work, HUAC's hammer needed an anvil. It was duly provided by other groups who willingly punished hostile or reluctant witnesses. American Legion publications spread the word about movies whose credits were fouled by subversion; Legionnaires (and other local true believers) could pressure theatre owners, if necessary, by trooping down to the Bijou to picket offending films. The mere threat of such forces soon choked off the supply of objectionable pictures at the source. Indeed, Hollywood, responding to broad hints from HUAC and to its own reading of the political climate, began making anti-Communist potboilers. These low-budget "B" pictures did poorly at the box office. They provided insurance, not profits.

Though entertainment industry moguls justified screening employees' politics by citing the threat from amateur censors, usually professional blacklisters made the system work. Blacklisting opened up business vistas on the Right. In 1950 American Business Consultants, founded by three ex-FBI agents, published *Red Channels*, a compendium listing 151 entertainers and their Communist-front links. *Counterattack*, an ABC publication started in 1947, periodically offered the same type of information. In 1953 an employee left ABC to establish Aware, Inc., which sold a similar service. Companies in show biz subscribed to these countersubversive finding aids and paid to have the names of those they might hire for a show or series checked against "the files." Aware charged five dollars to vet a name for the first time, two dollars for rechecks. It became habit for Hollywood, radio and TV networks, advertisers, and stage producers (though blacklisting had its weakest hold on Broadway) not to employ entertainers whose names cropped up in such files.

A few found ways to evade total proscription. Writers could sometimes submit work under pseudonyms. Studios asked some writers on the blacklist to doctor ailing scripts authored by others. The blacklisted writers received no screen credits and were paid a pittance, but at least they were working. Ostracized actors did not have this option. Said comedian Zero Mostel: "I am a man of a thousand faces, all of them blacklisted." A TV producer once called a talent agent to ask, "Who have you got like John Garfield?" He had Garfield himself, the agent exclaimed; but, of course, the blacklisted Garfield was taboo.

Unlike actors, blacklisted writers could also find work in television, which devoured new scripts ravenously. As in film, some used assumed names. Others worked through "fronts" (whence came the title of Woody Allen's 1976 movie). They wrote, but someone else put his name to the script (and might demand up to half of the income). Mistaken-identity plot twists worthy of a Restoration comedy resulted. One writer using a pseudonym wrote a script that he was asked, under a second pseudonym, to revise. Millard Lampell submitted a script under a phony name; the producers insisted that the script's writer appear for consultation; told that he was away and unavailable, they went for a quick fix: they asked Lampell to rewrite his own (unacknowledged) script.

The obverse of blacklisting was "clearance." Desperate actors or writers could seek absolution from a member of the anti-Communist industry. Often, not surprisingly, the person to see was one who had played a part in creating the blacklist. Roy Brewer, the chief of the International Alliance of Theatrical Stage Employees, had redbaited the leftist craft guilds, but helped rehabilitate blacklistees, as did several conservative newspaper columnists. The American Legion, which issued lists of Hollywood's undesirables, also certified innocence or repentance. A listee might get by with writing a letter to the Legion. Or he might be made to list suspect organizations he had joined and to tell why he joined, when he quit, who invited him in, and whom he had enticed. Thus the written route to clearance might also require naming names.

To regain grace, some sinners had to repent publicly, express robust patriotism in a speech or article, or confess to having been duped into supporting leftist causes. Typically, a blacklistee had to be willing to tell all to the FBI or to HUAC. Even liberal anti-Communists were "graylisted," and some had to write clearance letters. Humphrey Bogart had bought trouble by protesting the 1947 HUAC hearings against the Hollywood Ten. In his article, "I'm No Communist," he admitted he had been a "dope" in politics. Actor John Garfield, whose appearance before HUAC sent his career and life into a tailspin, was at the time of his death about to publish an article titled "I Was a Sucker for a Left Hook."[11]

Like teachers and entertainers, charitable foundations also triggered the suspicion of congressional anti-Communists. These products of capitalism plowed back into society some of the vast wealth of their Robber Baron founders, but conservatives found their philanthropic tastes too radical. In 1952 a special House committee led by Georgia conservative Eugene Cox inquired into the policies of tax-exempt foundations. Did not "these creatures of the capitalist system," asked Cox, seek to "bring the system into disrepute" and to assume "a socialistic leaning"?

Foundations had dipped their toes in swirling currents by focusing on such subjects as Soviet studies, improved race relations, education, and peace, and by subsidizing writers and artists. Grants that had occasionally gone to those who turned up on "lists" would return to haunt the donor. Cox bridled at the Rockefeller Foundation's twenty-five years of support for the IPR, at a Carnegie grant to Owen Lattimore, and at a Rockefeller stipend to Hanns Eisler, the left-wing composer and brother of reputed Comintern "rep" Gerhard Eisler. And why, the committee wondered, had the Carnegie Endowment hired Alger Hiss?

Foundation officers apologized for such "mistakes" but argued that they could avoid error only by never taking risks. None of them sounded radical. One claimed he knew the Attorney General's list by heart; others swore they never knowingly gave to groups on the list and never funded Communists. Paul Hoffman seconded a description of his Ford Foundation program as "somewhere near the middle of the road." Another witness soothed Cox's fears of radicalized college students, noting that the young liked to "shock" their elders, but five years out of school, with jobs, they "are all over" such youthful ailments.

Cox's probe drew no blood, but in the next four years the conflict sharpened. In 1953 conservative Tennessee Republican B. Carroll Reece aggressively renewed the inquiry. Based solely on the testimony of critics of the foundations, his panel's 1954 report damned much of recent history, including the New Deal and the "moral relativism" that went back to William James and John Dewey, and attacked the foundations that subsidized such trends.

The Fund for the Republic, incorporated in 1952, was a special goad to conservatives. Spun off by the parent Ford Foundation, the Fund owed its independence partly to Henry Ford II's wish to distance himself from a program so controversial that it sparked boycott threats against Ford showrooms. The Fund had a commitment to enhance American freedoms and fifteen billion dollars to carry it out. Paul Hoffman was its chairman; in 1954 Robert M. Hutchins became its president. The Right loathed Hoffman: he had run the Marshall Plan (Socialist globaloney), backed Ike (not Taft) in 1952, and opposed McCarthy. The presence of Hutchins, who when president of the University of Chicago in 1949 had defended civil liberties and tweaked the noses of clumsy anti-Communists on the Broyles commission, further guaranteed trouble from the Right.

The Fund for the Republic supported such projects as sober academic studies of communism, inquiries into the loyalty-security programs, efforts to build racial tolerance, studies of blacklisting and censorship, and a program to stimulate public discussion of the nation's "basic documents." Not all awards were so schoolish. An Iowa town got $10,000 after it found housing for a black Air Force officer who had moved to the all-white community.

The Fund gave a particularly controversial grant in 1955 to the Plymouth (Pennsylvania) Monthly Meeting. In 1953 that Quaker body hired a librarian named Mary Knowles, who had lost her previous job in Massachusetts by pleading the Fifth before the Internal Security

Subcommittee. FBI informant Herbert Philbrick had named her as a Red, and she had once worked for an agency named on the Attorney General's list. She refused to take a state loyalty oath or to revisit her past but stated that she had had no link with any left-wing or subversive groups since 1947 and that she adhered to her country and the Constitution. Further she would not budge.

Her stance stoked anger in the community. After the Plymouth Meeting hired her, local governments cut off funds to the library; schools halted class trips there. The American Legion, the Daughters of the American Revolution, and other pressure groups agitated, and petitions circulated. A group called Alerted Americans claimed that to keep Mrs. Knowles at the library "poses a possible future threat to our security." When the Plymouth Meeting refused to jettison her, the Fund for the Republic voted it a $5,000 award. The Right reacted angrily. Two committees of Congress again quizzed the librarian, and again she balked. In 1956 she was cited for contempt of Congress. She was fined and sentenced to 120 days in jail in 1957, but the verdict was over-turned on appeal in 1960.

Increasingly subject to attacks in 1955 and after, the Fund for the Republic had drawn a bead on "McCarthyism," and friends of that phenomenon struck back. McCarthy rightly suspected that the Fund's inquiries into the loyalty-security program aimed to criticize it. In 1956, when Hoffman was named to the nation's U.N. delegation, McCarthy exclaimed that Congress should address Hoffman's "activities as Chairman of the Ford Foundation Fund 'To Destroy the Republic.' " Other lawmakers lambasted the Fund; J. Edgar Hoover had tart words for it; the IRS scrutinized its tax exemption as a nonprofit organization; and rightist commentators and journalists led by Fulton Lewis, Jr., offered shrill criticism.

In June 1956, HUAC slated hearings on the Fund, then backed off. Soon after, however, the Fund-sponsored study *Report on Blacklisting* was published, and HUAC interrogated the author John Cogley, albeit ineptly. Then, for good measure, HUAC took another look at the grant to the Plymouth Monthly Meeting. It managed further to divide the community and antagonize local residents; the library board reaffirmed its faith in Mrs. Knowles. [12]

For the Fund, timing was all. Most of its major programs came to fruition after McCarthyism had hit the downswell, after the courts began to limit the second Red Scare, and while criticism of the loyalty-security mania was growing. Thus the 1956 HUAC hearings came as an ineffectual rearguard reaction to trends that were sapping the force of anti-communism.

HOW DEEPLY DID anti-communism gouge the social and political terrain of the 1950s? With dissent defined as dangerous, the range of political debate obviously was crimped. The number of times that books were labeled dangerous, thoughts were scourged as harmful, and speakers and performers were rejected as outside the pale multiplied. Anti-Communist extremism and accompanying pressures toward conformity had impact in such areas as artistic expression, the labor movement, the cause of civil rights, and the status of minorities in American life.

For some denizens of the Right, threats of Communist influence materialized almost anywhere. For instance, Illinois American Legionnaires warned that the Girl Scouts were being spoonfed subversive doctrines. Jack Lait and Lee Mortimer's yellow-journalistic *U.S.A. Confidential* warned parents against the emerging threat of rock and roll. It bred dope use, interracialism, and sex orgies. "We know that many platter-spinners are hopheads. Many others are Reds, left-wingers, or hecklers of social convention." Not every absurdity owed life to the vigilantes, however. A jittery Hollywood studio cancelled a movie based on Longfellow's "Hiawatha" for fear it would be viewed as "Communist peace propaganda."

Books and ideas remained vulnerable. It is true that the militant Indiana woman who abhorred *Robin Hood*'s subversive rob-from-the-rich-and-give-to-the-poor message failed to get it banned from school libraries. Other locales were less lucky. A committee of women appointed by the school board of Sapulpa, Oklahoma, had more success. The board burned those books that it classified as dealing improperly with socialism or sex. A spokesman claimed that only five or six "volumes of no consequence" were destroyed. A librarian in Bartlesville, Oklahoma, was fired for subscribing to the *New Republic*, *Nation*, and *Negro Digest*. The use of UNESCO materials in the Los Angeles schools became a hot issue in 1952. A new school board and superintendent were elected with a mandate to remove such books from school libraries.

Local sanctions against unpopular artists and speakers often were effective. In August 1950, a New Hampshire resort hotel banned a talk by Owen Lattimore after guests, apparently riled by protests of the Daughters of the American Revolution and others, remonstrated. Often local veterans—the American Legion and Catholic War Veterans—initiated pressures. The commander of an American Legion Post in Omaha protested a local production of a play whose author, Garson Kanin, was listed in *Red Channels*. A founder of *Red Channels* warned an American Legion anti-subversive seminar in Peoria, Illinois, that Arthur Miller's *Death of a Salesman*, soon to appear locally, was "a Communist-dominated play." Jaycees and Legionnaires failed to get the theatre to cancel the play, but the boycott they mounted sharply curbed the size of the audience.[13]

Libraries often became focal points of cultural anxieties. Not every confrontation ended like those in Los Angeles or Sapulpa, but librarians felt they were under the gun. "I just put a book that is complained about away for a while," said one public librarian. Occasionally, books were burned. "Did you ever try to burn a book?" asked another librarian. "It's *very* difficult." One-third of a group of librarians sampled in the late 1950s reported having removed "controversial" items from their shelves. One-fifth said they habitually avoided buying such books.

Academics, too, were scared. Many college and university social scientists polled in 1955 confessed to reining in their political views and activities. Twenty-seven percent had "wondered" whether a political opinion they had expressed might affect their job security or promotion; 40 percent had worried that a student might pass on "a warped version of what you have said and lead to false ideas about your political views." Twenty-two percent had at times "refrained from expressing an opinion or participating in some activity in order not to embarrass" their institution. Nine percent had "toned down" recent writing to avoid controversy. One teacher said he never expressed his own opinion in class. "I express the recognized and acknowledged point of view." Some instructors no longer assigned *The Communist Manifesto*.

About a hundred professors actually lost jobs, but an even greater number of frightened faculty trimmed their sails against the storm. Episodes far short of dismissal could also have a chilling effect. An economist at a Southern school addressed a business group, his talk, titled "Know Your Enemy," assessed Soviet resources and strengths. He was denounced to his president as a Communist. Another professor was assailed for advocating a lower tariff on oranges. "If I'd said potatoes, I wouldn't have been accused unless I had said it in Idaho." Some teachers got in mild trouble for such acts as assigning Robert and Helen Lynds' classic sociological study, *Middletown*, in class or listing the Kinsey reports on human sexuality as recommended reading. A professor once sent students to a public library to read works by Marx because his college's library had too few copies. Librarians logged the students' names. [14]

The precise effect of all this professed anxiety was fuzzy. Many liberals claimed that Americans had been cowed into silence, that even honest anti-Communist dissent had been stilled, and that basic freedoms of thought, expression, and association had languished. The worriers trotted out appropriate comparisons: the witch trials in Salem, the Reign of Terror in France, the Alien and Sedition Acts, Know-Nothingism, and the Palmer raids. Justice William O. Douglas warned of "The Black Silence of Fear." Prominent foreigners like Bertrand Russell and Graham Greene decried the pall of fear they observed in America. On July 4, 1951, a *Madison Capital-Times* reporter asked passersby to sign a paper containing the Bill of Rights and parts of the Declaration of Independence. Out of 112, only one would do so. President Truman cited the episode to show McCarthyism's dire effects. McCarthy retorted that Truman owed an apology to the people of Wisconsin in view of that paper's Communist-line policies. Some McCarthy allies upheld the wisdom of refusing to sign any statement promiscuously offered.

McCarthy's defenders ridiculed the more outlandish laments for vanished liberties. A New York rabbi who blamed "McCarthyism" for the current spree of college "panty raids" offered a case in point. Conservative journalist Eugene Lyons was amused by an ACLU spokesman, his tonsils flaring in close-up on television, arguing "that in America no one any longer dares open his mouth." Such talk, said Lyons, led to "hysteria over hysteria." In their apologia for McCarthy, William F. Buckley and L. Brent Bozell snickered at such silliness. They found it odd that, in a time when left-of-center ideas were supposedly being crushed, liberals seemed to monopolize symposia sponsored by the major universities, even in McCarthy's home state, and that Archibald MacLeish and Bernard De Voto, two of those who condemned the enervating climate of fear, had still managed to garner two National

Book Awards and a Pulitzer Prize. To Buckley and Bozell, the only conformity present was a proper one—a consensus that communism was evil and must be fought wholeheartedly.

But did such an argument miss the point? The successes enjoyed by prominent, secure liberals were one thing; far more numerous were the cases of those less visible and secure who lost entertainment and lecture bookings, chances to review books, teaching posts, even assembly-line jobs. The fight over the Communist menace had gone far beyond roistering debate or asserting the right of those who disagree with a set of views not to patronize them. People, a great number of whom had committed no crime, were made to suffer.[15]

RAMPANT ANTI-COMMUNISM narrowed the range of selection open to associations, utterances, and ideas. People were constrained by both external pressures and the inner checks with which they reactively restricted their own affairs. Fear was manifest in delicate matters of personal choice—such as what to read or think—as well as in more public behavior. In this latter respect, the collective result was a significant slowing of the momentum of change in a number of areas of American life.

In the 1930s, the civil-rights question had emerged from oblivion. FDR often ducked divisive race issues, but CIO unions, the Communist Party, and civil-rights activists pushed this American dilemma to the fore. By dramatizing the irony of battling Hitlerian racism at the same time that Jim Crow persisted, World War II heightened consciousness and hurried change. To blacks it brought occupational gains and augmented political leverage and assertiveness. Thus A. Philip Randolph's March on Washington Movement prodded FDR to create the Fair Employment Practices Commission.

This cantering change might have burst into a gallop after the war, but the rise of anti-communism inspired a new caution among mainstream civil-rights leaders. An old-time Socialist who had battled Communist efforts to infiltrate the March on Washington Movement and, earlier, the National Negro Congress, Randolph warned against dallying with the Communist conspiracy. (He also admonished that racism was a flaw vastly useful to the Soviets.) The Urban League also resisted any Communist influence in the civil-rights cause, and the 1948 national convention of the Congress of Racial Equality (CORE) went on record as opposing cooperation with Communist-front groups. In firing two professors who took the Fifth Amendment before HUAC, Fisk University proved no less timid than white colleges.

The NAACP, led by the Walter White, also preached anti-communism and worked to isolate black leaders who bucked the going trend. In 1950 its national board was authorized to expel any chapter that fell under Communist control. When in the same year the government lifted Paul Robeson's passport, the NAACP did not defend him. Its Legal Defense Fund also shunned W. E. B. Du Bois, once editor of the NAACP's journal but now linked to pro-Soviet causes. In 1951 the eighty-two-year-old Du Bois was arrested for failing to register as a leader of the Peace Information Center, an entity that aligned itself with Soviet-sponsored peace crusades. Claiming the government would successfully prove Du Bois's entanglement in conspiracy, Walter White convinced NAACP board members to remain aloof. The groundless case was later dismissed, however.

"By serving as the 'left wing of McCarthyism,' " Manning Marable has written, such leaders as Randolph and White "retarded the black movement for a decade or more." This criticism contains some truth but overlooks certain considerations. It is not clear that damn-the-torpedoes solidarity with Marxists or Popular Fronters would have advanced the civil-rights movement or that black public opinion would have supported it. As Marable notes, the Communists themselves squandered much of the sympathy they had won in the 1930s by taking pro-Soviet positions detrimental to black interests during the war. Randolph and other leaders had experienced Communists' efforts to join and exploit civil-rights groups for their own ends. CORE rejected alliance with Communists both because the latter often pursued conflicting goals and because such links would help foes to discredit CORE's cause. On balance the Communist issue operated as a retarding force, but even had it not been present, the civil-rights movement faced an uphill struggle against the tradition of American racism.

Soviet propaganda and the rise of anti-colonialism in Africa made U.S. race relations a sore point. Some American leaders came to see civil rights as at least a collateral Cold War priority. "We could not endorse a color line at home," wrote Harry Truman, "and still expect to influence the immense masses" of Asia and Africa. The greater leverage, however, lay with redbaiters and opponents of civil rights. Blacks could not, for example, use the Korean War as they had World War II as a fulcrum for change.[16]

Feminism also traveled a rough trail in the 1950s, but most of its hardships could not be ascribed to the Red Scare: the going had been rocky since 1920. Though World War II expanded women's job prospects—as for "Rosie the Riveter"—cultural expectations changed far less. The war's end brought what one historian terms a "vicious antifeminist backlash." The term "feminism" acquired increasingly negative connotations. What remained of a feminist presence was divided against itself: an old conflict pitted feminists who sought gains through union activities and government reforms against the National Woman's Party, whose single aim was to enact the Equal Rights Amendment. Rifts in the NWP itself were so wide in the late 1940s that they prompted party founder Alice Paul to disparage the loyalty of rivals to HUAC. (Some NWP members also applauded McCarthy and pointed knowingly to the Communist Party's opposition to the ERA.)

Political conservatism in the 1950s reinforced traditional female roles. So necessary was the home as a "symbol of security and stability" in that frightsome era that few dared question the reigning "domestic ideology." TV fare made the point. The mothers, like Harriet of "Ozzie and Harriet" or Mrs. Cleaver of "Leave it to Beaver," were able, steady, but clearly maternal figures. The effervescent Lucille Ball was something of an exception. Yet a typical "I Love Lucy" episode ended with discovery of her latest escapade, followed by her red-faced, keening apology ("Oooh Ricky") and a promise to shape up. She remained a housewife and eventually became a mother. In his analysis of 1950s anti-Communist movies, Michael Rogin finds "sexual politics" often depicted by a flawed mother figure (in such films as *My Son John*), who allows communism to intrude into the family.[17]

In the 1950s, practices deviating from the prescribed norms for family and sex were frowned on. When Alfred Kinsey's two famous studies of human sexual behavior revealed the prevalence of extramarital sex and of a great variety of sexual activity, traditionalists fumed. His *Sexual Behavior in the Human Female* (1953) impelled one cleric to detect a "fundamental kinship between that thing and Communism." A Catholic newspaper declared that the sex researcher's books "pave the way for people to believe in communism and to act like Communists." Lightheartedly, Senator Robert Kerr quipped that Dr. Kinsey and Joe Mc-

Carthy shared one trait: "They both claim to have uncovered a lot of domestic disloyalty." Morality's guardians were not amused. Congressman B. Carroll Reece's committee, which at the time was investigating charitable foundations and their support of subversive activities, assailed Kinsey's project. The general hostility to Kinsey's work, coupled with fears of what Reece might do, led the Rockefeller Foundation, already sensitive to criticisms of its funding activities, to end its grants to Kinsey.[18]

An age leery of excessive heterosexual activity had scant sympathy for homosexuality, which indeed was commonly viewed as a source of internal weakness analogous to communism. The 1950s brought heavy pressures upon gays and lesbians, who already faced severe social sanctions. The FBI watched gay bars, and local police often declared open season on them and lesbian hang-outs. The Post Office monitored recipients of "physique magazines" and entrapped them in various ways. From 1947 on, about five homosexuals were fired per month from federal jobs under the security program; the rate rose to sixty after an official testified in February 1950 that most of the ninety-one people recently fired by the State Department on moral grounds had been homosexuals. Indeed, that agency was thought to be especially rife with "sexual perverts."

These revelations threatened to make homosexuality a political issue in 1950. Republicans demanded an inquiry. In June, as Tydings's examination of McCarthy's charges ended, Senator Clyde Hoey launched a probe of homosexuality among federal employees. Hoey's panel questioned police and medical experts. It considered homosexuals in government a threat because they were vulnerable to manipulation and blackmail by Communist intriguers. (Its only evidence was a homosexual Austrian intelligence officer whom the Russians "turned" prior to World War I.) But Hoey's inquest was tame, with testimony taken in executive session, and a victory for restraint, especially given that McCarthy was a member of the parent committee. McCarthy himself often snickered about his targets' masculinity. He labeled Dean Acheson "the Red Dean of fashion" and belittled State Department anti-communism for slapping the Reds with a lace hanky at the front door while they bludgeoned one's grandmother at the back door. (Widespread rumors that he was himself a homosexual greatly vexed Joe. In fact, many witnesses have attested to his flagrant heterosexuality.)

World War II had accelerated single-sex congregation, geographic mobility, and thus the emergence of a growing number of gays and lesbians in America. The Mattachine Society, formed in 1951, was the first ongoing organization to advocate their interests. Founders included several current and former Communists. To prevent exposure. the Society was initially kept secret and patterned after the CP's "cell" structure. This precaution was based on both Party experience and a perception that McCarthyism embodied a trend toward repression that would encompass homosexuals as well as Reds. Had the guardians of public safety known of the founders' CP background or about the model the Society followed, they would have howled in anger.

But the main threat to the originators' vision came from within the Society itself. Early organizing success brought an influx of members who were unsympathetic to the founders' radical orientation and who wanted the Society to become open and respectable. In 1953 a newspaper column critical of the Society reported that one of its leaders had taken the Fifth Amendment before HUAC. Many newer members, sensitized to the dangers of a linkage between disloyalty and homosexuality, moved to take over and reshape the Society. Conceding the inevitable, the founders yielded control. Secrecy was ended. At its convention, the Society voted down a proposed loyalty oath, but its anti-Communist position was made clear. In so doing, the Society may have purchased slight immunity against anti-communism. (The FBI still saw fit to infiltrate the Mattachines and the Daughters of Bilitis, a lesbian organization.) But the Society had surrendered much of its militancy, dynamism, and early membership gains.[19] It thus repeated in its youth the pattern of older organizations. The times were so inhospitable, however, that quibbles about tactics or philosophy are beside the point. That, indeed, was the dilemma faced by all movements for change in this period.

Pacifists were a case in point. Having (like civil-rights activists) had disillusioning experiences, they sought to avoid links with Communists. The Cold War and especially the fighting in Korea destroyed any remaining romanticism among them about the Soviet Union. Though distancing themselves from the CP may have helped the pacifists to avert disaster, such prudence brought no appreciable gains, for at the height of the Cold War, peace groups had a hard time obtaining a hearing and were often redbaited—whether justifiably or not.

Later in the 1950s, a growing fear of radioactive fallout and of the nuclear arms race led to a rebirth of activism by peace groups. The strongest of these was SANE, the Committee for a Sane Nuclear Policy, founded in 1957. Sensitive to redbaiting, SANE's leaders adopted a resolution stating that the organization sought only members "whose support is not qualified by adherence to communist or other totalitarian doctrine." This action proved divisive and weakening—a sign itself of change—and a number of people resigned in protest at this revival of McCarthyism.[20]

Even the cause of Indian rights was marginally vulnerable to anti-Communist assaults. Advocates of Western economic growth and conservatives generally wanted to terminate tribal trust arrangements and open Indian reservations to economic development. The Eisenhower Administration was supportive: the property of several reservations was scheduled for release from tribal control. The terminationists viewed efforts to preserve traditional Native American communities and even the Bureau of Indian Affairs itself as socialistic, bureaucratic New Deal hangovers. One proponent of termination labeled John Collier, who had led New Deal Indian reform efforts, as "the voice of Russian Communists in their plans to capture the American Indian and thus start their world wide conspiracy to communize free America." An assimilated Klamath Indian called tribal government "communistic."[21]

Anti-communism had uses in local affairs too. For example, it was a recurrent element in the opposition to the adoption of a zoning ordinance for the city of Houston. In 1947 foes of zoning claimed that such planning "from Moscow . . . to Washington has backfired." It was a "legalistic monster, spawned in Europe and disguised in the slum-ridden eastern cities as a device to protect your homes." Oilman Hugh Roy Cullen (eventually a fervent McCarthy supporter) assailed zoning as "un-American and German." Such appeals persisted into the 1960s. In 1962 an opponent called zoning "socialized real estate."[22] Water flouridation was also termed by some critics a communist plot.

The ease with which redbaiting discredited so many causes showed how deeply anti-Communist assumptions permeated American culture. Indeed, they were a defining, rarely questioned characteristic of that culture. By and large, the debate over anti-communism among political and intellectual elites plumbed not goal but method. Liberal critics of McCarthy and of other extremists did not question the validity of anti-communism. Rather, they often began any exposition with the phrase, "I'm anti-Communist too, but. . . ." It has been suggested that a less apologetic—indeed, less anti-Communist—orientation would have better served liberalism. But inglorious though the liberal anti-

Communist posture sometimes appeared in the early 1950s, it is unlikely that a less pragmatic, more absolutist civil-libertarian position would have brought benefits. Such an argument assumes that the ultimate leverage in national politics at the Cold War's height was in the liberals' hands. Assuredly, it lay elsewhere.

7

"In Calmer Times. . . ."

In 1954 several developments combined to check the momentum of anti-Communist extremism. McCarthy's censure by the Senate was both a sign of and force for change. In the next three years, the atmosphere of the McCarthy era would dissipate. Many institutional underpinnings of the Red Scare endured, but the change was nonetheless profound.

Yet the anti-Communist posturing of the day often obscured this trend. Congress passed several anti-Communist measures in 1954. In August, as they moved gingerly to censure McCarthy, lawmakers posed as burly anti-Communists. The Senate moved to amend the McCarran Act to punish "Communist-infiltrated" bodies—meaning unions. After liberals failed to block this bill, Hubert Humphrey offered a substitute that labeled the CP as a conspiracy, not a party, and that would punish anyone who "knowingly and willfully" joined it. After years of anti-Red pallaver, said Humphrey, it was time "to quit 'horsing around' " and act. The two bills were combined, and this shotgun marriage was approved 85 to 1.

In the House, however, conservatives argued that Humphrey had gutted the McCarran Act. (That law stated that CP membership was *not* a crime; otherwise its registration requirement would open Communists to prosecution under the Smith Act.) When the bill went back to the Senate with new criminal penalties removed, liberals chided conservatives for their tepid anti-communism. Both chambers adopted the Communist Control Act by huge margins. Somewhat apologetically, Humphrey claimed he borrowed "only a few provisions" from a bill proposed by Martin Dies (who had returned to Congress in 1953 after having retired in 1945). He argued that his bill shifted the Communist issue from politics to the courts where it belonged. In fact, the law was a mere gesture that showed the grip of the anti-Communist consensus.

McCarthy's censure, as its supporters took pains to stress, implied no rejection of anti-communism. To prove it, early in 1955 the Senate passed a resolution reaffirming its committees' authority to investigate communism. Soon thereafter, McCarthy's subcommittee, now controlled by the Democrats after the 1954 election, again raked over the Army's handling of the Peress affair.

Other pursuers of communism kept busy even at the peak of McCarthy's notoriety. Investigating unions, churches, and the entertainment field, HUAC questioned over 650 witnesses in 1953–54. HUAC and SISS also made education a major focus in 1953 as over 100 college and university teachers were brought before the two panels (and sometimes McCarthy's).

Teachers who took the Fifth were usually fired, but outcomes varied. Public universities were likelier than well-endowed private schools to fire balky witnesses. Tenured faculty received formal hearings on their campuses. These proceedings often ratified removal but on occasion saved an instructor's job; still, trustees or presidents sometimes overrode a faculty recommendation for retention. Untenured teachers commonly were let go without due process.

Radical professors occupied "no ivory tower," in historian Ellen Schrecker's phrase. Academic communities often had surprisingly little knowledge of the Fifth Amendment or sympathy for its users. Having concluded by 1949 that Communists had forfeited the right to teach, by 1953 leaders of academe declared that teachers who took the Fifth had denied to colleagues the "complete candor" which academic life demanded. An atmosphere of anti-communism, consisting partly of conviction and partly of caution, prevailed on campus. In this climate, pressed by alumni, trustees, and state legislators, college presidents often tossed faculty mavericks over the side.

Yet the pattern was dappled. Rutgers University set precedent in 1952 by firing two teachers who cited the Fifth Amendment. Harvard kept tenured but dropped untenured Fifth-takers. University of Michigan faculty who invoked the Fifth were fired. Some schools managed to weather the era's political turbulence. Though some small colleges bent before the gale, liberal Reed College kept a professor who took the Fifth. The University of Wisconsin, despite its state's junior Senator, avoided controversy thanks to its canny president and the loyalty of many state politicians. Colorado College had no Reds or ornery witnesses, but vocal conservatives monitored the faculty and each year insisted on the ouster of teachers they deemed to be Communists. The college's president, a retired Major General loyal to his "troops," airily dismissed these demands. In all roughly a hundred college and university teachers lost jobs. An informal blacklist excluded most of them from other academic positions.[1]

Besides teachers, HUAC also harried liberal churchmen. Though cheered by the fundamentalist Right (then emerging as a source of hardshell anti-communism), HUAC Chairman Harold W. Velde's campaign against liberal and far-left clerics earned modest returns. Velde's chief mark was G. Bromley Oxnam, the liberal Methodist Bishop of Washington and a staunch foe of HUAC. (One committee member accused Oxnam of serving "God on Sunday and the Communist front for the balance of the week.") After Oxnam's effective rebuttal, HUAC soon moved on. Liberals could rejoice that the inept Velde chaired it in the Eighty-third Congress.

In 1955, with Congress under Democratic control, Francis Walter took over HUAC. Having viewed the committee's zanier antics with contempt, the potent Pennsylvania Democrat proceeded—sometimes, at least—more cautiously during his reign, which lasted until 1963. Hearings were fewer, but HUAC kept busy, and Walter was far from the savior some liberals had hoped for.

HUAC remained infatuated with entertainers and artists. In 1955 it called folksinger and songwriter Pete Seeger. He offered to discuss his music, including songs he learned from coal miners in Walter's district, but not the auspices under which he sang. Cited for contempt, he won a reversal in 1962, but his politics blighted his career. Folksong was ready to take off in the early 1950s. Seeger's group, the Weavers, had recorded a hit with "Good Night, Irene," but after *Counterattack* listed him, bookings sagged. After testifying, Seeger did not appear on network television until 1967, by which time he had become a hero to the folkishly inclined young. Rightists, however, still viewed folk music as a stigma of the Left.

HUAC was encountering a fundamental problem: pickings in its old haunts were growing slim. Amid the disillusionment prompted by Soviet Premier Nikita Krushchev's 1956 speech denouncing Stalinism, the already battered American Communist Party had become enfeebled. HUAC nevertheless continued its road-show hearings on Communist influences in various localities; twice in its proceedings, two FBI infiltrators surfaced to denounce each other as Communists.

The emerging civil-rights movement did offer redbaiters one growth sector in their dying enterprise. The Supreme Court's 1954 decision in *Brown v. Board of Education,* ruling that the doctrine of "separate but equal" was unconstitutional, tore up the foundations of American race law, and racial traditionalists scented the malign influence of communism. This was no sudden inspiration. For years Southern defenders of the status quo had lambasted New Dealers for encouraging black assertiveness. HUAC itself had always looked askance at groups that worked for civil rights.

Nor was the tie between racial unease and anti-communism unique to the South. In Northern and border states, as racial conflict flared along the frontiers of changing urban neighborhoods, anti-Communist rhetoric stoked turmoil. In Chicago's often violent battles over neighborhood turf, defenders of the existing race-segregated order leveled McCarthyite attacks at such foes as city housing planners—even before McCarthy's emergence. As the South saw its way of life menaced by a remote, "un-American" Supreme Court, so threatened neighborhoods reacted to distant housing bureaucrats.

In 1954 Louisville, Kentucky, witnessed an episode that combined racism and antiradicalism. A week before the *Brown* verdict, Carl and Anne Braden, two white radicals, bought a home in an all-white area, then resold it to black friends. Outrage festered. Soon after the blacks moved in, a local weekly asked whether Communists meant to "encourage panic, chaos, and riot to lower the morale of the American people?" After the house was bombed, local officials did not pursue the likeliest bombers, the enemies of integration, arguing instead that the crime may have been an "inside job," perhaps "Communistic-inspired." Indeed, Carl Braden was indicted for violating a state sedition law and conspiring to dynamite his friends' house. HUAC staffers aided the prosecutors, helping to procure the ex-Communists who testified for them. Convicted and sentenced to fifteen years in jail, Braden was freed after eight months only when the Supreme Court ruled in another case that federal anti-subversive measures overrode state sedition laws.

After the *Brown* ruling, Southern anti-communism took on a higher pitch, and Southern politicians, who previously had been least lured by McCarthy's appeal, now resorted more often to redbaiting. In 1954 Judge Tom Brady confided to the White Citizens Council of Indianola, Mississippi, that Communist influences had guided the Supreme Court to its decision. That theme became a staple of Southern anti-integration rhetoric and would buttress the 1960s campaign—launched by what came to be termed the radical Right—to "Impeach Earl Warren," the Chief Justice.

Once blasé, Southern state legislatures awoke to the Red menace. After *Brown*, they established variously named state commissions that often espied Communist conspiracy behind civil-rights agitation. Georgia's Attorney General charged that "either knowingly or unwittingly" the NAACP had "allowed itself to become part and parcel of the Communist conspiracy." South Carolina legislators called for its inclusion on the Attorney General's list. In 1957 Louisiana's Joint Legislative Committee to Maintain Segregation heard Manning Johnson, a busy ex-Communist (and black) informant, testify that the NAACP was "nothing more than a vehicle of the Communist Party." Johnson also appeared before a comparable committee in Arkansas, and J. B. Matthews testified similarly to panels in Mississippi, Arkansas, and Florida. Several states passed measures to outlaw or harass the NAACP in ways prefigured by earlier federal enactments. These efforts to redbait the civil-rights movement would persist into the 1960s. (Obviously, the pains civil-rights groups had taken to distance themselves from the Communists had made no impression on Southern racists.)[2]

In national politics, anti-communism and racism might have forged a potent alloy, but several factors—among them, fortuitous timing—prevented complete bonding. McCarthy's star was waning as distemper over civil rights rose. Nor was he a racist. Indeed, in 1953 opponents feared he might broaden his appeal by "going into the pro-Negro field." But in 1956, after the Supreme Court curbed state and federal anti-Communist activities, his interests converged with those of segregationists: both deplored the Court's trespass upon states' rights. At an Internal Security Subcommittee hearing, he sang a duet with Senator

James Eastland. When the latter taxed the Court with "one pro-communist decision after another," McCarthy said: "You are so right." When Eastland speculated that "some secret, but very powerful Communist or pro-communist influence" infected the Court, McCarthy merely suggested "incompetence beyond words" as an alternative.[3]

Though not its inventor, Eastland was a logical custodian of the union of civil rights and communism. The Mississippi conservative had sat on SISS from its birth and chaired it since 1955. Ten days after the *Brown* decision, he denounced the Supreme Court. It housed two character witnesses for Alger Hiss and honorees at testimonial dinners given by "Communist fronts like the Southern Conference for Human Welfare." Given the sources cited in *Brown*, Eastland saw nothing to prevent a future decision based on "the works of Karl Marx." Everyone knew that "the Negroes did not themselves instigate the agitation against segregation. They were put up to it by radical busybodies who are intent upon overthrowing American institutions."

The theme persisted. Eastland marked *Brown's* first anniversary by deploring the "dangerous influence and control exerted on the court by Communist-front pressure groups and other enemies of the American Republic." The ruling cited authorities whose ties to "the worldwide Communist conspiracy" shocked him. Thus the classic work on race relations, *An American Dilemma*, was written by "Swedish Socialist" Gunnar Myrdal in cahoots with the Carnegie Corporation "of Alger Hiss fame." Eastland saw no obligation to obey a ruling grounded on ideas of "pro-communist agitators" and anti-Americans. Senators Herman Talmadge and Strom Thurmond and Georgia Congressman E. L. Forrester also linked integration and communism.

Both SISS under Eastland and HUAC with its complement of Southern conservatives portrayed civil rights as a Red scheme. In 1954 Eastland held solo hearings in New Orleans to prove that the Southern Conference Education Fund (SCEF) had succeeded the much-maligned Southern Conference for Human Welfare and inherited its Communist liaisons. In 1958 Carl Braden, now working for SCEF, was called before HUAC. Uncooperative and scorning use of the Fifth, he was found guilty of contempt and jailed. In 1963 SCEF's leaders were arrested for violating a Louisiana anti-subversion law. Directed by Louisiana's Un-American Activities Committee, police tore apart SCEF's New Orleans office and seized its records; Eastland's subcommittee took custody of them. When SCEF sued for possession of the papers, they were spirited across the river out of Louisiana's jurisdiction.

Ultimately, SCEF won its legal battles. In 1965 the U.S. Supreme Court found Louisiana's anti-subversive law unconstitutional. However, SCEF survived Southern racism only to fall prey to sectarianism as the interracial civil-rights movement disintegrated. In the 1970s, it collapsed, succumbing to the centrifugal pull of black nationalists and white new-leftists.

The Highlander Folk School of Monteagle, Tennessee, also met Southern wrath. Founded in 1932, the school sought to catalyze social change by educating labor organizers and other leaders at integrated gatherings. A state of Georgia operative "infiltrated" such a meeting and snapped a photo that had political repercussions: he caught Rev. Martin Luther King, Jr., fresh from victory in the Montgomery bus boycott, seated near a *Daily Worker* writer. Hundreds of thousands of copies of the picture littered the South and crowded its billboards. Highlander became known as a "Communist training school." SISS summoned its director in 1954 and had him removed when he refused to testify. Hounded by the state of Tennessee, Highlander lost its charter and property in the early 1960s.

In such instances, the Communist issue and pertinent legal sanctions could have crushing impact civil-rights activists. National politicians played prominent, sometimes necessary, but seldom sufficient or solitary roles in countermoves against Southern civil-rights groups. Usually state-level harassment did more damage than the traveling inquisitors from Washington.

Paradoxically, at the national level efforts to merge racism and anti-communism probably tainted both causes. The outcome of Eastland's 1954 New Orleans hearings on SCEF hinted at this process. On one hand, the visit ruined the careers of a contractor and lawyer from Florida, and it wrecked the newspaper business of former New Dealer Aubrey Williams. On the other hand, SISS discredited itself by questioning Virginia Durr, a feisty SCEF board member. Mrs. Durr stood "mute" on questions about her associations. Ex-Communist paladin Paul Crouch then swore that the Durrs had advanced Communist causes.

But Williams, Virginia Durr, and her husband had unusual clout. Unprecedentedly, Eastland let Williams's lawyer, Clifford Durr, cross-examine Crouch whose flawed testimony left his credibility tattered; the government never again used him as a witness. Even newspapers opposed to integration termed the hearings shameful. Williams's and the Durrs' friendship with Lyndon Johnson assured that no contempt citations were issued and that Eastland never carried out his declared intent to hold more hearings in the South.

A changed atmosphere was also evident in the response to Dale Alford's maiden House speech in 1959. A newly elected segregationist, Alford ripped the "Warren-Myrdal court" and "racial agitation" like that taking place in his native Little Rock. Two Northern colleagues twitted the Arkansan, first making him concede that Commonwealth College, a defunct school in his home state, had been cited as subversive and then noting that Governor Orval Faubus, who had precipitated the 1957 Little Rock school crisis by resisting the integration of Central High, had attended the college. Though still a negotiable commodity in the proper local or regional setting, anti-communism had lost much of its national market.[4]

ANTI-COMMUNISM had by no means collapsed, but 1953–54 marked a multiple turning point as the underpinnings of the second Red Scare slowly eroded. About a year into Eisenhower's first term, the loyalty-security apparatus began to attract rising criticism, and by 1955 several congressional panels were at least skeptically examining it, although not with the intention of abolishing the system altogether. Previously, publicity had nourished Red-hunters like McCarthy; now it operated to highlight the system's harshness and to discredit, if not the premise of anti-communism, at least the methods by which (and the extremities to which) it was enforced.

In October 1953, Ed Murrow examined the case of Lt. Milo Radulovich on the television show "See It Now." A meteorologist in the Air Force Reserve, Radulovich was charged as a security risk because of his sister's and father's Communist associations. The show conveyed Radulovich's eloquent defense, his family's anger, and his hometown's support. The Secretary of the Air Force was at length persuaded that Radulovich was no security risk. More broadly, the show spelled out to the public the injustices the security program sometimes visited upon ordinary folks next door.

When the GOP began playing a "numbers game" with the results of Ike's security program late in 1953, Democrats were angered. The bandying of these figures convinced many Democrats that the Republicans had appropriated McCarthy's issue and tactics. They were further outraged in November when Attorney General Herbert Brownell attacked Truman for not firing the suspected Communist Harry Dexter White in 1946. When HUAC's Chairman Harold Velde subpoenaed Truman to respond to the charge, however, the ex-President ignored the summons and assailed the Eisenhower Administration for embracing McCarthyism.

Several controversial cases focused additional criticism on the security program. A particularly agonizing case in 1954 was that of J. Robert Oppenheimer. The rising star of American theoretical physics in the 1930s, "Oppie" had run the Manhattan Project's Los Alamos lab during the war. But the "father" of the A-bomb viewed his destructive child with misgivings, and his expressed doubts, as well as his leftist associations during the 1930s, kindled suspicions in more committed cold warriors. Indeed, propelled by anti-fascism into the Popular Front, he had hobnobbed with Communists, who included his brother, wife, several friends, and some of his graduate students. At Los Alamos, he never compromised security but sometimes deceived security officers about his contacts and indiscretions. As sleuths tapped his phone and watched his movements, his dossier grew to a height of four and a half feet.

In wartime Oppenheimer was deemed indispensable, so his errant ways had been excused, but later his sometimes abrasive manner and his brooding concern over the arms race won him enemies in the nuclear establishment. Then, Soviet conquest of the atom led U.S. leaders, in 1950, to press ahead on development of the H-bomb. Oppie's doubts about the project dismayed enthusiasts like fellow physicist Edward Teller; William Borden, former executive director of the Joint Congressional Committee on Atomic Energy (JCAE); and Admiral Lewis Strauss, a member and later chairman of the Atomic Energy Commission (AEC). Oppenheimer's skepticism about the H-bomb and the prevailing faith in strategic bombing also earned him the enmity of important Air Force leaders.

By 1953 Oppenheimer served only as an occasional consultant to the AEC. His contract was to expire in June 1954, but events were not allowed to run their course. Late in 1953, William Borden warned J. Edgar Hoover that "more probably than not J. Robert Oppenheimer is an agent of the Soviet Union." Ike thereupon ordered the physicist separated from AEC secrets by a "blank wall." Oppenheimer chose to contest the charges. A Personnel Security Board headed by former Army Secretary Gordon Gray heard the case at vast length in April and May of 1954 (while the Army-McCarthy hearings ground on).

On June 1, the Gray Board by a 2-to-1 vote ruled Oppenheimer a security risk. The AEC general manager's concurring report dwelt on Oppenheimer's past involvements in communism, his ongoing ties with people of dubious political reliability, his questionable "veracity," and his "obstruction and disregard of security." With just eighteen days to consider the report before Oppie's contract expired, four of the AEC's five commissioners voted to deny him clearance. Chairman Strauss rested his majority opinion on Oppenheimer's "fundamental defects of character and imprudent dangerous associations."

Critics of the verdict suspected that Oppie's views on the H-bomb were what primarily underlay the government's determination to break his influence. After all, almost every other aspect of the case involved events prior to 1947, when the AEC's own security program had cleared him. In subsequent conflicts between (and among) the scientists and the military over nuclear and defense policies, Oppenheimer was a central actor and symbol. His fate was also snarled in more current politicking. Could the Eisenhower Administration wink at his indiscretions after all its anti-Communist posturing? McCarthy was nosing about; in April 1954, he had charged deliberate delays in the H-bomb project. Only assurances of swift action—and his own problems—kept him from meddling further. Senator Clinton Anderson, a member of the JCAE, theorized that going after Oppenheimer "was only a move to win Joe McCarthy's silence toward Admiral Strauss."

The Oppenheimer case prompted many doubts about the security system. Oppenheimer's record was questionable, but as Dr. Ward Evans, dissenting from the Gray Board's majority view, put it, "All people are somewhat of a security risk." Many observers believed Oppenheimer's past service and future usefulness far outweighed the negative indications. A Herblock cartoon showed the scientist sitting pensively on one side of a rising cinderblock barrier. The caption asked, "Who's Being Walled Off From What?"[5]

Other cases also stimulated debate. In late 1954, the plight of Wolf Ladejinsky became public. A land reform expert who served ably in Japan, Ladejinsky was seeking to transfer from the State Department to the Department of Agriculture, but the Secretary of Agriculture found him to be a security risk. He had relatives in the USSR who, it was claimed, enabled Moscow to hold sway over him. Indeed, it was even suggested that his *anti*-Bolshevik writings proved he was under Soviet control. These postulates sparked criticism in the press and Congress. The situation was resolved in 1955 when another agency, the Foreign Operations Administration, employed Ladejinsky's talents in crisis-ridden Vietnam. (In 1956 he had to resign over a perfectly capitalist conflict of interest.)

Meant to quell cricitism, the Eisenhower security program only bred it. Journalists exposed injustices committed in its name. A 1955 study sponsored by the Fund for the Republic offered a sample of cases. There were horror stories of guilt by familial relationship and by early, casual, even inadvertent radical ties. One man in a government agency was accused of associating with someone known as "J," who had quit the same agency while under scrutiny and who allegedly had "communist tendencies." For a friend known as "K," who resigned in similar straits, the employee had penned a tribute and attended a farewell party. In another tale, a government employee was accused of owning "Communist art," apparently meaning reproductions of Modigliani, Renoir, Picasso, and Matisse. Another was said to have cohabited with a woman not his wife (true, but they were now married). At times questions outdid charges in inventiveness. Did he ever buy the *New York Times* regularly? a geographer was asked. Did he have favorite columnists? Did he attend church or give his children religious training? Did he favor government ownership of utilities?

The Military Personnel Security Program earned demerits too. Many men received unwelcome draft notices only to face disciplinary proceedings based on their lives prior to induction. Some whose loyalty was impeached were kept in uniform but assigned meaningless duties; many received unfavorable discharges. The activities that flagged a GI's file typically occurred in his teens, but in one case, the inductee's age at the time of his alleged subversion was eight. In other cases, three soldiers encountered trouble because their stepmothers assertedly belonged to the CP. Another was said to have a Communist mother-in-law who was "lying low" but was soon to become active again. In fact, she had died in 1940, when the draftee was ten—a decade before he would meet his wife.

The nation boasted still other security programs. The Defense Department checked out employees working for all its contractors, scrutinizing perhaps three million workers by 1955. The Korean War and fear of Harry Bridges's influence over the Longshoremen's Union prodded Congress to enact a Port Security Program under which the Coast Guard barred some 2,500 workers from ships or restricted waterfront areas. U.N. employees, union officers, employees of twenty-four states and many localities, teachers, attorneys in a number of places, some physicians, even boxers in Indiana—all fell under various loyalty programs. The Bell phone companies made employees foreswear membership in any group on the Attorney General's list. The accounting firm of Arthur Andersen and Co., required a loyalty statement. Author Ralph S. Brown, Jr., estimated that some 13,500,000 employees—roughly one out of every five in America—came under the toils of such programs.[6]

The Democrats wearied of the issue. Senate Majority Leader Lyndon Johnson's staff warned that if the trend persisted, "The Democrats are almost certain to become embroiled in a number of 'numbers game' investigations. *These are extremely dangerous to the party.*" Hubert Humphrey also feared Republicans would "continue to use the security issue as a political club."

When the Democrats regained control of the Senate in January 1955, three of them—Olin Johnston, Thomas Hennings, and Hubert Humphrey—launched investigations of the security programs. They unearthed cases of injustice, inefficiency, and excessive zeal. Hennings's group heard the mayor of New Rochelle concede that his suburb's 1950 ordinance requiring Communist residents to register was "really meaningless"; enacted at a moment of "public pressure," it had netted not a single Red. The implications of these probes were clear to Joe McCarthy. He showed up at several hearings of the Humphrey panel and blasted Hennings's inquiry.[7]

The security system also sprang a leak at its weakest point—the use of ex-Communists as informants, secret or otherwise. Former Party members had always played key roles in the politics of denunciation, but it took Harvey Matusow to devalue his profession's reputation for veracity. Matusow had joined the CP in 1947; disillusioned, he became an undercover FBI informant. In 1952 he broke cover as a witness in a Smith Act trial. Soon he was serving as an expert and finger-man for the Justice Department, the Subversive Activities Control Board, the McCarthy subcommittee, HUAC, SISS, and other watchdogs; he also wrote for the Hearst papers, gave speeches, and campaigned for

Republicans—on a for-hire basis. Then, in February 1955, Matusow confessed that his testimony at various trials and hearings had been perjured. He even wrote a book merchandizing his admissions, which included the claim that he had testified falsely at the trial of unionist Clinton Jencks in Texas.

Other "kept witnesses" had blotched records as well. Paul Crouch admitted to having a fanciful memory. Louis Budenz had raised eyebrows with his opportune ability to recall new names (like Owen Lattimore's) after failing to mention them in extensive prior debriefings. It became clear that, whether resulting from error or malice, fallacious identifications of accused persons as Communists had been going on for some time. Indeed, the whole informer system was politically vulnerable. On call for trials, immigration hearings, and legislative probes, these ex-Communists were, after all, paid for their services. "This is a good racket, being a professional witness," Matusow boasted. To prosper, one obviously had to keep on supplying the sort of tidbits prosecutors wanted to hear. By 1954 the Justice Department had a list of over eighty witnesses in current use. Thus, when Matusow exposed the program's seedy mercenary side, embarrassing prosecutors and legislators who owned stock in the Communist issue, an effort was made to discredit his confession. SISS held an inquiry, which promptly concluded that the only lie Matusow ever told was the one he was telling *now*—about having lied in the past.

Though collectively they fell short of the "Hiss-case-in-reverse" that journalist Joseph Alsop predicted the security program would eventually produce, Matusow's apostasy and the dubious cases against Oppenheimer, Ladejinsky, and others began to take their toll. In March 1955, Attorney General Brownell announced palliative reforms in the security program. Senator Humphrey proposed the appointment of a Commission on Government Security. Sponsored by the liberal Humphrey and the conservative John Stennis, the resolution passed in August with bipartisan support. Chosen by the House, Senate, and Executive Branch, the commission's members were empaneled in November.

In spite of its auspicious, bipartisan beginnings, however, the commission was not fated to bring real change. Fundamentally conservative, it was headed by West Coast attorney Loyd G. Wright; its members included Senator Stennis and HUAC Chairman Francis Walter, and its staff director was an ex-aide to J. Edgar Hoover. Issued in 1957, the commission's report disappointed reformers. It advocated a broader and tighter security program and a return to separate loyalty hearings. Its advocacy of the right to confront and cross-examine accusers was hedged by its strictures against compromising intelligence sources. Its recommendations were generally ignored.

Ultimately it took the Supreme Court to bedevil security's guardians into submission. Although the security program remained a part of government, it was bridled by many of the Court's rulings in the late 1950s.[8]

IN FACT, if anti-Communist extremism was the Dracula prowling the mid-century darkness of American politics, it was the Supreme Court that drove the fatal stake through its heart. At first, the Court seldom championed individual rights over the demands of national security. It mandated use of the Smith Act against Communist Party chiefs; it (narrowly) upheld the loyalty program; it permitted enforcement of immigration and passport regulations against radicals; it approved Taft-Hartley Act sanctions against Communist union chiefs; and it let stand most state and local anti-subversive measures.

The situation changed after 1953 when Earl Warren succeeded the late Fred Vinson as Chief Justice. Warren's past did not foreshadow clearly his subsequent course. As California's Governor he was a liberal, but he had also been a hardnosed prosecutor. He had endorsed relocating Japanese-Americans during World War II yet later had guilty second thoughts. Though he orated against the Red menace as the 1948 GOP vice-presidential nominee, on occasion he also criticized McCarthy. Only after his succession as Chief Justice did his support of individual rights become fully clarified. William Brennan's elevation to the High Court in 1956 would add another vote in favor of civil liberties.

In 1955 the Supreme Court began to put modest obstacles in the way of investigative committees. Eventually, three opinions warned that HUAC's inquiries could not simply harass people; they must have a legislative aim. The Court also ruled that the Loyalty Review Board (which Eisenhower's 1953 security program had abolished) had wrongly assumed the power to reverse favorable lower board rulings.

Change quickened in 1956. In *Cole v. Young,* the Court reversed the security firing of a food and drug inspector on the grounds that the Department of Health, Education and Welfare was not a "sensitive" agency as enumerated in the 1950 law that undergirded the security program; the program had thus exceeded its statutory authority in dismissing the inspector. In response, the court's minority view deplored the majority's premise that sensitive positions were easily identified, arguing that a janitor could as easily betray as a department head. Eisenhower and several members of Congress protested this curb on the war against subversion.

Pennsylvania v. Nelson stirred deeper ire. CP leader Steve Nelson had been convicted under Pennsylvania's sedition law, but Warren held in 1956 that by its own internal-security measures Congress had preempted the field from the states. Anti-Communists, who had long policed Americanism in amicable partnership with state authorities, seethed over the ruling. Conservative Southerners, already rubbed sore by the *Brown* decision, also protested the invasion of states' rights. The case cemented the McCarthy-Eastland alliance.

The Court also upheld the right against self-incrimination, reversing a decision against a Brooklyn College professor fired for using the Fifth before SISS. In 1957 the Court ruled that bar associations could not reject admissions applicants solely for refusing to testify about political affiliations.

That same year, the Court swiped at HUAC. Union leader John Watkins testified freely that, though not a Party member, he had cooperated with Communists; refusing to discuss anyone he did not think was currently a CP member, he challenged HUAC's authority to make him do so. He was cited for contempt. The Warren Court argued that congressional power to investigate was not boundless: committees could not "expose for the sake of exposure." An actual legislative function was required.

Government's power to use untested contents of secret files or to act on the word of ex-Communists was also curtailed. Testimony by two witnesses (including Matusow) had convicted Clinton Jencks of perjury in signing the Taft-Hartley Act's non-Communist oath. The trial judge denied Jencks's request to see FBI files that might refute the witnesses' memories, but the Supreme Court held for Jencks. The ruling shocked lawmakers, Eisenhower, and J. Edgar Hoover, who feared a future in which his secret files would lack their sacrosanct status.

The Court even hobbled use of the Smith Act, negating convictions of fourteen "second-string" Communists in *Yates v. U.S.* Unlike earlier defendants, particularly those in the *Dennis* case, this group forsook a "labor defense," instead stressing civil liberties and a devotion to peaceful change. The High Court upheld them, ruling that the statute of limitations now covered the 1945 act of reestablishing the CPUSA and that the lower court erred in not distinguishing between "advocacy of abstract doctrine and advocacy of action." Justice Tom Clark and other critics of the Court's majority ruling rightly warned that the Smith Act had been gutted. Eighty-one other indictments of CP leaders were dismissed. By 1957 such prosecutions had ended, although the government did use the Smith Act's membership clause against eight Party members. The Supreme Court confirmed the conviction of Junius Scales in 1961, but later that year it found that, without evidence of personal commitment to forcible overthrow of the government, mere Party membership did not afford grounds for a conviction.

On June 17, 1957, besides *Yates, Watkins,* and its reversal of John Stewart Service's firing, the Court also curbed state anti-subversionists again. In *Sweezy v. New Hampshire,* it struck down a contempt verdict against a Marxist professor who had refused to answer the queries of New Hampshire's one-man inquisition, Attorney General Louis Wyman, about the professor's connections, beliefs, and even the contents of his lectures at the state university. Horrified critics of these decisions termed the date "Red Monday."

Warning darkly of Communist influences on the Court, some conservatives urged action to countermand these rulings. Columnist David Lawrence proposed a loyalty program for Supreme Court law clerks and—startlingly for a conservative—the election of judges. One Congressman considered *Jencks* and *Watkins* a greater victory for the Soviets than they had won "on any battlefield since World War II." Critical rumblings issued from the American Bar Association. Eisenhower later told Warren of his displeasure with all these "Communist cases." When Warren asked how he would deal with the Communists, Ike replied: "I would kill the S.O.B.s."

Lawmakers pondered remedies. Some would strip the Court of jurisdiction over various internal-security matters. Representative Howard Smith proposed to negate the doctrine of federal preemption of state authority to act in any field unless Congress specifically mandated it. Passed by the House, this bill lost, thanks to Lyndon Johnson, by a single Senate vote in 1958, in what may have been the last floor battle of the McCarthy era. Congress did pass a law to limit the *Jencks* ruling; while it reserved the defendant's right of discovery, the new law prevented fishing expeditions through FBI files.

Though other bills to curb or chastise the Court foundered, the Court handled internal-security issues more gingerly after 1957. It pulled back from *Nelson's* fuller implications in 1959 by letting states combat subversion aimed at their own governments. In 1958 it interpreted broadly the congressional power to investigate—a retreat from *Watkins*. In 1961 the Court let stand the contempt citations voted against two foes of HUAC who had refused to testify.

Yet the Warren Court kept hacking at the props of Cold War repression. For years the State Department withheld passports from critics of U.S. policy. In several decisions, notably in the 1958 case of pro-Soviet artist Rockwell Kent, the Court affirmed the right to travel. The State Department continued to deny passports to those whose travel it deemed harmful to the nation, but it usually lost on appeals to the courts. By the mid-1960s, the right to a passport was firmly established. Even Paul Robeson finally got his back.

With the Smith Act wrecked, the McCarran Act remained anti-communism's last legal artillery, but eventually it misfired as well. It empowered the Subversive Activities Control Board to identify Communist-action and front groups and to make them register. However, countless hearings, delays, court appeals, and remands ensued after passage of the act in 1950. Three times the SACB held the CP to be a Communist-action entity. Finally, in 1961 the Supreme Court found the registration provision constitutional, but the ruling proved an empty victory. In 1965 the Court ruled that making Party leaders register violated their Fifth Amendment immunity from self-incrimination. Two years later, a lower court found the registration requirement unconstitutional; the government did not appeal. Beyond the legal harassment it wrought, the McCarran Act proved fangless.

Along with McCarthy's fall, Democratic control of Congress, and growing criticism of the security programs, the Supreme Court played a central role in deflating "McCarthyism." In his *Dennis* dissent in 1951, Justice Hugo Black had offered the hope that "in calmer times," the Court would "restore the First Amendment liberties to the high preferred place where they belong to a free society." By 1957 those times had arrived. But given the fact that the McCarthy era amounted to so much more than the Senator's antics, including legal, bureaucratic, and informal sanctions against dissent, it is daunting to ponder what might have happened had different judges sat on the High Court in the 1950s. It was a happy accident that Eisenhower made what he called his biggest error, appointing "that dumb son of a bitch Earl Warren" as Chief Justice.[9]

AFTER ANTI-COMMUNIST extremism was dispersed from the surface of public life, it coursed with hidden potency below ground. The microphone had been its tool, but so had the manila folder. Anticommunism had always had a strong bureaucratic component, and so its files and their keepers endured after outward, public McCarthyism passed. In addition, federal government agencies undertook a set of clandestine activities worthy of the secret police of the czars.

Aliens suspected of disloyalty sensed none of the greater placidity of American political life. Though hostility to foreigners had somewhat softened at the plight of the many refugees uprooted by World War II and the Cold War, and asssimilation was proceeding apace, xenophobia persisted. Some foes of immigration feared that subversives marched in the ranks of displaced persons. A Texas Congressman termed DPs "a new fifth column." Just as Martin Dies and Ham Fish sought to curb immigration in the 1930s, so such prominent anti-Communists in the 1950s as Congressman Francis Walter and Senator Pat McCarran bugled the threat of alien radicalism. The McCarran Act of 1950 denied entry to foreigners who had had Communist or Fascist affiliations, and the 1952 McCarran-Walter Immigration Act refined these sanctions.

The laws and the times prompted sharp growth in the number of allegedly subversive aliens who were excluded from the United States. The number denied entry in the 1940s totaled 29; in the 1950s, the annual average exceeded 140, and in the peak year 1957, 302 were excluded. The same decade saw a rise in the number of aliens deported as subversives or anarchists. Only 17 had been sent away in the 1940s. After 1950 the yearly average was 24—higher in the earlier years.

The government often tried to deport CP chiefs who were aliens and to denaturalize Communists or members of their families who had become U.S. citizens. The numbers, far below those of the first Red Scare and the 1920s, were unimpressive. From 1945 to 1954, only 163 subversives were deported, and just a few denaturalization proceedings proved successful. Since Iron Curtain countries of origin did not accept American deportees, the latter rarely left the United States. Yet the new laws of 1950 and 1952 and the Justice Department's broad discretion in immigration matters served as heavy weapons against the foreign-born.

The power to threaten and harass could also hurt: there were many more deportation proceedings than deportees. Soon after passage of the McCarran Act, the Attorney General issued warrants for eighty-six alien Communists. Far left labor leaders often fell afoul of immigration law.

Guardians against the alien menace swept exceeding fine. In 1951 Benny Saltzman, a fifty-six-year-old Bronx house painter who had emigrated from Russian Poland in 1913, was ordered deported because of a 1936–37 Communist Party membership. "This is my home and the land that I love," he told the court in a voice cracking with emotion. "Everything is here"—including a son killed in World War II "who is resting here." Though ordered deported, Saltzman remained in the United States because his native land would not take him.

Sometimes the law moved too slowly for the Immigration authorities. In 1958 they snatched William Heikkila on his way home from work in San Francisco, tossed him on a plane and, ignoring a restraining order, flew him to Finland with only pocket change and the light clothes he wore. At midnight they told his wife he was gone but would not say where. Heikkila, who quit the CP in 1939, had fought deportation since 1947; he had recently lost an appeal, but local Immigration officials acted before due process had run its course. The judge in the case ripped these "Gestapo" methods. Facing bad publicity and possible contempt citations, the Immigration Service relented and brought Heikkila home. In 1960 Heikkila, under a new order to depart, died in his adopted country of fifty-four years. [10]

In the ever more bureaucratic battle against communism, the FBI's and J. Edgar Hoover's role grew relatively and absolutely. The FBI had always used covert surveillance and disruptive tactics against Communists and other radicals. By one estimate, FBI infiltrators made up a sixth of the CP's membership in the early 1960s. Even as the Supreme Court buttressed the rights of radicals, the FBI stepped up its subterranean activities against them—perhaps in part because of the growing obstacles to prosecution. Paradoxically, as the Communists' legal status improved, their susceptibility to extralegal harassment deepened.

Hoover's August 1956 initiation of what the FBI termed a COINTELPRO against the CPUSA produced this perverse result. Though labeled a counterintelligence program, it was in fact a series of actions (of which 1,338 have been documented) aimed at convulsing the CP and punishing its members. In 1958 Hoover told Eisenhower of the program's existence in a vague, pro-forma fashion. COINTELPRO was novel less for its content (the FBI had carried on such actions for years) than for its formalization as a program.

In coming years, other groups became targets of COINTELPROs. The Socialist Workers Party was bracketed in 1961. In 1964 Hoover launched a COINTELPRO against white hate groups. Black Nationalist-Hate Groups (among whom the FBI included Martin Luther King, Jr.'s Southern Christian Leadership Conference [SCLC]) and New Left groups received similar treatment. The later COINTELPROs owed much to White House pressures. Lyndon Johnson's desire to end racist attacks on civil-rights workers prompted the campaign against the Ku Klux Klan. Johnson was also keen to secure proof of links (never found) between communism and the growing movement against the Vietnam War. By 1970 FBI surveillance had extended to the women's liberation movement and even to Earth Day rallies.

The initial COINTELPRO against the Communist Party was driven by the FBI's ideological loathing rather than by any perceived threat to national security. The CP was feeble. Already damaged by the Cold War and hounded by the government, the Party was wracked by internal crisis as well. Nikita Khrushchev's shattering address to the Twentieth Soviet Party Congress on "The Crimes of the Stalin Era" provoked soul-searching, factional strife and mass resignations that left the CPUSA anything but a threat to the standing order.

COINTELPROs involved far more than surveillance. Their aim was to discredit or otherwise weaken the targeted organization. Tactics included leaking information to journalists, Legionnaires, university officials, or other wielders of influence. FBI agents also mailed anonymous letters to members of affected groups to whet their paranoia with warnings of imaginary threats. Agents tried repeatedly to get the wife of a Wisconsin CP leader fired from her job. After sending Party literature to her fellow employees, they succeeded. In a car carrying William Albertson, an FBI man planted a phony document insinuating that the Party leader was an FBI informant. The ploy had the desired effect: the veteran Communist was drummed out of the Party to which he had devoted his life.

In subsequent years, COINTELPRO techniques were steadily refined. The wife of a St. Louis black leader was sent an unsigned letter accusing her husband of extramarital affairs. The husband of a civil-rights and peace activist received a letter ostensibly from a jealous black woman who speculated that his "old lady doesn't get enough at home or she wouldn't be shucking and jiving with our Black Men. . . ." A subsequent report proudly noted the break-up of this marriage. The FBI planted a gossip column item attributing actress Jean Seberg's pregnancy to a Black Panther. A Panther sympathizer, Seberg won a libel suit, but she suffered a miscarriage and a mental breakdown, and some years later committed suicide. The FBI also tried without success to set off strife between the Communist Party and the Mafia. It had more success in embroiling various black groups against each other, and FBI informants played roles in various efforts to harass the Black Panthers, several of which ended in loss of life.[11]

While keeping close watch on Martin Luther King, Jr., the FBI learned that two of his allies had had ties to the CP. In 1962 a COMINFIL (Communist Infiltration) probe of SCLC was activated. King and his associates became the object of illegal phone taps and bugs. Pressed by the Kennedy Administration, King broke off relations with the two men, but Hoover's animosity only grew. The director loathed most civil-rights activists; King's occasional criticisms of the FBI were a further irritant. Gleanings from FBI surveillance outraged Hoover, who considered King a "tom cat" and sought to discredit him. The FBI began bugging King's hotel rooms. Surveillance of one of his visits to Washington picked up the sounds of what one historian describes as a "lively party." The FBI's most notorious trick was to mail excerpts from these recordings, along with a threatening note, to King's home shortly before he was to accept the Nobel Peace Prize in 1964.

Secret, illegal political surveillance was no FBI monopoly, however. As the onrushing 1960s brought vehement, sometimes violent, dissent over the Vietnam War and unleashed turmoil in U.S. cities and campuses, other intelligence agencies broadened their activities, sometimes at the urging of Lyndon Johnson. Breaching the charter that confined it to foreign intelligence, the CIA mounted operation CHAOS against the antiwar groups in 1967. The National Security Agency, specializing in electronic intelligence, began to focus on the communications of civil-rights and antiwar activists. Military intelligence and even the Internal Revenue Service entered the field. Such enterprises reached a peak in the Nixon era, when they were counterpoint to the "dirty tricks" and "enemies lists" that the President was prone to keep tabs on, but they originated before—sometimes long before—Nixon.[12]

Thus, while anti-Communist extremism receded from outward public life, it had not ended. Indeed, the activities of the FBI and other intelligence agencies escalated sharply. On the surface, the 1960s manifested political pluralism and yeasty radicalism, but the decade's underside was marked by ramifying political repression. The secrecy of the COINTELPRO activities and similar programs made them the more chilling. One mystery of the 1960s is the extent to which the era's more outrageous radicalism was the product of fertile minds of agents-provocateurs in America's domestic intelligence agencies.

The radicals of the 1960s have sometimes ascribed the failure of "the Movement" in part to these secret disruptive tactics. Others blamed McCarthyism in its broad sense for suppressing the Left in the postwar era, opening a gap between the ferment of the 1930s and 1960s and depriving younger radicals of guidance and continuity. Historian H. Stuart Hughes lamented the "religious and philosophical fatalism" of the 1950s intellectuals, their "substantial reconciliation" with the status quo, and the *"privatization"* of life in the decade as factors in their succumbing to McCarthyism and to the era's dull political flatness.[13]

However, such unloved but potent social forces of the 1950s as consumerism and suburbanization may in some ways have helped cool the fever of McCarthyism. It is too much to say that people simply abandoned fear of communism because they had better things to do, but William Levitt's remark that homeowners had no time to be Communists might apply as well to some of those who might otherwise be inclined toward extremist anti-communism. Neighborhoods in roiling cities or small towns whose way of life was being eroded were likelier to be infected by fears of "communism" in several guises than were most suburbs. In fact, socioeconomic groups least amenable to McCarthy's appeal tended to concentrate in the suburbs. Such traits of restraint may have migrated with them, but perhaps the suburbs, with the centrifugal force of privatization and the social sanctions of "togetherness," encouraged a blandness that, though maddening to young 1960s radicals, also frustrated right-wing extremists.

Epilogue

Where We Came Out

BY THE 1956 election campaign, preoccupation with the Red menace had measurably declined in party politics. In 1954 Richard Nixon celebrated the exodus of Communists from government, but McCarthy was disappearing and the genre was dying. Two years later, it barely breathed. Republicans raised the ghost of Alger Hiss, but this theme owed its brief and only prominence to ex-President Truman's snap remark that he did not think Hiss had been a spy. Adlai Stevenson, the Democratic candidate for President, was taxed to disown Truman. Once Stevenson affirmed Hiss's guilt, Nixon commended his "forthright, direct statement" and the story faded. In the 1956 Idaho Senate race, McCarthy's pal Herman Welker reverted to redbaiting but lost to the liberal Frank Church. Anti-communism was even less evident in 1958, when a more potent election totem was the "labor boss." The late Joseph Stalin had one weird cameo role in Arizona's Senate race. Anonymous pamphlets depicted the grinning dictator asking, "Why Not Vote for Goldwater?" The conservative Goldwater could hardly be redbaited, and his opponent disavowed the handbills.

The identity of the 1960 presidential candidates might have heartened the nostalgic. Nixon was an old anti-Communist pro. John F. Kennedy had once assailed Yalta and China's fall; he had tiptoed around the McCarthy issue; his family had befriended McCarthy. Yet the dead domestic Red menace did not revive. In their first TV debate, the two candidates barely nudged the bait. Quizzed about the domestic Communist menace, Kennedy pledged to "be continually alert" but located the chief peril abroad. "Maintaining a strong society" at home would spike any internal danger. "Generally" agreeing with JFK, Nixon noted that Moscow's schemes did not spare the home front, but he too preached the need to combat "injustices" on which communism fed.[1]

Thus while anti-communism did frame the rhetoric of 1960, both candidates agreed that the danger flowed from Moscow, not from some federal agency. After eight years of GOP rule, Red infiltration was a forgotten issue. Cuba, however, was not, having been taken over by Fidel Castro in 1959. For a change Democrats could ascribe a "loss" to the Republicans, although the Right did levy blame on those who duped Americans into thinking Castro was a reformer, not a Communist. *New York Times* reporter Herbert Matthews, who had interviewed Castro in 1957, was the Right's prime target. Said William F. Buckley, Jr.: Castro could claim "I got my job through the New York Times." Still, "Who lost Cuba?" never rivaled the China postmortem as a political issue.

Indeed, both candidates did their best to edge away from the McCarthy legacy in 1960. Kennedy worked hard at wooing liberal Democrats to whom McCarthyism had been a gut issue. Alluding to his Pulitzer Prize-winning book, Eleanor Roosevelt wished he had shown less profile and more courage during McCarthy's heyday. As for the Republican candidate, he became reincarnated as a "new Nixon" and shunned the stridency of old. Once HUAC foe rejoiced that Nixon, "a shrewd ear-to-the-grounder[,] has suddenly remembered that he told McCarthy to change his ways and no longer talks about how he (Nixon) caught the wicked Alger Hiss." Contrasting his Communist-hunting with McCarthy's, Nixon termed it vital "to shoot with a rifle in this area and not a shotgun." Some Republicans did claim that JFK's constant "running down" of America aided the Soviets. Ex-Governor Thomas Dewey said Kennedy "echoed communist propaganda" in claiming that the Soviets were overtaking America's economy. However, the domestic Communist issue hardly flickered in opinion polls.[2]

The Red menace retained marginal utility on some issues. It tinted Hawaii's politics. Prior to becoming a state, that territory had enough

Communists, notably in the ILWU, to rate a Smith Act trial and visits by HUAC and SISS, which provided ammunition to opponents of statehood. A 1950 draft of a statehood bill banned Reds from public office. Senator Joseph O'Mahoney hoped thus to "solve the most difficult question" about Hawaiian statehood. Yet critics kept flailing at communism. In 1958 Congressman John Pillion charged that Harry Bridges "rules a Communist collectivized kingdom in Hawaii." Statehood would "invite four Soviet agents to take seats in our Congress." Pillion also opposed Alaskan statehood lest that territory "run interference" for Hawaii; even in Alaska, Bridges had created "a Communist beachhead" and was biding his time. Nonetheless, Hawaii and Alaska joined the Union in 1959.[3]

By the 1960s, the domestic Communist issue had grown quaint, and momentum had shifted to foes of virulent anti-communism. Senator J. William Fulbright won kudos for criticizing Army-sponsored seminars mounted by anti-communist extremists. Where once conspiracy theories had been the domain of the Right, now liberals saw bogeymen in the sometimes secretive rightist groups that flourished in the 1960s. The ultra-conservative John Birch Society, with its cell-like organization and infiltration tactics, became liberalism's equivalent of the Communist Party.

Old Red-hunters fell on evil days. At its 1960 San Francisco hearings, HUAC met with massive student opposition. Rehearsing for the coming decade, police used fire hoses and billy clubs and dragged students down steps. Through the distorted film *Operation Abolition* HUAC portrayed the riots as Red-inspired, but the film only added to the ranks of committee critics, particularly on college campuses. "We are indebted to the Committee for that film," said a leader of the emerging radical group, Students for a Democratic Society.

HUAC's 1962 hearings on Women Strike for Peace also earned ridicule. Members of that group showed up in force to cheer subpoenaed witnesses, presented them with bouquets, nursed babies, and by acting in a fashion that was stagily feminine and motherly as well as politically astute, got the committee's goat. Eric Bentley, a noted scholar of the history of drama, called the episode "the fall of HUAC's Bastille." These tactics in some ways foreshadowed the costumed, burlesque appearances of New Left leaders Abbie Hoffman and Jerry Rubin later in the decade.

Several groups worked, none too cooperatively, to abolish HUAC, and James Roosevelt led critics inside Congress, but their efforts alone achieved nothing dramatic. As one HUAC opponent put it, progress was "due, not so much to the hard work so many civil liberties agencies have done, but to the stupidity and ineptness of HUAC itself!" In 1966, ninety-two Congressmen voted against its appropriation. In 1969, trying to molt its scruffy past, the committee renamed itself the House Internal Security Committee. It was finally abolished in 1975, its duties inherited by the Judiciary Committee. The Senate Internal Security Subcommittee's formal existence ended in 1977.[4]

Other monuments of McCarthyism crumbled. The Smith Act fell into ruin, and the Subversive Activities Control Board registered not a single soul under the McCarran Act. In 1971 SACB's chairman testified, "We do not have enough to fill our time." President Nixon tried to broaden its duties, but the Senate balked at the change; in 1973 Nixon abolished the board. As antiwar and civil-rights dissent grew in the 1960s, militants feared that the McCarran Act's Title II emergency detention provisions might be employed on them. Their fears were unwarranted, however, and in 1971 Congress repealed Title II. (J. Edgar Hoover had had his own round-up lists before the McCarran Act and maintained them even after repeal. Remarkably, Senator Paul Douglas, coauthor of Title II, was listed for pick-up; Lee Harvey Oswald was not.)[5]

IN THE LATE 1950s, the stormcellars began disgorging their occupants as the blacklist in entertainment unraveled. The 1956 Academy Award for best script went to *The Brave One*, whose author, Robert Rich, nobody could locate. "Robert Rich" was Dalton Trumbo's pseudonym. At the same time, several films were released without an author's credit or with an incorrect one, because the real writers were on the blacklist. In 1960 Otto Preminger ostentatiously hired Trumbo to script *Exodus* under his real name.

John Henry Faulk, a folkloric talk-show host, struck a heavy psychological blow against the blacklist. Faulk belonged to a faction of AFTRA (American Federation of Television and Radio Actors), which resisted the blacklisters. For his part in the faction, Faulk was targeted, and he lost his CBS show in 1956. He sued both Laurence Johnson, a

Syracuse grocery store owner and active amateur blacklister, and Vincent Hartnett, proprietor of Aware, Inc., for whom blacklisting people was business. In 1962 a jury found the defendants guilty of libel and awarded Faulk an unprecedented judgment of $3,500,000 (much reduced on appeal).

The 1960s brought rehabilitation for other people as well. In 1963 J. Robert Oppenheimer received the AEC's Enrico Fermi Award. As events matured in Asia, the China Hands also won redemption. Some already had achieved legal redress. John Stewart Service's dismissal was voided by the Supreme Court in 1957. In 1969 John Paton Davies won back his security clearance, but by then it was a mere gesture. As Nixon began preparations to go to China, it made little sense to keep these experts in internal exile. Some testified regarding China before the Senate Foreign Relations Committee and were interviewed on television. In 1973 the survivors were honored at a State Department luncheon. Old foes persisted, however. SISS rushed an edition of the "*Amerasia* Papers" to press in 1969, as Nixon initiated secret contacts with the Chinese, and rightist leaflets were scattered at the China Hands' luncheon.

This rehabilitation of the Asia experts whom McCarthy and McCarran had hounded came too late to mitigate America's agony in Vietnam. The roots of that conflict ran deep but owed at least something to the rancor of the McCarthy era. Democrats who experienced the onslaught that followed the "loss" of China had learned a bitter lesson. Kennedy reportedly said in 1963 that if he withdrew entirely from Vietnam, "we would have another Joe McCarthy red scare on our hands." Lyndon Johnson expressed similar fears.[6]

By the 1970s, blacklistees had become cultural heroes. In 1971 Ring Lardner, Jr., of the Hollywood Ten won an Oscar for the script of *M.A.S.H.* Charles Chaplin, who had left America in 1952 after being accused of harboring Communist sympathies, received a special Oscar in 1973. Television dramatized Faulk's story and ran a documentary on the Hollywood writers. In the late 1960s Pete Seeger returned to TV as a fixture on "Sesame Street," but many stations would not carry the anti-Vietnam protest song he sang in his prime-time debut. Woody Allen's 1976 movie *The Front* presented a view of the blacklist that was at once poignant and zany. Many of those featured in the film's credits, including Zero Mostel, had been blacklisted. Lillian Hellman's 1976 memoir *Scoundrel Time* heaped scorn on those who abetted or knuckled under to the investigators. Author Victor Navasky's *Naming Names* indicted informers as a species.

Critics have argued that these productions shamefully ignored communism's dark side and its apologists' guilt. More recently, Peter Collier and David Horowitz, two former 1960s radicals, have objected to the way in which the Left abuses the term "McCarthyism" against those views it opposes, and have said that the term is employed as "a political blunt instrument, an aggressive symbol forcibly deforming our view of the world." The word "is now equated with anti-Communism itself and is invoked to interdict discussion."[7]

But rife with bad memories, "McCarthyism" became a byword even to conservatives. Defending HUAC in 1965, Congressman Richard Ichord avowed that "McCarthyism is definitely a thing of the past." In 1968 Vice President-to-be Spiro Agnew called Democratic candidate Hubert Humphrey "squishy soft" on communism. Amid the outcry, Agnew was contrite: he "would have turned five somersaults" to avoid the crack had he known it would make him "the Joe McCarthy of 1968."

Routinely "McCarthyism" was attributed to all sectors of the political spectrum and all manner of activities. New York Mayor John V. Lindsay ascribed "McCarthyism" to critics of his appointment of people with police records to neighborhood youth centers. New York's police commissioner decried a survey of police corruption as "McCarthyism all over again." Author Truman Capote called a review of a book of his "McCarthy-like." The *New York Times* called *Izvestia*'s attacks on two jailed Soviet writers "Soviet McCarthyism." Columnist Joe Alsop espied "left-wing McCarthyism" in criticisms of defense policies in 1971. The term "McCarthyism" thus enriches our language—with a sloppiness worthy of its origins.[8]

Considering the profoundly negative judgment the language pronounces, one would think that any phenomenon resembling McCarthyism would receive short shrift from the American people. Or would it? In the 1970s, with the rise of terrorism, the internal-security bugaboo enjoyed partial rebirth. Congress eyed the phenomenon, and some members drew an exaggerated linkage of communism with terrorism. (The Symbionese Liberation Army's kidnapping of Patty Hearst gave such claims a shot in the arm.) The House Internal Security Committee heard psychologists speculate on the terrorist's mental profile. This was all well and good, but some members wanted to get on to the real business—how terrorism was tied up with Marxist-Leninism. Yet that old horse would no longer run.

In the era of Ronald Reagan, there were fears that a "new McCarthyism" had emerged. The conservative tide that swept Reagan into the White House offered hope to those who sought a revival of the old-time religion of anti-communism, and the world in which America found itself when Reagan took office in 1981—what with the hostage crisis in Iran, the Soviet invasion of Afghanistan, and proxy wars elsewhere—had a gloomy cast.

Reagan had long affected muscled anti-communism. He decried Communist activities in America and the disarming of agencies tasked with monitoring them. In the 1970s, he argued that Moscow guided "a subtle campaign to make anticommunism unfashionable." He understood the anti-nuclear and peace causes to be infiltrated with Reds. As President he called the USSR an "evil empire" and accepted the premise of some authorities that the Soviets were responsible for most terrorist activities in the world. Interviewed by the editor of the rightist *Washington Times*, Reagan saw a strong Soviet "disinformation campaign" at work in the media and in Congress, where, he agreed, "pro-Soviet agents of influence" operated. Once Congress investigated communism; now, sadly, "they've done away with those committees." His Secretary of the Interior, James Watt, labeled "extreme environmentalists" a "left-wing cult" hostile to "our very form of government." A Watt lieutenant suggested that the Sierra Club and Audubon Society were "infiltrated" by sympathizers with socialism and communism. Like Reagan, Watt also charged that the nuclear freeze movement was Soviet-inspired.

The observant shivered when a Subcommittee on Security and Terrorism of the Senate Judiciary Committee was established in 1981. Led by Senator Jeremiah Denton, the panel set out to publicize the premise that the Soviets were behind worldwide "disinformation" and terrorism campaigns. The panel also seemed ready to act on recommendations in a "blueprint" drafted by the right-wing Heritage Foundation, which called for removing the restraints placed on the FBI and CIA as a consequence of congressional inquiries in the 1970s. Early hearings elaborated these themes, and at first it looked like old times. Chairman Denton opened his shirt at the first hearing to scotch rumors that he wore a bullet-proof vest. A peace group called Mobilization for Survival was accused of affiliation with a Soviet front. Veterans of the age of McCarthy and HUAC might well "get a queasy feeling," wrote columnist Tom Wicker.

Yet the worst fears were not borne out. Hearings were few, undramatic, and little noted. Indeed, after a bomb exploded in the Capitol in November 1983, Denton berated the media for not giving his hearings adequate coverage. But Denton had stated, "I am no Joe McCarthy," and he was not. He even criticized one administration anti-terrorist bill as too broad-gauged. A Democratic Senator noted with relief that Denton "can't get his subcommittee off the ground." Said an American Civil Liberties Union spokesman: "it seems to be a play without a script."

Incendiary talk continued, and the Reagan Administration made several efforts to limit the 1974 Freedom of Information Act, which allows public access to governmental records, and to strengthen curbs on the unauthorized disclosure of restricted information. Evidence emerged that the FBI still monitored the activities of groups critical of government policies (as in Central America). Wiretaps were on the increase. The McCarran-Walter Immigration Act was invoked to exclude critics of American policies and even "anti-American" movies from our midst. Libertarians were properly concerned over these developments, but they did not quite bring a return to the 1950s.[9]

Several reasons account for the absence of a fullblown new red scare. Americans have simply become more skeptical about Communist plots. Indeed, they are less credulous about the global threat posed by communism. They trust communism no more than in the past, but in the aftermath of Vietnam, they are disinclined to chase the menace around the globe, as the persistent lack of public support for the Reagan Administration's program in Nicaragua has indicated. Critics of the American temper bemoan a "new isolationism" and the "Vietnam Syndrome." Moreover, it has become difficult to promote extreme anti-communism in an age of summit conferences, General Secretary Mikhail Gorbachev and various manifestations of *glasnost*, the signing of the Intermediate Nuclear Forces Treaty, and Soviet withdrawal from Afghanistan.

Other circumstances have changed too. The press, once a megaphone for charges like McCarthy's, is now more skeptical as well and at times even "adversarial" of government activity, as Senator Denton might attest. The fact that the Republican Party—indeed, the Right—

held power in the 1980s also militated against a strong anti-Communist reaction. It would be hard to hypothecate a politics of frustration or revenge by the Right when it occupies the White House. The appeal of a conspiracist, anti-Communist view of world events is further limited by the fact that the party likeliest to advocate it has had charge of American foreign policy for most of the past two decades. Some attacks on Democratic foes of aid to the Nicaraguan *contras* have sounded the old theme of softness on communism. The keynoter at the 1988 Republican National Convention even accused the Democrats of "pastel patriotism." Liberalism has in some circles become the dreaded "L-word," and in the 1988 presidential campaign it was thoroughly panned, but while this may amount to a disturbing absence of comity in American politics, it does not represent a new McCarthy era.[10]

Public sensitivity to civil-liberties issues was notoriously limited in the second Red Scare. As early as the 1930s, majorities expressed support for the drastic treatment of radicals that politicians of the Cold War era would later enact. Indeed, poll respondents often advocated rougher justice than did the political elite. This low public tolerance for political deviance, along with the rhythms of party politics and the anxieties driven by events of the Cold War, has been a central theme in explaining the onset of the second Red Scare. McCarthyism was an elite phenomenon, but any explanation of it must in some way account for the existence of consistently high levels of public support for repression of Communists.

In this regard, the 1960s, with their "do your own thing" ethic and their encouragement of anti-Establishment sentiments, brought about greater public tolerance of political and cultural diversity. The rise of the Black Power movement and such axioms as "Black is Beautiful" and a corresponding growth in other varieties of group pride reflected some degree of broadened tolerance of, if not always a taste for, alternative viewpoints. One might tentatively venture that the obverse side of the criticism that neoconservatives have leveled against the rise of "pressure groups" in American politics is the tendency of more Americans to see themselves, at least potentially, as members of nonmajority groupings.

Recent years supply ample evidence of persisting social strains in America. Vietnamese shrimpers have been attacked in Texas. The Ku Klux Klan has had something of a rebirth (one of several). Right-wing extremist and Fascist organizations have advanced calls for a white, Gentile America and have sometimes resorted to violence. Abortion clinics have been bombed. (Such episodes were not included in the Reagan Administration's enumerations of "terrorism.")[11] Yet these activities represent the views of a small fringe. Most Americans are now less gullible about the Red menace and slightly more attuned to civil liberties than in the past.[12] This is not the firmest stay against a new time of troubles, but it may have to do.

Notes·

Chapter 1

1. Richard Polenberg, *One Nation Divisible: Class, Race, and Ethnicity in the United States since 1938* (New York, 1980), p. 128; Eric F. Goldman, *The Crucial Decade—And After: America, 1945–1960* (New York, 1961), p. 305; Douglas T. Miller and Marion Nowak, *The Fifties: The Way We Really Were* (Garden City, N.Y., 1977), pp. 47, 97.

2. "Political" interpretations of McCarthyism include Earl Latham, *The Communist Controversy in Washington from the New Deal to McCarthy* (Cambridge, Mass., 1966); Michael Paul Rogin, *The Intellectuals and McCarthy: The Radical Specter* (Cambridge, Mass., 1967); Nelson W. Polsby, "Towards an Explanation of McCarthyism," *Political Studies* 8 (October 1960): 250–71; and Robert Griffith, *The Politics of Fear: Joseph R. McCarthy and the Senate* (Lexington, Ky., 1970) (quote from p. ix).

3. For the sociological perspective, see Daniel Bell, ed., *The Radical Right* (Garden City, N.Y., 1963). Among accounts critical of Truman, liberals, and Democrats are Athan Theoharis's many works, including *Seeds of Repression: Harry S. Truman and the Origins of McCarthyism* (Chicago, 1971); Richard M. Freeland, *The Truman Doctrine and the Origins of McCarthyism: Foreign Policy, Domestic Politics, and Internal Security, 1946–1948* (New York, 1972); and Mary Sperling McAuliffe, *Crisis on the Left: Cold War Politics and American Liberals, 1947–1954* (Amherst, Mass., 1978).

4. Seymour Martin Lipset and Earl Raab, *The Politics of Unreason: Right-*

Notes

Wing Extremism in America, 1790–1970 (New York, 1970), p. 238. A valuable work on American political culture is Louis Hartz, *The Liberal Tradition in America: An Interpretation of American Political Thought since the Revolution* (New York, 1955).

5. Al Richmond, *A Long View from the Left* (Boston, 1973), p. 73; Sidney Lens, *Unrepentant Radical* (Boston, 1980); Vivian Gornick, *The Romance of American Communism* (New York, 1977), pp. 16, 32, 113, 132.

6. Robert Bendiner, *Just Around the Corner* (New York, 1968), p. 103; Irving Howe and Lewis Coser, *The American Communist Party: A Critical History* (New York, 1962), p. 232; Harvey Klehr, *The Heyday of American Communism: The Depression Decade* (New York, 1984), pp. 113–15.

7. Lawrence A. Wittner, *Rabels Against War: The American Peace Movement, 1941–1960* (New York, 1969) pp. 20, 23–24, 286; Howe and Coser, *American Communist Party*, p. 415; Nancy Lynn Schwartz, *The Hollywood Writers' Wars* (New York, 1982), p. 173; Bert Cochran, *Labor and Communism: The Conflict that Shaped American Unions* (Princeton, N.J., 1977), pp. 200, 208, 226–27, 230.

8. Joseph E. Davies, *Mission to Moscow* (New York, 1941), pp. 356–57; *New York Times* quoted in John Lewis Gaddis, *The United States and the Origins of the Cold War, 1941–1947* (New York, 1972), p. 38.

9. J. Edgar Hoover to George E. Allen, May 29, 1946, Box 167, President's Secretary's File; John Cronin, "The Problem of American Communism in 1945," n.d. [November 1945], mimeographed, Box 10, Francis P. Matthews Papers, both at Harry S Truman Library (HSTL), Independence, Mo. The most important source on Hiss is Allen Weinstein, *Perjury: The Hiss–Chambers Case* (New York, 1978).

10. Notes for Lincoln Day Talk, February 14, 1950, Karl Mundt MSS, Mundt Library, Madison, S.D.; *Milwaukee Journal*, October 25, 1950, Sec. 2, p. 2; *New York Times*, November 4, 1950, p. 43; Richard M. Fried, *Men Against McCarthy* (New York, 1976), pp. 232, 234.

11. For most quotations in this section, see U.S. Senate, Subcommittee of the Committee on Foreign Relations, *State Department Loyalty Investigation*, 81st Cong., 2nd sess. (Washington, D.C., 1950), pp. 84–87, 293–312, 1855–61, and Esther Brunauer, "To My Friends and Former Colleagues," December 8, 1952, Box 30, Fund for the Republic MSS, Firestone Library, Princeton University. See also Betty Miller Unterberger, "Brunauer, Esther Delia Caukin," in *Notable American Women: The Modern Period*, ed. Barbara Sicherman and Carol Hurd Green (Cambridge, Mass., 1980), pp. 114–16; *Congressional Record*, 80th Cong., 1st sess., 1947, vol. 93, pp. 5296–5300 (Fred Busbey charges); and William F. Buckley, Jr., and L. Brent Bozell, *McCarthy and His Enemies: The Record and Its Meaning* (Chicago, 1954), pp. 125–35 (quote from p. 133).

12. Elmer Davis, *But We Were Born Free* (Indianapolis, 1954), pp. 18–19; August Raymond Ogden, *The Dies Committee* (Washington, D.C., 1945), p. 48.

Notes

This section relies heavily on Jane De Hart Mathews, "Art and Politics in Cold War America," *American Historical Review* 81 (October 1976): 762–87. See also Eva Cockcroft, "Abstract Expressionism, Weapon of the Cold War," *Artforum* 12 (September 1973): 39–41.

13. Mathews, "Art and Politics in Cold War America"; *Congressional Record*, 81st Cong., 1st sess., 1949, vol. 95, p. 11584; U.S. House of Representatives, Subcommittee of the Committee on Appropriations, Hearings, *Department of State Appropriation Bill for 1948*, 80th Cong., 1st sess. (Washington, D.C., 1947), pp. 412–19; Sidney Hyman, *The Lives of William Benton* (Chicago, 1969), p. 381; Emily Genauer, "Still Life with Red Herring," *Harper's*, August 1949, p. 89.

14. William Hauptman, "The Suppression of Art in the McCarthy Decade," *Artforum* 12 (October 1973): 50; James Truett Selcraig, *The Red Scare in the Midwest, 1945–1955: A State and Local Study* (Ann Arbor, 1982), p. 57; Mathews "Art and Politics in Cold War America," pp. 764–70, 778–90; HUAC, Hearings, *The American National Exhibition, Moscow, July 1959*, 86th Cong. 1st sess. (Washington, D.C., 1959), pp. 900, 914–15, 917, 931.

15. Selcraig, *Red Scare in the Midwest*, p. 84; Goldman, *Crucial Decade—and After*, pp. 101, 213; Eddie Stanky, "All Out for 'Beizbol,'" *Saturday Review*, October 4, 1952, pp. 24–25.

16. Amicus curiae brief of National Union of Marine Cooks and Stewards, quoted in Jerold Lee Simmons, "Operation Abolition: The Campaign to Abolish the House Un-American Activities Committee, 1938–1965" (Ph.D. diss., University of Minnesota, 1971), p. 68.

Chapter 2

1. See Robert K. Murray, *Red Scare: A Study in National Hysteria* (New York, 1955), pp. 64–65, 127, 129, 155–156 and passim; Stanley Coben, *A. Mitchell Palmer: Politician* (New York, 1963); William Preston, Jr., *Aliens and Dissenters: Federal Suppression of Radicals, 1903–1933* (Cambridge, Mass., 1963), p. 198; and Theodore Draper, *The Roots of American Communism* (New York, 1957), p. 139.

2. Irving Bernstein, *The Lean Years* (Baltimore, 1966), pp. 237, 247; J. Stanley Lemons, *The Woman Citizen: Social Feminism in the 1920s* (Urbana, Ill., 1973), chap. 8; Philip L. Cantelon, "In Defense of America: Congressional Investigations of Communism in the United States, 1919–1935" (Ph.D. diss., Indiana University, 1971), pp. 48, 52.

3. Cantelon, "In Defense of America," pp. 56–59, 61, 66–68, 92, 159–69, 197.

4. Cantelon, "In Defense of America," pp. 264–80; Arthur M. Schlesinger, Jr., *The Coming of the New Deal* (Boston, 1958), p. 457–58.

Notes

5. Cantelon, "In Defense of America," chap. 8; William F. Lucitt to Representative John McCormack, July 5, 1934; Samuel Dickstein to McCormack, September 19, 1934, both in Box 1, Dickstein MSS, American Jewish Archives, Hebrew Union College, Cincinnati.

6. Walter Goodman, *The Committee: The Extraordinary Career of the House Committee on Un-American Activities* (New York, 1968), pp. 13–23; Cantelon, "In Defense of America," pp. 307–8; Martin Dies to Franklin Delano Roosevelt, September 13, 1935; release, Dies speech, April 24, 1936; clipping, Beaumont *Enterprise*, September 1, 1935, all in President's Personal File 3438, Franklin Delano Roosevelt Library (FDRL), Hyde Park, N.Y. The following coverage of the Dies Committee relies heavily on Goodman's work.

7. Hadley Cantril, ed., *Public Opinion, 1935–1946* (Princeton, N.J., 1951), pp. 130, 164; Goodman, *Committee*, p. 55.

8. Edwin M. Watson memorandum, September 10, 1940, Official File (OF) 1661, FDRL; Francis Biddle, *In Brief Authority* (Garden City, N. Y., 1962), p. 107; Stephen Vincent Benet et al., *Zero Hour: A Summons to the Free* (New York, 1940), p. 6; Lewis Mumford, *Faith for Living* (New York, 1940), pp. 116, 314.

9. On the "red fascism" metaphor, see Les K. Adler and Thomas G. Paterson, "Red Fascism: The Merger of Nazi Germany and Soviet Russia in the American Image of Totalitarianism, 1930's–1950's," *American Historical Review* 75 (April 1970): 1046–64, and Thomas R. Maddux, "Red Fascism, Brown Bolshevism: The American Image of Totalitarianism in the 1930s," *Historian* 40 (November 1977): 85–103 (quote from p. 91).

10. Kenneth O'Reilly, "A New Deal for the FBI: The Roosevelt Administration, Crime Control, and National Security," *Journal of American History* 69 (December 1982): 638–58 (esp. p. 646); Federal Bureau of Investigation, "Present Status of Espionage and Counter Espionage Operations of the Federal Bureau of Investigation," October 24, 1940, OF 10-B, FDRL; FDR to J. Edgar Hoover, December 3, 1940, President's Secretary's File (PSF): Justice Department, J. Edgar Hoover; blind memorandum, April 2, 1942, PSF: Justice Department, Francis Biddle, all at FDRL. Many examples of Hoover's political reporting to FDR can be found in OF 10-B, FDRL.

11. Harry F. Ward et al. to FDR, March 17, 1936; FDR to Ward, March 23, 1936, both in OF 2111, FDRL.

12. Memorandum, Frank Murphy to FDR, July 26, 1939, PSF: Hatch Bill (1939), FDRL; Zechariah Chafee, Jr., *Free Speech in the United States* (Cambridge, Mass., 1941), pp. 441–42; *Congressional Record*, 76th Cong., 1st sess., 1939, vol. 84, pp. 8535–36; *Congressional Record*, 76th Cong., 1st sess., 1939, vol. 84, pp. 10367, 10370–78; *Congressional Record*, 76th Cong., 2nd sess., 1940, vol. 85, p. 9034; FDR to Adolph Sabath, August 27, 1940, OF 133, FDRL; Michal R. Belknap, *Cold War Political Justice: The Smith Act, the Communist Party, and American Civil Liberties* (Westport, Conn., 1977), chap. 1.

Notes

13. Roger Keeran, *The Communist Party and the Auto Workers Unions* (Bloomington, Ind., 1980), p. 213; Harold L. Ickes, *The Secret Diary of Harold L. Ickes*, vol. 3, *The Lowering Clouds, 1939–1941* (New York, 1955), p. 536.

14. Irving Howe and Lewis Coser, *The American Communist Party: A Critical History* (New York, 1957), pp. 418, 431; FDR press release, May 16, 1942, OF 3977, FDRL.

15. Eleanor Bontecou, *The Federal Loyalty-Security Program* (Ithaca, N.Y., 1953), p. 14; Richard Polenberg, *War and Society: The United States, 1941–1945* (Philadelphia, 1972), p. 50; telephone conversation, Henry Morgenthau to Francis Biddle, October 18, 1941, Henry Morgenthau Diary; Biddle to Congress, September 1, 1942, Herbert Gaston MSS; FBI, "[Report] Prepared Pursuant to Public Law No. 135, 77th Congress," August 22, 1942, ibid.; Edwin D. Dickinson, memorandum to "Executive heads of departments . . . ," May 12, 1942, ibid., all at FDRL.

16. Interdepartmental Committee on Employee Investigations, "Outline of Policy and Procedure," September 1, 1943; Herbert Gaston to Biddle, February 12, 1944, October 4, 1945; report, Interdepartmental Committee on Investigations to Biddle, June 30, 1942, all in Gaston MSS; Morgenthau Diary, May 19, 1941; telephone call, Biddle to Morgenthau, October 13, 1941, Morgenthau Diary.

17. *New York Times*, September 26, 1944, p. 1, October 6, 1944, p. 14, October 8, 1944, p. 36, October 26, 1944, p. 15, October 31, 1944, p. 14, November 2, 1944, p. 1; clipping, *Philadelphia Inquirer*, September 27, 1944, Box 25, Samuel I. Rosenman Papers; Fred Busbey, franked handbill, "Wake Up America!" Box 14; Hopkins memorandum, November 10, 1944, Box 335, both in Harry L. Hopkins Papers; Oscar Ewing speech, October 27, 1944, Box 1159, Democratic National Committee Papers; DNC press release, October 10, 1944, Box 6, Rosenman Papers; Harold Ickes speech, September 24, 1944, Box 1163; DNC Publicity Bureau press release, Blue Network, NBC, November 1, 1944, both in Democratic National Committee Papers; DNC radio script, CBS, November 6, 1944, Box 33, Stephen T. Early Papers, all at FDRL.

18. Arthur M. Schlesinger, Jr., *The Vital Center: The Politics of Freedom* (Boston, 1949, 1962), p. 203.

Chapter 3

1. Athan Theoharis, "The Rhetoric of Politics: Foreign Policy, Internal Security, and Domestic Politics in the Truman Era, 1945–1950," in *Politics and Policies of the Truman Administration*, eds Barton J. Bernstein (Chicago, 1970); Theoharis, *Seeds of Repression: Harry S. Truman and the Origins of McCarthyism* (Chicago, 1971); Richard M. Freeland, *The Truman Doctrine and the Origins of McCarthyism: Foreign Policy, Domestic Politics, and Internal Security, 1946–1948* (New York, 1972).

2. Hadley Centril, ed., *Public Opinion, 1935–1946* (Princeton, N.J., 1951),

Notes

pp. 130–32; *Public Opinion Quarterly* 10 (Fall 1946): 437; (Winter 1946–47): 608; *Public Opinion Quarterly* 11 (Summer 1947): 281; *Public Opinion Quarterly* 12 (Fall 1948): 537.

3. Harvey Klehr and Ronald Radosh, "Anatomy of a Fix," *New Republic*, April 21, 1986, pp. 18–21; E. J. Kahn, Jr., *The China Hands: America's Foreign Service Officers and What Befell Them* (New York, 1975).

4. Allen Weinstein, *Perjury: The Hiss-Chambers Case* (New York, 1978), pp. 356–59, 365 and passim; Memorandum, J. Anthony Panuch to Russell, July 19, 1946, Box 7; Panuch, "Report on Office of Assistant Secretary of State as of Jan. 31, 1947," Box 9; [Panuch], "The Marzani Case . . . ," n.d., Box 9, all in Panuch Papers, HSTL.

5. James R. Boylan, *The New Deal Coalition and the Election of 1946* (New York, 1981), pp. 91, 134–39, 142; Earl Mazo and Stephen Hess, *Nixon: A Political Portrait* (New York, 1968), pp. 39–40; Ronald Wayne Johnson, "The Communist Issue in Missouri: 1946–1956" (Ph.D. diss., University of Missouri, 1973), p. 9; *New York Times*, May 29, 1946, p. 2, June 2, 1946, p. 12; *Washington Post*, November 2, 1946, p. 2, November 5, 1946, p. 2, November 6, 1946, p. 8, January 4, 1947, p. 3; *Milwaukee Journal*, September 13, 1946, p. 1, October 2, 1946, p. 1, October 3, 1946, p. 1, October 4, 1946, p. 1.

6. Alonzo L. Hamby, *Beyond the New Deal: Harry S. Truman and American Liberalism* (New York, 1973); Mary Sperling McAuliffe, *Crisis on the Left: Cold War Politics and American Liberals, 1947–1954* (Amherst, Mass., 1978).

7. "RB," "Memorandum for Mr. Connelly," October 1, 1946, Box 117, President's Secretary's File, HSTL.

8. Minutes of the President's Temporary Commission on Employee Loyalty (PTCEL), January 13, 1947; Spingarn, note on minutes of subcommittee meeting of January 23, 1947, both in Stephen J. Spingarn Papers, PTCEL, vol. II, folder 1, HSTL; Spingarn Oral History Interview, p. 790, HSTL.

9. Freeland, *Truman Doctrine and the Origins of McCarthyism*, p. 130; Spingarn, "Memorandum for the Loyalty Commission File," February 24, 1947, Treasury Department File, Spingarn Papers; *Washington Post*, March 6, 13, 1947; Richard M. Fried, *Men Against McCarthy* (New York, 1976), p. 26; Clark Clifford, "Confidential Memorandum for the President," November 19, 1947, Clark Clifford Papers, HSTL.

10. Eleanor Bontecou, *The Federal Loyalty-Security Program* (Ithaca, N.Y., 1953), pp. 69–70, 85, 87–88, 109, 175, 200, 204; Adam Yarmolinsky, *Case Studies in Personnel Security* (Washington, D.C., 1955), pp. 12, 75, 81, 101.

11. Robert Griffith, "American Politics and the Origins of McCarthyism," in *The Specter: Original Essays on the Cold War and the Origins of McCarthyism*, ed. Robert Griffith and Athan Theoharis (New York, 1974), p. 13; William R. Tanner, "The Passage of the Internal Security Act of 1950," (Ph.D. diss., University of Kansas, 1971), p. 136.

Notes

12. Walter Goodman, *The Committee: The Extraordinary Career of the House Committee on Un-American Activities* (New York, 1968), pp. 86, 101–2; August Raymond Ogden, *The Dies Committee: A Study of the Special House Committee for the Investigation of Un-American Activities, 1938–1944* (Washington, D.C., 1945), p. 212; Larry Ceplair and Steven Englund, *The Inquisition in Hollywood: Politics in the Film Community, 1930–1960* (Garden City, N.Y., 1980), pp. 65–66, 160–61.

13. HUAC, *Hearings Regarding the Communist Infiltration of the Motion Picture Industry*, 80th Cong., 1st sess., 1947, pp. 111–12 (cited hereafter as *Hollywood Hearings*); Stefan Kanfer, *A Journal of the Plague Years* (New York, 1973), pp. 28–29, 84; John Cogley, *Report on Blacklisting* (New York, 1956), vol. 1, p. 43; Ceplair and Englund, *Inquisition in Hollywood*, p. 50.

14. Ceplair and Englund, *Inquisition in Hollywood*, p. 209; *Hollywood Hearings*, pp. 11–14, 76, 84–90, 217–18, 224.

15. Nineteen unfriendly witnesses were subpoenaed, but eight were not heard in 1947. The eleventh witness was the renowned German playwright and poet Bertolt Brecht, who managed to answer all questions yet befuddle the committee.

16. *Hollywood Hearings*, pp. 291, 293–94, 296, 334, 365–66, 384, 482.

17. Cogley, *Report on Blacklisting*, vol. 1, p. 4; Ceplair and Englund, *Inquisition in Hollywood*, pp. 289, 291, 356.

18. Ceplair and Englund, *Inquisition in Hollywood*, pp. 328–30, 362, 445; Kanfer, *Journal of the Plague Years*, pp. 85, 87; Dorothy Jones, "Communism and the Movies: A Study of Film Content," in Cogley, *Report on Blacklisting*, vol. 1, p. 216; Les K. Adler, "The Politics of Culture: Hollywood and the Cold War," in Griffith and Theoharis, *Specter*, p. 257.

19. HUAC, *Hearings Regarding Communist Infiltration of Minority Groups—Part 1*, 81st Cong., 1st sess. (Washington, D.C., 1949), pp. 481, 492; "V.F.W. Youth Baseball Team Program Helps Build Better Citizens," *VFW Magazine*, April 1959, p. 19; David M. Oshinsky, *A Conspiracy So Immense: The World of Joe McCarthy* (New York, 1983), p. 218; *Los Angeles Times*, November 3, 1946, p. 11.

20. David E. Lilienthal, *The Journals of David E. Lilienthal*, vol. 2, *The Atomic Energy Years, 1945–1950* (New York 1964), p. 155; Goodman, *Committee*, pp. 197, 231–39; Arthur M. Schlesinger, Jr., *The Imperial Presidency* (Boston, 1973), pp. 153–54; George M. Elsey to Steven J. Spingarn, September 9, 1948, Subject File, "Int. Sec.–Cong. Loyalty Investigations," Elsey Papers, HSTL.

21. Goodman, *Committee*, p. 252; Adolph A. Berle to Jesse H. Jones, November 23, 1953, Box 97; AP clipping, "Mundt Says He Saw U.S. Hiss Evidence," July 29 [1962], both in Berle MSS, FDRL.

22. *Public Papers of the Presidents, Harry S. Truman, 1948* (Washington, D.C., 1964) pp. 433, 860; memoranda [George Elsey], "Spies," August 9, 1948, and "Random Thoughts 26 August" [1948], Subject File, "Int. Secy.–Cong. Loyalty Investigations," Elsey Papers; Clifford, "Confidential Memorandum for the Presi-

dent," November 19, 1947, pp. 15, 22–23; McAuliffe, *Crisis on the Left*, pp. 38–39; Tom Clark speech to Jewish War Veterans, September 18, 1948, White House Assignment File, Spingarn Papers.

23. Goodman, *Committee*, p. 207; Freeland, *Truman Doctrine and the Origins of McCarthyism*, pp. 217–19, 298, 302, 337–38; Michal R. Belknap, *Cold War Political Justice: The Smith Act, the Communist Party, and American Civil Liberties* (Westport, Conn., 1977).

24. Stanley I. Kutler, *The American Inquisition: Justice and Injustice in the Cold War* (New York, 1982), p. 153; Belknap, *Cold War Political Justice*, pp. 45–47; John F. X. McGohey handwritten notes, "Memo of Conferences on F.B.I. brief," n.d. [1948], Box 1, John F. X. McGohey Papers, HSTL.

25. Theoharis, *Seeds of Repression*, pp. 153–56, and "Rhetoric of Politics," pp. 221–22; Allen Yarnell, *Democrats and Progressives: The 1948 Presidential Election as a Test Case for Liberalism* (Berkeley, 1974), pp. 85, 107; Fried, *Men Against McCarthy*, pp. 18–19.

26. *Public Opinion Quarterly* 12 (Spring 1948): 150; (Fall 1948): 537; (Winter 1948–49): 756.

27. Kenneth O'Reilly and Athan Theoharis, "The FBI, the Congress, and McCarthyism," in *Beyond the Hiss Case: The FBI, Congress, and the Cold War*, ed. Athan Theoharis (Philadelphia, 1982), p. 372.

28. Arthur L. Conrad to Francis P. Matthews, March 16, 1948, and attachment, Box 10, Francis P. Matthews Papers, HSTL; George Lipsitz, *Class and Culture in Cold War America: "A Rainbow at Midnight"* (South Hadley, Mass., 1982), chap. 8.

Chapter 4

1. *Time*, April 25, 1949, p. 19; Cedric Belfrage, *The American Inquisition, 1945–1960* (Indianapolis, 1973), p. 104; *New York Times*, March 4, 1949; *Congressional Record*, 81st Cong., 1st sess., 1949, vol. 95, p. 12878; Thomas G. Paterson, *On Every Front: The Making of the Cold War* (New York, 1979), pp. 119–20; *Public Opinion Quarterly* 14 (Spring 1950): 175–76; George H. Gallup, *The Gallup Poll: Public Opinion, 1935–1971* (New York, 1972), pp. 808, 853.

2. *Time*, August 15, 1949, p. 24, October 24, 1949, p. 40; Eric F. Goldman, *The Crucial Decade—And After: America, 1945–1960* (New York, 1960), p. 116; *Time*, August 15, 1949, p. 11; *Congressional Record*, 81st Cong., 2nd sess., 1950, vol. 96, p. 298.

3. *Time*, October 3, 1949, p. 7, August 7, 1950, p. 17, October 2, 1950, pp. 12, 14; Douglas T. Miller and Marion Nowak, *The Fifties: The Way We Really Were* (Garden City, N.Y., 1977), p. 47; Gregg Herken, *The Winning Weapon: The Atomic Bomb in the Cold War, 1945–1950* (New York, 1980), pp. 284–85.

Notes

4. David E. Lilienthal, *The Journals of David E. Lilienthal*, vol. 2, *The Atomic Energy Years, 1945–1950* (New York, 1964), pp. 528–32, 558; Walter Goodman, *The Committee: The Extraordinary Career of the House Committee on Un-American Activities* (New York, 1968), pp. 274–78.

5. Goodman, *Committee*, pp. 279–82; *Time*, December 12, 1949, p. 19. Congressman John McDowell of HUAC had announced in August 1948 that a "mystery witness" would expose the uranium transfers. Perhaps because of the hullabaloo over the Hiss–Chambers episode, this opening was not pursued (*Seattle Post-Intelligencer*, August 7, 1948, p. 1).

6. Athan Theoharis, *Spying on Americans: Political Surveillance from Hoover to the Huston Plan* (Philadelphia, 1978), pp. 100–104; Stanley I. Kutler, *The American Inquisition: Justice and Injustice in the Cold War* (New York, 1982), p. 39; *Time*, July 11, 1949, p. 18, August 8, 1949, p. 13; Athan Theoharis, "In-House Coverup: Researching FBI Files," in *Beyond the Hiss Case: The FBI, Congress, and the Cold War*, ed. Athan Theodoris (Philadelphia, 1982), pp. 27–28; Percival R. Bailey, "The Case of the National Lawyers Guild, 1939–1958," in Theodoris, *Beyond the Hiss Case*, pp. 129–75; Kenneth O'Reilly, *Hoover and the Un-Americans: The FBI, HUAC, and the Red Menace* (Philadelphia, 1983), pp. 5–6.

7. Goodman, *Committee*, p. 260; HUAC, *Hearings Regarding Communist Espionage in the United States Government*, 80th Cong., 2nd sess., 1948, p. 548; Karl Mundt to Casper Nohner, January 8, 1949, "Un-American Activities, Favorable [1949]" folder, Karl Mundt MSS, Mundt Library; Paul Douglas to Mrs. N. S. Haselton [1951], Douglas MSS, Chicago Historical Society; *Seattle Times*, October 1, 1952, p. 22; Leslie Fiedler, "Hiss, Chambers, and the Age of Innocence," in *An End to Innocence* (Boston, 1955), p. 24; Alonzo L. Hamby, *Beyond the New Deal: Harry S. Truman and American Liberalism* (New York, 1973), pp. 383–88; Kenneth O'Reilly, "Liberal Values, the Cold War, and American Intellectuals: The Trauma of the Alger Hiss Case, 1950–1978," in Theoharis, *Beyond the Hiss Case*, pp. 313–15, 326.

8. Michal R. Belknap, *Cold War Political Justice: The Smith Act, the Communist Party, and American Civil Liberties* (Westport, Conn., 1977), pp. 58–60, 77, 85ff; *Time*, June 27, 1949, p. 18; David Caute, *The Great Fear: The Anti-Communist Purge Under Truman and Eisenhower* (New York, 1978), pp. 192–93; Peter L. Steinberg, *The Great "Red Menace": United States Prosecution of American Communists, 1947–1952* (Westport, Conn., 1984), pp. 108, 148–49, 166, 193; *New York Times*, July 18, 1949, p. 17.

9. Steinberg, *Great "Red Menace,"* pp. 42, 126–27, 149, 172; Caute, *Great Fear*, pp. 164–65; Belfrage, *American Inquisition*, pp. 85–86; James Truett Selcraig, *The Red Scare in the Midwest, 1945–1955: A State and Local Study* (Ann Arbor, 1982), pp. 132–33.

10. Selcraig, *Red Scare in the Midwest*, p. 89; Harvey A. Levenstein, *Communism, Anticommunism, and the CIO* (Westport, Conn., 1981), p. 289; *Time*,

Notes

February 21, 1949, p. 26; *New York Times*, February 11, 1949, p. 13; George Lipsitz, *Class and Culture in Cold War America: "A Rainbow at Midnight"* (South Hadley, Mass., 1982), pp. 154–63.

11. Paterson, *On Every Front*, chap. 6; *Hollywood Hearings*, p. 453; Kenneth O'Reilly and Athan Theoharis, "The FBI, the Congress, and McCarthyism," in Theoharis, *Beyond the Hiss Case*, p. 372; Seattle *Post-Intelligencer*, August 8, 1948, p. 1.

12. Richard M. Freeland, *The Truman Doctrine and the Origins of McCarthyism: Foreign Policy, Domestic Politics, and Internal Security, 1946–1948* (New York, 1972), pp. 231–34; Wayne C. Grover to Senator Olin D. Johnston, January 24, 1949; stenographic transcript, Hearings before Subcommittee of the Senate Committee on Post Office and Civil Service, on S.J. Res. 31, January 28, 1949; interim report, Thomas D'Arcy Brophy to Trustees of the American Heritage Foundation, "The Freedom Train: Highlights of the First Year . . . ," November 4, 1948, all in Box 19, Scott W. Lucas MSS, Illinois State Historical Library, Springfield.

13. Ronald W. Johnson, "The Communist Issue in Missouri: 1946–1956" (Ph.D. diss., University of Missouri, 1973), pp. 60–63; Thomas Michael Holmes, "The Specter of Communism in Hawaii, 1947–1953" (Ph.D. diss., University of Hawaii, 1975), p. 239; Mosinee *Times*, April 26, May 3, 1950; *New York Times*, May 15, 1950, p. 11; Des Moines *Register*, June 15, 1950, p. 3; Indianapolis *Star*, December 2, 1951, sec. 2, p. 1.

14. Bert Cochran, *Labor and Communism: The Conflict that Shaped American Unions* (Princeton, N.J., 1977). See also Harvey A. Levenstein, *Communism, Anticommunism, and the CIO* (Westport, Conn., 1981).

15. Lawrence A. Cremin, *The Transformation of the School: Progressivism in American Education, 1876–1957* (New York, 1961), chap. 9; David Lane Marden, "The Cold War and American Education" (Ph.D. diss., University of Kansas, 1975), pp. 23–24, 104, 109–114 and passim; John B. Chapple, *The LaFollette Road to Communism* (n.p., 1936).

16. Jane Sanders, *Cold War on Campus: Academic Freedom at the University of Washington, 1946–1964* (Seattle, 1979), p. 28 and passim; Raymond B. Allen, "Communists Should Not Teach in American Colleges," *Educational Forum*, May 1949, p. 440; Ellen W. Schrecker, *No Ivory Tower: McCarthyism and the Universities* (New York, 1986), pp. 94–105.

17. Schrecker, *No Ivory Tower*, pp. 116–25; David P. Gardner, *The California Oath Controversy* (Berkeley, 1967).

18. Marden, "Cold War and American Education," pp. 137, 141; Sidney Hook, "Academic Integrity and Academic Freedom," *Commentary*, October 1949, p. 334; *New York Times*, June 9, 1949, p. 11; Caute, *Great Fear*, p. 406; Committee A Report, *AAUP Bulletin* 34 (1947): 126–27; Francis Biddle, *The Fear of Freedom* (Garden City, N.Y., 1951), pp. 156–57; Sigmund Diamond, "The Arrangement:

Notes

The FBI and Harvard University in the McCarthy Period," in Theoharis, *Beyond the Hiss Case*, pp. 341–71.

19. Lawrence H. Chamberlain, *Loyalty and Legislative Action* (Ithaca, N.Y., 1951), pp. 54–55 and passim; Schrecker, *No Ivory Tower*, pp. 76–83.

20. Edward L. Barrett, Jr., "California: Regulation and Investigation of Subversive Activities," in *The States and Subversion*, ed. Walter Gellhorn (Ithaca, N.Y., 1952), pp. 7, 14; M. J. Heale, "Red Scare Politics: California's Campaign Against Un-American Activities, 1940–1970," *Journal of American Studies* 20 (April 1986): 5–32; Ingrid Winther Scobie, "Jack B. Tenney and the 'Parasitic Menace': Anti-Communist Legislation in California, 1940–1949," *Pacific Historical Review* 43 (May 1974): 188–211.

21. E. Houston Harsha, "Illinois: The Broyles Commission," in Gellhorn, *States and Subversion*, pp. 73, 75, 80–82, 99, 104.

22. Vern Countryman, *Un-American Activities in the State of Washington* (Ithaca, N.Y., 1951); Caute, *Great Fear*, p. 409; Melvin Rader, *False Witness* (Seattle, 1979).

23. James A. Robinson, *Anti-Sedition Legislation and Loyalty Investigations in Oklahoma* (Norman, Okla., 1956), pp. 14, 27, 29, 34 and passim.

24. Robert J. Mowitz, "Michigan: State and Local Attack on Subversion," in Gellhorn, *States and Subversion*, pp. 191–92; Selcraig, *Red Scare in the Midwest*, pp. 6–9.

25. William B. Prendergast, "Maryland: The Ober Anti-Communist Law," in Gellhorn, *States and Subversion*, p. 149 and passim; Walter Gellhorn, "A General View," in Gellhorn, *States and Subversion*, p. 363; Countryman, *Un-American Activities in the State of Washington*, p. 329; Selcraig, *Red Scare in the Midwest*, pp. 12, 32–34; Don E. Carleton, *Red Scare! Right-wing Hysteria, Fifties Fanaticism, and Their Legacy in Texas* (Austin, 1985), pp. 96–97.

26. Mowitz, "Michigan," pp. 204–16; Selcraig, *Red Scare in the Midwest*, pp. 46, 48, 59, 62; Caute, *Great Fear*, pp. 341–42, 345.

27. Gellhorn, "General View," p. 361; Michael O'Brien, *McCarthy and McCarthyism in Wisconsin* (Columbia, Mo., 1980), pp. 192–202; Dale Sorensen, "The Anticommunist Consensus in Indiana, 1945–1958" (Ph.D. diss., Indiana University, 1980), pp. 27, 90–91, 194–98; Selcraig, *Red Scare in the Midwest*, p. 42; Arnold A. Rogow, "The Loyalty Oath Issue in Iowa, 1951," *American Political Science Review* 55 (December 1961): 861–69.

28. Gellhorn, "General View," p. 388; Countryman, *Un-American Activities in the State of Washington*, pp. 95–96; Holmes, "Specter of Communism in Hawaii."

29. Stephen J. Spingarn, "Memorandum for the File on Internal Security and Individual Rights," July 22, 1950, Chronological File, Box 13, Stephen J. Spingarn Papers, HSTL; *New York Times*, July, 19, 1950, p. 8, August 1, 1950, p. 18, August 4, 1950, pp. 1, 22, August 14, 1950, p. 1, August 24, 1950, p. 30,

Notes

September 23, 1950, p. 6; Selcraig, *Red Scare in the Midwest*, pp. 8–14, 33–34, 39–40; Sorenson, "Anticommunist Consensus in Indiana," pp. 125–26.

30. Belknap, *Cold War Political Justice*, pp. 130–31, 152–54; Caute, *Great Fear*, p. 219; Steinberg, *Great "Red Menace*," pp. 198, 223–24, 226, 232; *New York Times*, August, 2, 1950, p. 6; Felix Frankfurter to Robert H. Jackson, February 27, 1952, Box 19, Frankfurter MSS, Library of Congress (LC); Ronald Radosh and Joyce Milton, *The Rosenberg File: A Search for the Truth* (New York, 1983).

31. Wayne Morse to J. F. Lawry, August 21, 1950, Box A25, Morse MSS, University of Oregon; John W. McCormack to Scott Lucas, July 10, 1950, General File, Box 128, Truman Papers, PSF, HSTL; Karl Mundt to Everett Dirksen, August 4, 1950, Mundt MSS; Spingarn, Memorandum for the Record, July 21, 1950, Chronological File, Spingarn Papers.

32. Wayne Morse to Reverend and Mrs. Mark A. Chamberlin, May 25, 1952, Box A25, Morse MSS. Sites were Florence and Wickenburg, Arizona; Allenwood, Pennsylvania; Avon Park, Florida; El Reno, Oklahoma; and Tule Lake, California. James V. Bennett, Director, Bureau of Prisons, to Morse, April 28, 1952, Box A25, Morse MSS; Richard Longaker, "Emergency Detention: The Generation Gap, 1950–1971," *Western Political Quarterly* 27 (September 1974): 395–408.

Chapter 5

1. Robert Chadwell Williams, *Klaus Fuchs, Atom Spy* (Cambridge, 1987), p. 153. On "Dinner at the Colony," see Eric F. Goldman, *The Crucial Decade—and After: America, 1945–1960* (New York, 1961), pp. 139–41; Drew Pearson, *Washington Post*, March 14, 1950; Donald Crosby, *God, Church, and Flag: Senator Joseph R. McCarthy and the Catholic Church, 1950–1957* (Chapel Hill, N.C., 1978), pp. 47–52; Michael O'Brien, *McCarthy and McCarthyism in Wisconsin* (Columbia, Mo., 1980), pp. 91–96.

2. Thomas C. Reeves, *The Life and Times of Joe McCarthy: A Biography* (New York, 1982), pp. 223–25, 248–49; Richard M. Fried, *Men Against McCarthy* (New York, 1976), p. 43; "The Reminiscences of Robert E. Lee" (1978), Columbia University Oral History Project, p. 14, courtesy of Professor James L. Baughman.

3. On McCarthy's life, see O'Brien, *McCarthy and McCarthyism*; Reeves, *Life and Times of Joe McCarthy*; and David M. Oshinsky, *A Conspiracy So Immense: The World of Joe McCarthy* (New York, 1983) (quote from p. 8).

4. Robert Griffith, *The Politics of Fear: Joseph R. McCarthy and the Senate* (Lexington, Ky., 1970), pp. 40–41, 48–51; Fried, *Men Against McCarthy*, pp. 46–49; Edwin R. Bayley, *Joe McCarthy and the Press* (Madison, 1981), pp. 18, 36; Oshinsky, *Conspiracy So Immense*, p. 111.

Notes

5. Griffith, *Politics of Fear*, pp. 54–57, 103–4, 196–97; Kenneth Wherry to Thomas J. Sheehan, Jr., April 13, 1950, Wherry MSS, University of Nebraska; Oshinsky, *Conspiracy So Immense*, p. 134.

6. Walter Judd to John Cowles, May 8, 1950, Box 145, Walter Judd MSS, Minnesota Historical Society, St. Paul. Millard Tydings narrowly avoided hearing Patrick Hurley testify on the fall of China. Telephone conversations, Hurley and Tydings, June 2, 5, 1950, Hurley MSS, Western Historical Collections, University of Oklahoma.

7. Annotated clipping, "Truman to Open Loyalty Files to Senate in State Dept. Inquiry," New York *Herald-Tribune*, March 2, 1950; memorandum, "The Possible Republican Complaints . . . ," May 10, 1950, both in Elsey Papers, Internal Security—McCarthy Charges, HSTL.

8. George Elsey to Clark Clifford, September 19, 1949; Elsey to Stephen J. Spingarn, January 9, 1950; memorandum [Elsey?], "Employee Loyalty," February 22, 1950, all in Elsey Papers, Internal Security—Federal Employee Loyalty Program; Charles S. Murphy and Spingarn to Truman, May 24, 1950, OF 252-K, HSTL; Truman to Philip L. Graham, June 13, 1950, Box 121, General File, PSF, HSTL.

9. U.S. Senate, *State Department Employee Loyalty Investigation*, 81st Cong., 2nd sess., Rept. No. 2108 (Washington, D.C., 1950), p. 167; Millard Tydings to Fritz Moses, September 11, 1952, Tydings MSS, University of Maryland.

10. Fried, *Men Against McCarthy*, chap. 4; Elmer Davis radio script, June 27, 1950, Box 20, Davis MSS, LC; Kenneth Hechler memorandum, "The 1950 Elections," Nov. 15, 1950, Elsey Papers.

11. Unsigned (State Department) memorandum for the President, "Subject: McCarthyism," n.d. (July–August 1951), General File 1951, Alben Barkley MSS, University of Kentucky.

12. *Washington Post*, March 25, 1953, p. 13; Dorothy Thompson to Ralph Flanders, April 3, 1953, Box 111, Flanders MSS, Syracuse University; Bayley, *Joe McCarthy and the Press*, p. 67; Hubert Humphrey to Frederick J. Kottke, March 8, 1954, Box 109, Humphrey MSS, Minnesota Historical Society.

13. *New York Times*, January 17, 1953, p. 12; *Washington Post*, May 1, 1953, p. 14.

14. Excerpts, diary of a newsman accompanying Adlai Stevenson tour (1953), Box 32, Name Series, Ann Whitman Files, Dwight D. Eisenhower Library (DDEL), Abilene, Kan.

15. Eisenhower to William E. Robinson, March 23, 1954, Box 29, Name Series, Whitman Files; Eisenhower Diary, April 1, 1953, DDEL; Fred I. Greenstein, *The Hidden-Hand Presidency: Eisenhower as Leader* (New York, 1982); draft greeting to National Civil Liberties Clearing House, March 16, 1954, President's Personal File 47, DDEL.

Notes

16. Thomas C. Hennings to John Foster Dulles, June 25, 1953, Box 29, Hennings MSS, Western Historical Manuscript Collection/State Historical Society of Missouri Joint Collection, University of Missouri; *Washington Post,* April 10, 1953, p. 26; "Johnny" to "Pete" [Raymond Brandt?], March 21, 1954, "Political 1952, McCarthy" File; Leland Stowe manuscript, "Regarding McCarthyism," n.d. [Summer 1953], both in Adlai E. Stevenson MSS, Illinois State Historical Library, Springfield.

17. G. D. Wiebe, "The Army-McCarthy Hearings and the Public Conscience," *Public Opinion Quarterly,* 21 (Winter 1958–59): 490–502. Welch may have been primed for McCarthy's thrust. McCarthy had threatened several times to "tell the 'Fisher story.' " After defending Fisher at the hearings, Welch exited tearfully; once reporters left him, he asked a companion, "Well, how did it go?" Yet he told Fisher the attack "caught me completely unprepared." (Fred Fisher, "Joseph N. Welch," May 20, 1963 [copy kindly provided by Professor David Oshinsky]; Griffith, *Politics of Fear,* p. 260; Welch to Fisher, June 9, 1954, Box 6, Welch MSS, Boston Public Library.)

18. Henry Cabot Lodge, Jr., to Eisenhower, December 11, 1953, Administration Series, Whitman Files; George N. Craig to Eisenhower, March 19, 1954, Box 7, Name Series, Whitman Files; George H. Bender to Eisenhower, May 7, 1954, OF 138, all at DDEL.

19. Arthur V. Watkins to M. E. Dalton, December 9, 1954, Box 23, Watkins MSS, Brigham Young University.

20. Oshinsky, *Conspiracy So Immense,* p. 503; William F. Buckley, Jr., ed., *Odyssey of a Friend: Whittaker Chambers' Letters to William F. Buckley, Jr., 1954– 1961* (New York, 1969), p. 52.

Chapter 6

1. Elmer Davis radio script, January 16, 1951, Box 21, Davis MSS, LC.

2. U.S. Senate, Internal Security Subcommittee of the Committee on the Judiciary, Hearings, *Institute of Pacific Relations,* 82nd Cong., 2nd sess., 1952, p. 1894; E. J. Kahn, Jr., *The China Hands: America's Foreign Service Officers and What Befell Them* (New York, 1975), p. 92.

3. Pat McCarran in *Congressional Record,* 82nd cong., 2nd sess., 1952, vol. 98, pp. 8858–59, 8862; Earl Latham, *The Communist Controversy in Washington from the New Deal to McCarthy* (Cambridge, Mass., 1966), pp. 313–14; Kahn, *China Hands,* pp. 166, 234–35, 238, 247.

4. Internal Security Subcommittee, Hearings, *IPR,* pp. 2905, 3154–55, 3177, 3199, 3200–3201, 3387–88, 3495–96, 3574, 3674, 3676–77. On the weight given to Lattimore's failure to mention the meeting with Truman, see Senator Willis Smith to Hornell Hart, May 29, 1952, Box 6, Smith MSS, Duke University.

Notes

5. Stanley I. Kutler, *The American Inquisition: Justice and Injustice in the Cold War* (New York, 1982), pp. 203–14; William L. O'Neill, *A Better World—The Great Schism: Stalinism and the American Intellectuals* (New York, 1982), pp. 275–83.

6. David Halberstam, *The Best and the Brightest* (New York, 1972), pp. 113, 130, 188.

7. Walter Goodman, *The Committee: The Extraordinary Career of the House Committee on Un-American Activities* (New York, 1968), pp. 316–18; Ronald Wayne Johnson, "The Communist Issue in Missouri: 1946–1956" (Ph.D. diss., University of Missouri, 1973), pp. 174–76; Ronald W. Schatz, *The Electrical Workers: A History of Labor at General Electric and Westinghouse, 1923–60* (Urbana, Ill., 1983), pp. 201–3. Schatz notes that "local factors" may have affected the outcome as much as did the Communist issue (pp. 203–4).

8. Harvey A. Levenstein, *Communism, Anticommunism, and the CIO* (Westport, Conn., 1981), chap. 17 and p. 300; George N. Green, "McCarthyism in Texas: The 1954 Campaign," *Southern Quarterly* 16 (April 1978): 259, 262.

9. David Caute, *The Great Fear: The Anti-Communist Purge Under Truman and Eisenhower* (New York, 1978), pp. 437, 439, 445; SISS, *Subversive Influence in the Education Process*, 83rd Cong., 1st sess., 1953, pp. 466, 543, 648, 653, 998ff.

10. HUAC, *Communist Infiltration of Hollywood Motion-Picture Industry—Part 1*, 82nd Cong., 1st sess., 1951, pp. 89, 93, 107, 189–90, 227, 586–91; Larry Ceplair and Steven Englund, *The Inquisition in Hollywood: Politics in the Film Community, 1930–1960* (Garden City, N.Y., 1980), pp. 371, 373, 383; Stefan Kanfer, *A Journal of the Plague Years* (New York, 1973), p. 196.

11. Ceplair and Englund, *Inquisition in Hollywood*, pp. 399–400, 406; Victor Navasky, *Naming Names* (New York, 1980), p. 178; Kanfer, *Journal of the Plague Years*, pp. 110, 269; Merle Miller, "Trouble on Madison Avenue, N.Y.," *Nation*, June 28, 1952, p. 631; John Cogley, *Report on Blacklisting* (New York, 1956), vol. 1, p. 156.

12. U.S. Senate, Select Committee to Investigate Tax-Exempt Foundations and Comparable Organizations, Hearings, *Tax-Exempt Foundations*, 82nd Cong., 2nd sess., 1953, pp. 140, 188, 236; Thomas C. Reeves, *Freedom and the Foundation: The Fund for The Republic in the Era of McCarthyism* (New York, 1969); Joe McCarthy to Paul Hoffman, December 3, 1956, Box 84, Hoffman MSS, HSTL. On the Knowles episode, see Reeves, *Freedom and the Foundation*, pp. 117–24 and passim.

13. *New York Times*, August 28, 1950, p. 1, September 14, 1950, p. 15, September 17, 1950, sec. 4, p. 2, February 12, 1952, p. 29; Kanfer, *Journal of the Plague Years*, p. 120–21, 151; Lait and Mortimer quoted in Douglas T. Miller and Marion Nowak, *The Fifties: The Way We Really Were* (Garden City, N.Y., 1977) p. 304;

Notes

James Truett Selcraig, *The Red Scare in the Midwest, 1945–1955: A State and Local Study* (Ann Arbor, 1982), pp. 90–91, 94–95.

14. Marjorie Fiske, *Book Selection and Censorship: A Study of School and Public Libraries in California* (Berkeley, 1959), pp. 48–50, 64–65; Paul F. Lazarsfeld and Wagner Thielens, Jr., *The Academic Mind: Social Scientists in a Time of Crisis* (Glencoe, Ill., 1958), pp. 55–56, 65, 76, 78, 123, 197.

15. McCarthy to Truman, August 3, 1951, President's Personal File 200, Truman Papers, HSTL; William F. Buckley, Jr., and L. Brent Bozell, *McCarthy and His Enemies: The Record and Its Meaning* (Chicago, 1954), pp. 308–12; Eugene Lyons, "Is Freedom of Expression Really Threatened?" *American Mercury*, January 1953, pp. 22–33.

16. Manning Marable, *Race, Reform and Rebellion: The Second Reconstruction in Black America, 1945–1982* (Jackson, Miss., 1984), pp. 21, 28–30, 32–33; Wilson Record, *Race and Radicalism: The NAACP and the Communist Party in Conflict* (Ithaca, N.Y., 1964), pp. 162–63; August Meier and Elliott Rudwick, *CORE: A Study in the Civil Rights Movement, 1942–1968* (Urbana, Ill., 1975), pp. 31–32, 63–65; Harry S. Truman, *Memoirs*, vol. 2, *Years of Trial and Hope* (Garden City, N.Y., 1956), p. 183; Harvard Sitkoff, *The Struggle for Black Equality, 1954–1980* (New York, 1981), p. 18.

17. Leila J. Rupp, "The Survival of American Feminism: The Women's Movement in the Postwar Period," in *Reshaping America: Society and Institutions, 1945–1960*, ed. Robert H. Bremner and Gary W. Reichard (Columbus, 1982), pp. 40, 44, 55; Sara Evans, *Personal Politics: The Roots of Women's Liberation in the Civil Rights Movement and the New Left* (New York, 1979), pp. 11–12; Michael Rogin, "Kiss Me Deadly: Communism, Motherhood, and Cold War Movies," *Representations* 6 (Spring 1984): 1–36.

18. Wardell B. Pomeroy, *Dr. Kinsey and the Institute for Sex Research* (New Haven, Conn., 1982), pp. 366, 368, 374ff; Cornelia V. Christenson, *Kinsey: A Biography* (Bloomington, Ind., 1971), p. 166.

19. John D'Emilio, *Sexual Politics, Sexual Communities: The Making of a Homosexual Minority in the United States, 1940–1970* (Chicago, 1983); U.S. Senate, Subcommittee on Investigations of the Committee on Expenditures in the Executive Departments, Interim Report, *Employment of Homosexuals and Other Sex Perverts in Government*, 81st Cong., 2nd sess., 1950; Stephen J. Spingarn Oral History Interview, pp. 800–801, HSTL.

20. Lawrence S. Wittner, *Rebels Against War: The American Peace Movement: 1941–1960* (New York, 1969), pp. 258–61.

21. Larry W. Burt, *Tribalism in Crisis: Federal Indian Policy, 1953–1961* (Albuquerque, 1982), pp. 5, 41, 98.

22. Barry A. Kaplan, "Urban Development, Economic Growth and Personal Liberty: The Rhetoric of the Houston Anti-Zoning Movement, 1947–1962," *Southwestern Historical Quarterly* 84 (October 1980): 152, 154–156, 159–61.

Notes

Chapter 7

1. Ellen W. Schrecker, *No Ivory Tower: McCarthyism and the Universities* (New York, 1986), pp. 178, 188, 218 and passim; Michael O'Brien, *McCarthy and McCarthyism in Wisconsin* (Columbia, Mo., 1980), pp. 196–200; Elaine Yaffe, "Days of Suspicion—Acts of Courage," *Colorado College Bulletin*, January 1986, pp. 5–8.

2. Walter Goodman, *The Committee: The Extraordinary Career of the House Committee on Un-American Activities* (New York, 1968), pp. 200, 334–41, 374, 378–79; Arnold R. Hirsch, *Making the Second Ghetto: Race and Housing in Chicago, 1940–1960* (Cambridge, England, 1983), p. 174 and passim; Anne Braden, *The Wall Between* (New York, 1958), pp. 89–92, 185 and passim; Wilma Dykeman and James Stokely, "McCarthyism under the Magnolias," *Progressive*, July 1959, p. 6; Numan V. Bartley, *The Rise of Massive Resistance: Race and Politics in the South During the 1950's* (Baton Rouge, 1969), pp. 182, 185–88.

3. Max Kampelman to George Weaver, July 27, 1953, Box 97, Humphrey MSS, Minnesota Historical Society; Maurice Rosenblatt to Gifford Phillips, August 31, 1953, File 4, Drawer 1, National Committee for an Effective Congress MSS, Washington, D.C.; Walter F. Murphy, *Congress and the Court: A Case Study in the American Political Process* (Chicago, 1962), pp. 88–89.

4. *Congressional Record*, 83rd Cong., 2nd sess., 1954, vol. 100, pp. 7252–57; 84th Cong., 1st sess., 1955, vol. 101, pp. 6963–64, 7119–24; 84th Cong., 2nd sess., 1956, vol. 102, p. 3207; 86th Cong., 1st sess., 1959, vol. 105, pp. 2545–46; Wayne Clark, "An Analysis of the Relationship Between Anti-Communism and Segregationist Thought in the Deep South, 1948–1964" (Ph.D. diss., University of North Carolina–Chapel Hill, 1976), pp. 84–86; SISS, Hearings, *Southern Conference Educational Fund, Inc.*, 83rd Cong., 2nd sess., 1954; Goodman, *Committee*, pp. 420–22; Arthur Kinoy, *Rights on Trial: The Odyssey of a People's Lawyer* (Cambridge, Mass., 1983), pp. 215–30, 283; Irwin Klibaner, "The Travail of Southern Radicals: The Southern Conference Educational Fund, 1946–1976," *Journal of Southern History* 49 (May 1983): 179–202; Howell Raines, *My Soul Is Rested* (New York, 1983), pp. 395–400; John A. Salmond, " 'The Great Southern Commie Hunt': Aubrey Williams, the Southern Conference Educational Fund, and the Internal Security Subcommittee," *South Atlantic Quarterly* 77 (Autumn 1978): 433–52.

5. Philip M. Stern, *The Oppenheimer Case: Security on Trial* (New York, 1969), pp. 155–56, 204, 398–99, 406, 426 and passim; draft letter, Clinton P. Anderson to Dorothy Schiff, June 14, 1956, Box 435, Anderson MSS, LC; U.S. Atomic Energy Commission, *In the Matter of J. Robert Oppenheimer* (Cambridge, Mass., 1971), p. 1020 and passim.

6. Adam Yarmolinsky, ed., *Case Studies in Personnel Security* (Washington, D.C., 1955), pp. 2–3, 146, 177, 206, 209; Rowland Watts, *The Draftee and*

Notes

Internal Security: A Study of the Army Military Personnel Security Program (New York, [1955]), pp. 26, 40, 47; Ralph S. Brown, Jr., *Loyalty and Security: Employment Tests in the United States* (New Haven, Conn., 1958), pp. 70–72, 92, 140, 173, 181.

7. Memorandum [January 1955], attached to Lyndon Johnson to Hubert Humphrey, January 17, 1955, Box 117; Humphrey to Olin Johnston, November 28, 1955, Box 96, both in Humphrey MSS; U.S. Senate, Subcommittee on Constitutional Rights, Hearings, *Security and Constitutional Rights*, 84th Cong., 2nd sess., 1956, pp. 319–27; U.S. Senate, Subcommittee on Reorganization of Committee on Government Operations, Hearings, *Commission on Government Security*, 84th Cong., 1st sess., 1955, pp. 1, 143 and passim.

8. Richard Rovere, "The Kept Witnesses," *Harper's*, May 1955, pp. 25–34; *Washington Post*, June 20, 1955, clipping, Box 121, Humphrey MSS; Donald J. Kemper, *Decade of Fear: Senator Hennings and Civil Liberties* (Columbia, Mo., 1965), pp. 93–99; *Report of the Commission on Government Security* (Washington, D.C., 1957); Athan Theoharis, *Spying on Americans: Political Surveillance from Hoover to the Huston Plan* (Philadelphia, 1978), pp. 212ff. Harry Cain, a McCarthyite Senator until 1953 and then a member of the Subversive Activities Control Board, added his second thoughts about recent security cases to the criticism.

9. Paul L. Murphy, *The Constitution in Crisis Times, 1918–1969* (New York, 1972), pp. 322–37; G. Theodore Mitau, *Decade of Decision: The Supreme Court and the Constitutional Revolution, 1954–1964* (New York, 1967), chap. 1; Walter F. Murphy, *Congress and the Court: A Case Study in the American Political Process* (Chicago, 1962), pp. 112, 130 and passim; Earl Warren, *The Memoirs of Chief Justice Earl Warren* (Garden City, N.Y., 1977), pp. 5–6; Stanley I. Kutler, *The American Inquisition: Justice and Injustice in the Cold War* (New York, 1982), chap. 4; William R. Tanner, "The Passage of the Internal Security Act of 1950" (Ph.D. diss., University of Kansas, 1971), pp. 490, 496–99; Robert W. Mollan, "Congressional Policy-Making During the Eisenhower Administration Regarding Internal Security" (Ph.D. diss., University of Minnesota, 1967), p. 94; Stephen E. Ambrose, *Eisenhower*, vol. 2, *The President* (New York, 1984), p. 190.

10. Robert A. Divine, *American Immigration Policy, 1924–1952* (New Haven, Conn., 1957), p. 118; *Annual Report of the Immigration and Naturalization Service, 1959* (Washington, D.C., 1959), pp. 52, 58; David Caute, *The Great Fear: The Anti-Communist Purge Under Truman and Eisenhower* (New York, 1978), pp. 227, 229, 230, 241; *New York Times*, January 26, 1951, p. 4, February 1, 1955, p. 12, April 22, 1958, p. 3, April 23, 1958, p. 20, April 26, 1958, p. 6, May 8, 1960, p. 88.

11. Theoharis, *Spying on Americans*, chap. 5 (esp. pp. 135–37); Kenneth O'Reilly, *Hoover and the Un-Americans: The FBI, HUAC, and the Red Menace* (Philadelphia, 1983), p. 198, Frank J. Donner, *The Age of Surveillance: The Aims and Methods of America's Political Intelligence System* (New York, 1981), pp. 184, 237; Caute, *Great Fear*, p. 116.

Notes

12. David J. Garrow, *The FBI and Martin Luther King, Jr.: From "Solo" to Memphis* (New York, 1981), p. 105 and passim; Theoharis, *Spying on Americans*, pp. 121, 178 and passim.

13. H. Stuart Hughes, "Why We Had No Dreyfus Case," *American Scholar* 30 (Fall 1961): 478.

Epilogue

1. *New York Times*, April 16, 1956, p. 15, September 4, 1956, p. 1, September 5, 1956, p. 20, September 13, 1956, p. 1, September 15, 1956, p. 8, September 18, 1956, p. 1, September 19, 1956, p. 1, September 27, 1960, p. 29; Leroy Ashby, "Frank Church Goes to the Senate: The Idaho Election of 1956," *Pacific Northwest Quarterly* 78 (January–April 1987): 26, 28; Ross R. Rice, "The 1958 Election in Arizona," *Western Political Quarterly* 12 (March 1959): 271.

2. Richard E. Welch, Jr., "Herbert L. Matthews and the Cuban Revolution," *Historian* 47 (November 1984): 1–18; Dorothy Marshall to Frank Wilkinson, August 27, 1957, Box 8, National Committee Against Repressive Legislation MSS, State Historical Society of Wisconsin; *New York Times*, May 16, 1960, p. 20; Democratic National Committee, *Correction, Please!* (October 5, 1960).

3. Honolulu *Advertiser*, May 23, 1950, pp. 1, 8; *Congressional Record*, 85th Cong., 2nd sess., 1958, vol. 104, pp. 8126–27; ibid., p. 9506; Roger Bell, *Last Among Equals: Hawaiian Statehood and American Politics* (Honolulu, 1984).

4. Jerold Lee Simmons, "Operation Abolition: The Campaign to Abolish the House Un-American Activities Committee, 1935–1965" (Ph.D. diss., University of Minnesota, 1971), chap. 6, pp. 292–95 and passim; George Thayer, *The Farther Shores of Politics: The American Political Fringe Today*, 2nd ed. (New York, 1968), p. 401; Amy Swerdlow, "Ladies' Day at the Capitol: Women Strike for Peace Versus HUAC," *Feminist Studies* 8 (Fall 1982): 492–520; Eric Bentley, ed., *Thirty Years of Treason: Excerpts from Hearings before the House Committee on Un-American Activities, 1938–1968* (New York, 1971), p. 951; Frank Wilkinson to Clarence Pickett, March 29, 1963, Box 1, National Committee Against Repressive Legislation MSS, State Historical Society of Wisconsin.

5. Richard Longaker, "Emergency Detention: The Generation Gap, 1950–1971," *Western Political Quarterly* 27 (September 1974): 395–408; Frank J. Donner, *The Age of Surveillance: The Aims and Methods of America's Political Intelligence System* (New York, 1981), pp. 164–65, 409–10.

6. E. J. Kahn, Jr. *The China Hands* (New York, 1975), chaps. 12, 13; Kenneth P. O'Donnell and David F. Powers, with Joe McCarthy, *"Johnny, We Hardly Knew Ye": Memories of John Fitzgerald Kennedy* (Boston, 1972), p. 16; Doris Kearns, *Lyndon Johnson and the American Dream* (New York, 1976), p. 252.

7. Peter Collier and David Horowitz, "McCarthyism: The Last Refuge of the Left," *Commentary* 85 (January 1988): p. 41. Cf. William L. O'Neill, *A Better*

Notes

World: The Great Schism: Stalinism and the American Intellectuals (New York, 1982).

8. Quoted in Simmons, "Operation Abolition," p. 286; Toledo *Blade*, September 14, 1968, p. 1, October 25, 1969, p. 1; *New York Times*, January 16, 1966, sec. 4, p. 12, March 27, 1966, p. 85, September 6, 1970, p. 52; *Washington Post*, May 25, 1971, p. 15.

9. Donner, *Age of Surveillance*, pp. 398–99, 455–58; House Internal Security Committee, Hearings, *Terrorism—Part 1*, 93rd Cong., 2nd sess., 1974, pp. 3021, 3045; Ronnie Dugger, *On Reagan: The Man & His Presidency* (New York, 1983), pp. 273–77 and passim; *Chicago Tribune*, October 2, 1987, p. 3, January 29, 1988; *New York Times*, April 21, 1981, p. B12, April 25, 1981, p. 10, May 5, 1981, p. 23, May 10, 1982, p. 18, June 6, 1984, p. 7.

10. The recent emergence of the flag as a political issue might appear to belie this unworried estimate. In 1989 in *Texas v. Johnson*, the Supreme Court held that a far-left demagogue's burning of the American flag was an action protected by the constitutional right of free speech. The ruling stirred a counterdemagoguery by both the far Right and mainstream politicians, including President Bush, who rushed to propose a Twenty-seventh Amendment to the Constitution which would crimp the freedoms protected by the First. Since the eruption which greeted the Court's decision, emotions seem to have cooled slightly.

11. Beau Grosscup, *The Explosion of Terrorism* (Far Hills, N.J., 1987), pp. 102–4.

12. For an attempt to analyze changes in American attitudes, see James A. Davis, "Communism, Conformity, Cohorts, and Categories: American Tolerance in 1954 and 1972–73," *American Journal of Sociology* 81 (November 1975): 491–513.

Bibliographical Essay

The literature on "McCarthyism"—that is, mid-century varieties of extremist anti-communism, generally attended by forms of political repression—is vast. Historians at first tended to concentrate on McCarthy himself, on national rather than local politics, on political leaders rather than institutions, and on politics rather than culture. Although recent scholarship has gone far to rectify these imbalances, there is room for more studies that relate individual facets of McCarthyism to the longer tradition of American anti-radicalism.

Valuable treatments of American anti-radicalism can be found in David Brion Davis, *The Fear of Conspiracy: Images of Un-American Subversion from the Revolution to the Present* (Ithaca, N.Y., 1971), and John Higham, *Strangers in the Land* (New York, 1965). David H. Bennett's *The Party of Fear: From Nativist Movements to the New Right in American History* (Chapel Hill, N.C., 1988), especially good on the nineteenth century, appeared too late to assist me. Robert Justin Goldstein's *Political Repression in Modern America from 1870 to the Present* (Cambridge, Mass., 1978) sees antiradical outbursts as functional expressions of the interests of groups opposing change.

In the 1950s, social scientists sought to locate McCarthy and his appeals in a tradition of conspiracy-minded, "populist" social movements and his followers among social and ethnic groups, often "status-deprived," that had deep-seated grievances against the Establishment. See Daniel Bell, ed., *The Radical Right* (Garden City, N.Y., 1963), an updated version of *The New American Right* (New York, 1955), and Seymour Martin Lipset and Earl Raab, *The Politics of Unreason: Right-Wing Extremism in America, 1790–1970* (New York, 1970).

Bibliographical Essay

By the 1960s, most interpreters of McCarthyism had come to reject this sociological analysis. Nelson W. Polsby, "Towards an Explanation of McCarthyism," *Political Studies* 8 (October 1960); Earl Latham, *The Communist Controversy in Washington from the New Deal to McCarthy* (Cambridge, Mass., 1966); and Michael P. Rogin, *McCarthy and the Intellectuals: The Radical Specter* (Cambridge, Mass., 1967), offered important critiques of that approach. They ascribed McCarthy's influence to the conventional workings of partisan politics and to the frustrations of Republican Party conservatives. This "political" interpretation has shaped most subsequent writings, but scholars disagree sharply about which "conventional" politicians were to blame for the onset of McCarthyism.

Anti-communism, however, was not invented during the Cold War. The events of 1919–20 set important patterns for subsequent outbursts. Useful on this first Red Scare are Robert K. Murray, *Red Scare* (Minneapolis, 1955); Stanley Coben, *A. Mitchell Palmer: Politician* (New York, 1963), and "A Study in Nativism: The American Red Scare of 1919–1920," *Political Science Quarterly* 79 (March 1964); and William Preston, *Aliens and Dissenters: Federal Suppression of Radicals, 1903–1933* (Cambridge, Mass., 1963).

Historians have given little focused coverage to the anti-communism that endured, despite its demise as a burning national issue, in the 1920s. Hints of its cultural hardiness can be found in studies of anti-alien sentiment, cited above; of labor, for instance, Irving Bernstein, *The Lean Years: A History of the American Worker, 1920–1933* (Boston, 1960); and of reform movements such as feminism, for which see J. Stanley Lemons, *The Woman Citizen: Social Feminism in the 1920s* (Urbana, Ill., 1973), and Joan M. Jensen, "All Pink Sisters: The War Department and the Feminist Movement in the 1920s," in *Decades of Discontent: The Women's Movement, 1920–1940*, ed. Joan M. Jensen and Lois Scharf (Westport, Conn., 1983).

In the 1930s, anti-communism was revitalized thanks to the rise of conservative opposition to Franklin D. Roosevelt's New Deal, the increased activism and visibility of the Communists themselves, and the growth of totalitarianism abroad. The use of "fifth-column" methods of subversion in Europe stoked generalized worry that those whose loyalties were externally directed might try to subvert American institutions; the Nazi-Soviet Pact heightened already active fears of the designs of American Communists.

Congress took an increasingly active role in investigating communism. Walter Goodman, *The Committee: The Extraordinary Career of the House Committee on Un-American Activities* (New York, 1968), deals with that key institution of the second Red Scare. See also Michael Wrezin, "The Dies Committee," in *Congress Investigates, 1792–1974*, ed. Arthur M. Schlesinger, Jr., and Roger Bruns (New York, 1975), and Richard Polenberg, "Franklin D. Roosevelt and Civil Liberties: The Case of the Dies Committee," *Historian* 30 (February 1968). Philip L. Cantelon's "In Defense of America: Congressional Investigations of Communism

Bibliographical Essay

in the United States, 1919–1935" (Ph.D. diss., Indiana University, 1971) is an important study of Dies's predecessors. For the right wing's anti-New Deal *angst*, see George Wolfskill and John A. Hudson, *All But the People: Franklin D. Roosevelt and his Critics, 1933–1939* (London, 1969). Les K. Adler and Thomas G. Paterson, "Red Fascism: The Merger of Nazi Germany and Soviet Russia in the American Image of Totalitarianism, 1930's–1950's," *American Historical Review* 75 (April 1970), and Thomas R. Maddux, "Red Fascism, Brown Bolshevism: The American Image of Totalitarianism in the 1930s," *Historian* 40 (November 1977), offer two viewpoints on the American penchant for lumping communism with Nazism.

Since the 1960s, many historians have dated the germination of the loyalty-security state in the Truman years, yet the political, legislative, and bureaucratic roots of this phenomenon sprouted immediately before and during World War II. See Richard Polenberg, *War and Society: The United States, 1941–1945* (Philadelphia, 1972); William Preston, Jr., "The 1940s: The Way We Really Were," *Civil Liberties Review* 2 (Winter 1975); Leo P. Ribuffo, *The Old Christian Right: The Protestant Far Right from the Great Depression to the Cold War* (Philadelphia, 1983); Geoffrey S. Smith, *To Save a Nation: American Countersubversives, the New Deal, and the Coming of World War II* (New York, 1973); and Carmen Notaro, "Franklin D. Roosevelt and the American Communists: Peace-time Relations, 1932–1941" (Ph.D. diss., State University of New York-Buffalo, 1969).

Books that focus on (and criticize) the Truman presidency include Athan Theoharis, *Seeds of Repression: Harry S. Truman and the Origins of McCarthyism* (Chicago, 1971); Richard M. Freeland, *The Truman Doctrine and the Origins of McCarthyism: Foreign Policy, Domestic Politics, and Internal Security, 1946–1948* (New York, 1972); and Mary Sperling McAuliffe, *Crisis on the Left: Cold War Politics and American Liberals, 1947–1954* (Amherst, Mass., 1978). A more sympathetic analysis is found in Alonzo L. Hamby, *Beyond the New Deal: Harry S. Truman and American Liberalism* (New York, 1972), and Alan D. Harper, *The Politics of Loyalty: The White House and the Communist Issue, 1946–1952* (Westport, Conn., 1969). On the McCarran Act, see William Randolph Tanner, "The Passage of the Internal Security Act of 1950" (Ph.D. diss., University of Kansas, 1971).

More recent works have highlighted the FBI's role in the advent of the Red Scare: Athan Theoharis, *Spying on Americans: Political Surveillance from Hoover to the Huston Plan* (Philadelphia, 1978); Frank J. Donner, *The Age of Surveillance: The Aims and Methods of America's Political Intelligence System* (New York, 1980); and Kenneth O'Reilly, *Hoover and the Un-Americans: The FBI, HUAC, and the Red Menace* (Philadelphia, 1983). Two recent biographies of J. Edgar Hoover are Richard Gid Powers, *Secrecy and Power: The Life of J. Edgar Hoover* (New York, 1987), and Athan Theoharis and John Cox, *The Boss: J. Edgar Hoover and the American Inquisition* (Philadelphia, 1988). The Smith Act trial of the eleven top Communists was one of several major cases that helped fix the atmosphere of anti-communism. For the Truman Administration's (and the FBI's) legal attack on the Communist Party, see Michal R. Belknap, *Cold War Political Justice: The Smith Act, the Communist Party, and American Civil Liberties* (Westport, Conn., 1977), and Peter L. Steinberg, *The Great "Red Menace": United States Prosecution of American Communists, 1947–1952* (Westport, Conn., 1984).

The best book on the Hiss case is Allen Weinstein, *Perjury: The Hiss-Chambers Case* (New York, 1978). Compare John Chabot Smith, *Alger Hiss, the True Story* (New York, 1976), and two essays in Athan Theoharis, ed., *Beyond the Hiss Case: The FBI, Congress, and the Cold War* (Philadelphia, 1982). Similar controversy surrounds the conviction of Julius and Ethel Rosenberg. See especially Ronald Radosh and Joyce Milton, *The Rosenberg File: A Search for the Truth* (New York, 1983). A dissenting view is presented in Walter Schneir and Miriam Schneir, *Invitation to an Inquest* (New York, 1983). On the Fuchs case, see Robert Chadwell Williams, *Klaus Fuchs, Atom Spy* (Cambridge, Mass., 1987).

A wealth of scholarship on Joseph R. McCarthy now burdens library shelves. There are two excellent, exhaustive biographies: Thomas C. Reeves. *The Life and Times of Joe McCarthy* (New York, 1982), and David M. Oshinsky, *A Conspiracy So Immense: The World of Joe McCarthy* (New York, 1983). Richard Rovere's *Senator Joe McCarthy* (Cleveland, 1959) is insightful but impressionistic and shows its age. Also see Fred J. Cook, *The Nightmare Decade: The Life and Times of Senator Joe McCarthy* (New York, 1971).

Monographs that treat important aspects of the McCarthy story include Robert Griffith, *The Politics of Fear: Joseph R. McCarthy and the Senate* (Lexington, Ky., 1970); Michael O'Brien, *McCarthy and McCarthyism in Wisconsin* (Columbia, Mo., 1980); Fr. Donald F. Crosby, *God, ·Church, and Flag: Senator Joseph R. McCarthy and the Catholic Church, 1950–1957* (Chapel Hill, N.C., 1978); Richard M. Fried, *Men Against McCarthy* (New York, 1976); and Edwin R. Bayley, *Joe McCarthy and the Press* (Madison, 1981).

Several wider ranging assessments of McCarthyism deserve note. David Caute, *The Great Fear: The Anti-Communist Purge Under Truman and Eisenhower* (New York, 1978), surveys the exertions of more anti-Communist entrepreneurs (at the local and state as well as national levels) over a longer period, and directed at a vaster company of victims, than ordinarily receive attention. The work's broad reach comes at the price of occasional inaccuracies. Stanley I. Kutler's *The American Inquisition: Justice and Injustice in the Cold War* (New York, 1982) reveals the legal, bureaucratic, and political roots of that era's injustices. Several essays in Athan Theoharis and Robert Griffith, eds., *The Specter: Original Essays on the Cold War and the Origins of McCarthyism* (New York, 1974), also point up the institutional and interest-group bases of anti-Communist activism. This institutional or sectoral approach to McCarthyism constitutes an important trend in recent scholarship.

Several works weigh the impact of the federal loyalty and security programs.

Bibliographical Essay

Besides Caute, these include Ralph S. Brown, Jr., *Loyalty and Security: Employ-ment Tests in the United States* (New Haven, Conn., 1958); Eleanor Bontecou, *The Federal Loyalty-Security Program* (Ithaca, N.Y., 1953); and Adam Yarmo-linsky, ed., *Case Studies in Personnel Security* (Washington, D.C., 1955).

The entertainment field, Hollywood in particular, has received much atten-tion. The best book is Larry Ceplair and Steven Englund, *The Inquisition in Hollywood: Politics in the Film Community, 1930–1960* (Garden City, N.Y., 1980). Victor Navasky's *Naming Names* (New York, 1980) treats the film industry purge in leveling a broader indictment of the informers generally and of their interrogators and apologists. See also John Cogley, *Report on Blacklisting*, 2 vols. (New York, 1956), and Stefan Kanfer, *A Journal of the Plague Years* (New York, 1973).

Numerous works assay the impact of anti-communism on educational institu-tions. Ellen Schrecker's *No Ivory Tower: McCarthyism and the Universities* (New York, 1986) is the best introduction. Also useful are Jane Sanders, *Cold War on the Campus: Academic Freedom at the University of Washington, 1946–64* (Seattle, 1979); David P. Gardner, *The California Oath Controversy* (Berkeley, 1967); and David Lane Marden, "The Cold War and American Education" (Ph.D. diss., University of Kansas, 1975).

The McCarthy literature deals with the fates of some of those whose government careers he shortened. For the Red-hunters' inroads on the Foreign Service, see E. J. Kahn, Jr., *The China Hands* (New York, 1975), and Gary May, *China Scapegoat: The Diplomatic Ordeal of John Carter Vincent* (Washington, D.C., 1979). Aspects of the attack on charitable foundations are treated in Thomas C. Reeves, *Freedom and the Foundation: The Fund for the Republic in the Era of McCarthyism* (New York, 1969).

It is widely, and not unreasonably, assumed that McCarthyism had a chilling effect on reform, liberalism, and radicalism in the postwar period. The treatment of this phenomenon as it relates to a number of areas—civil rights, for instance—tends to be scattered. See the citations for appropriate topics in the notes for Chapters 4 and 6. Particularly pertinent is Manning Marable, *Race, Reform and Rebellion: The Second Reconstruction in Black America, 1945–1982* (Jackson, Miss., 1984). On labor, see Harvey A. Levenstein, *Communism, Anticommunism, and the CIO* (Westport, Conn., 1981), and Bert Cochran, *Labor and Communism: The Conflict that Shaped American Unions* (Princeton, N.J., 1977).

Local and state-level activities are crucial for appraising anti-communism's overall impact. Two fine local studies are Don Carleton, *Red Scare! Right-wing Hysteria, Fifties Fanaticism, and Their Legacy in Texas* (Austin, 1985), and Charles H. Mc-Cormick's *This Nest of Vipers* (Urbana, Ill., 1989). For the state and regional level, see George H. Calcott, *Maryland and America, 1940–1980* (Baltimore, 1985); James Truett Selcraig, *The Red Scare in the Midwest, 1945–1955: A State and Local Study* (Ann Arbor, 1982); M. J. Heale, "Red Scare Politics: California's Campaign Against Un-American Activities, 1940–1970," *Journal of American Studies* 20 (April

Bibliographical Essay

1986); Wayne Johnson, "The Communist Issue in Missouri: 1945–1956" (Ph.D. diss., University of Missouri, 1973); Thomas Michael Holmes, "The Specter of Communism in Hawaii, 1947–1953" (Ph.D. diss., University of Hawaii, 1975); and Dale Sorenson, "The Anticommunist Consensus in Indiana, 1945–1958" (Ph.D. diss., Indiana University, 1980). Of the state studies published in the 1950s, see especially Walter Gellhorn, ed., *The States and Subversion* (Ithaca, N.Y., 1952).

The period after McCarthyism passed its zenith has received little attention. The burgeoning field of works on President Dwight D. Eisenhower mostly ignores it, concentrating instead on Ike's role in undermining McCarthy. Highly laudatory treatments include Fred I. Greenstein, *The Hidden-Hand Presidency: Eisenhower as Leader* (New York, 1982), and William Bragg Ewald, Jr., *Who Killed Joe Mc-Carthy?* (New York, 1984). Steven E. Ambrose, *Eisenhower*, vol. 2, *The President* (New York, 1984), renders a more measured verdict.

Post-McCarthy McCarthyism receives scrutiny in exposés of the FBI's ongoing exertions in surveillance and infiltration, which postdated McCarthy's (not to mention the Communist Party's) decline. Previously cited works by David Caute, Stanley Kutler, and Ralph S. Brown, Jr., provide coverage too. See also Robert W. Mollan, "Congressional Policy-Making During the Eisenhower Administration Regarding Internal Security" (Ph.D. diss., University of Minnesota, 1967). After 1954, much of the controversy was centered in the courts, for which Paul L. Murphy, *The Constitution in Crisis Times, 1918–1969* (New York, 1972), and Walter Murphy, *Congress and the Court: A Case Study in the American Political Process* (Chicago, 1962), are valuable.

Other works that suggest some of the civil-liberties issues remaining unsettled after the "McCarthy era" are David J. Garrow, *The FBI and Martin Luther King, Jr.: From "Solo" to Memphis* (New York, 1981); Alan Rogers, "Passports and Politics: The Courts and the Cold War," *Historian* 47 (August 1985); Richard Longaker, "Emergency Detention: The Generation Gap, 1950–1971," *Western Political Quarterly* 27 (September 1974); Hugh T. Lovin, "Lyndon B. Johnson, the Subversive Activities Control Board, and the Politics of Anti-Communism," *North Dakota Quarterly* 54 (Winter 1986); and Jerold Lee Simmons, "Operation Abolition: The Campaign to Abolish the House Un-American Activities Committee, 1935–1965" (Ph.D. diss., University of Minnesota, 1971). Richard O. Curry, ed., *Freedom at Risk: Secrecy, Censorship, and Repression in the 1980s,* (Philadelphia, 1988), appeared too late to be of use for this book.

The moral issues of the 1950s, bitter enough then, resurfaced in the 1970s as many of the victims of the earlier age gained rehabilitation. Lillian Hellman's memoirs, particularly *Scoundrel Time* (Boston, 1976), evoked especially spirited debate, as did Navasky's *Naming Names* (previously cited). A useful and astringent appraisal of these and other participants in the controversy is William L. O'Neill, *A Better World: The Great Schism: Stalinism and the American Intellectuals* (New York, 1962). Also useful is Richard H. Pells, *The Liberal Mind in a Conservative*

Age: American Intellectuals in the 1940s and 1950s (New York, 1985). A recent polemic is Peter Collier and David Horowitz, "McCarthyism: The Last Refuge of the Left," *Commentary* 85 (January 1988).

This is by no means a complete bibliography. It omits much of the biographical literature and memoirs of the main actors of the second Red Scare, as well as the growing primary and secondary literature on the Communist Party and the Left at mid-century. Many valuable works on smaller segments of the larger picture have been omitted, and I have not included manuscript sources in this essay, because the chapter notes indicate my scholarly debts in these regards. A useful bibliographical work on this subject is John Earl Haynes, *Communism and Anti-Communism in the United States: An Annotated Guide to Historical Writings* (New York, 1987).

Index

Abstract expressionism, 30–32
Acheson, Sec'y of State Dean G., 93, 148, 167
Adams, John G., 138, 139
Addams, Jane, 44
Advertising Council, 98
Agricultural Adjustment Administration, 18, 45
Albertson, William, 190
Alford, Rep. Dale, 178
Allen, Raymond B., 101
Allen, Woody, 157, 197
Alsop, Joseph, 183, 198
Amerasia case, 60–61, 147
American Association of University Professors, 103
American Business Consultants, 157
American Artists Professional League (AAPL), 30, 31, 33
American Civil Liberties Union (ACLU), 52, 66, 106, 163, 200
American Federation of Labor (AFL): Communists and, 12; and Seattle general strike, 39; anti-communism of, 44, 45, 48; and Bucyrus-Erie strike, 96; CIO rejoins, 153

American Federation of State, County, and Municipal Employees, 110
American Federation of Teachers, 103
American Labor Party, 66
American League for Peace and Democracy, 14
American Legion: and baseball, 34, 79; and Americanism movement, 41; Hamilton Fish and, 45; miscellaneous anti-Communist efforts of, 78, 84, 98, 161, 162; and Peekskill, 97; and education, 100; and state-level anti-Communism, 106, 108, 110; and Tule Lake camp, 118; and blacklist, 156, 158
Americans for Democratic Action, 65, 82
Anderson, Sen. Clinton P., 180
Anti-communism: socioeconomic basis of, 8; cultural basis of, 9, 29–35; political elites and, 16; public opinion and, 16, 49, 59–60, 87–88; "functional" aspects of, 35–36; consensus on, 36; rise of, 38ff.; in 1920s, 43–44; in localities, 95–97; and CIO, 99–100; and education, 100–103, 162–63; in states, 104–14, 175; and foundations, 158–61; and lib-

231

Anti-communism (*continued*)
  eral causes, 161, 163–64; impact on culture, 161–63, 166; and civil-rights movement, 164–66, 174–78; and feminism,
  166; and gays and lesbians, 167–68; and
  peace movement, 168–69; and Indian
  policy, 169; and zoning, 169; and Hawaiian statehood, 194–95
Anti-radicalism, 37–39, 42. *See also* Anti-
  communism
Army, Department of, 137–39
Atomic bomb, 6, 19
Atomic Energy Commission (AEC), 25, 80,
  90, 179–80
Attorney General's list, 55, 68, 70–71, 97,
  108, 112, 125, 159, 160
Aware, Inc., 157, 197

Bailey, Dorothy, 71
Bakewell, Rep. Claude, 64
Ball, Sen. Joseph, 28
Ball, Lucille, 166
Barkley, Sen. Alben, 64
Baseball, and anti-communism, 34–35, 79
Beck, Dave, 110
Bender, Rep. George H., 140
Benet, Stephen Vincent, 50
Bentley, Elizabeth, 19, 81, 62
Bentley, Eric, 195
Benton, William B., 32, 79, 140
Berkeley, Martin, 154
Berle, Adolph A., 18
Berlin airlift, 7, 84
Bessie, Alvah, 76
Biberman, Herbert, 76
Biddle, Att'y Gen. Francis, 51, 56
Bingham, Hiram, 133, 147
Black, Justice Hugo, 114, 187
Blacklist, 77–78, 156–58, 196–98
Black Panther Party, 191
Blau v. U.S., 154
Bobrowicz, Edmund V., 64
Bogart, Humphrey, 57, 77, 158
Bolshevik Revolution, 11, 39–40
Borden, William L., 179
Bowron, Mayor Fletcher, 79

Bozell, L. Brent, 28, 163
Braden, Anne, 174
Braden, Carl, 174–75, 176
Brennan, Justice William, 184
Brewer, Roy, 75, 158
Bricker, Gov. John W., 57
Bridges, Harry Renton: efforts to deport, 35,
  152; attacks on, 48, 56, 195; and Team-
  sters, 110; bail revoked, 113, 115; and
  Port Security Program, 182
Bridges, Sen. Styles, 89, 121, 125
Browder, Earl, 12; and united front, 13, 15;
  mentioned, 22, 61, 121; jailed, 54; as
  campaign issue, 57
Brown, Ralph S., Jr., 182
*Brown v. Board of Education of To-
  peka, Kan.*, 174–76, 185
Brownell, Att'y Gen. Herbert, Jr., 149, 179
Broyles, State Sen. Paul, 106–7, 112
Broyles Commission, 106–7, 111, 112
Brunauer, Esther C., 23–29, 125
Brunauer, Stephen, 23–28, 125
Buckley, William F., Jr., 28, 163, 194
Budenz, Louis, 15, 94, 126, 146, 148, 183
Bureau of Immigration (U.S. Dept. of La-
  bor), 38–39, 42
Bureau of Investigation, 41, 43. *See also*
  Federal Bureau of Investigation
Bureau of Prisons (U.S.), 118
Busbey, Rep. Fred, 25, 132
Bush, Pres. George H., 222 *n*.10
Butler, Sen. John M., 151
Byrnes, James F., 19, 62, 63, 65, 123

Cagney, Jimmy, 57
California, anti-communism in, 105–6,
  110, 112
California Joint Fact-Finding Committee
  on Un-American Activities, 105–6, 110,
  111
Cannon, James, 11
Canwell, Albert, 101, 107–8, 111, 112
Canwell Committee, 101, 107–8, 112
Capote, Truman, 198
Carey, James C., 66, 151–52

Index

Carnegie Endowment for International
  Peace, 19, 158
Castro, Fidel, 194
Catholic Church, 16, 97
Catholic War Veterans, 162
Catholics, and McCarthyism, 8
Celler, Rep. Emanuel, 53, 116
Central Intelligence Agency, 31, 134, 191
Ceplair, Larry, 74
Chambers Whittaker: and Hiss case, 18–21,
  62, 81, 92, 112; books purged by IIA,
  136; on McCarthy, 143
Chaplin, Charles, 197
Chicago Tribune, 25
Childs, Marquis, 130
China Hands, 61, 89, 146–50, 197
China Lobby, 89, 125, 126, 147, 148
Chinese Nationalists, 61, 147
China policy: and *Amerasia* case, 61–62; as
  political issue, 88–89, 145–50, 197; Mc-
  Carthy on, 121, 125
Cincinnati Reds, 34–35
CIO-PAC (CIO Political Action Commit-
  tee), 57, 63–64
City College of New York, 104
Civil defense, 89–90, 99
Civil liberties: public opinion on, 9–10, 36;
  in World War I era, 38–42
Civil rights, anti-communism's impact on,
  164–66, 175–78
Civil Service Commission (U.S.), 55, 70
Clark, Att'y Gen. Tom C.: and *Amerasia*
  case, 61; and loyalty program, 67, 69;
  anti-Communist rhetoric of, 82–83; and
  Dennis case, 83–84; and Freedom
  Train, 97–98; on *Yates*, 186
Cleaver, June, 166
Cogley, John, 160
Cohn, Roy M., 134, 136, 137, 139
COINTELPRO, 189–92
Cold War: and origins of McCarthyism, 3,
  8, 9; anxieties raised by, 6; origins of, 7–
  8; and Communist issue, 19, 59; and
  U.S. liberalism, 64–65; and civil-rights
  movement, 165–66
Cole, Lester, 76, 77

Cole v. Young, 184–85
Collier, Peter, 198
Colorado College, 173
Conant, James B., 103
Comintern, 15, 39
Commission on Government Security
  (U.S.), 183–84
Committee for the First Amendment, 77, 78
Communism (domestic): fears of, 3, 7; dur-
  ing 1930s, 10–14; issue in 1944 election,
  56–58; in 1946 election, 63–64; in 1948
  election, 81–84; in 1950 election, 129–
  30; and labor unions, 151–53; in 1954–
  60 campaigns, 193–94
Communism (foreign), threat of, 7–8
Communist Control Act (1954), 171–72
Communist Labor Party, 40, 42
Communist Party (CP, CPUSA): early
  years, 11–12, 40, 42; in 1930s, 12–14;
  and Popular Front, 13–14; and Nazi-
  Soviet Pact, 14; in World War II, 14–15;
  and Hiss, 19; public opinion of, 60; and
  Hollywood, 73–74; and *Dennis* case, 93–
  95; goes underground, 95; vigilantism
  against, 95–96; and McCarran Act, 118;
  and civil rights, 164, 165; and de-
  Stalinization, 174, 190; and *Yates*, 185;
  and deportations, 188–89; FBI programs
  against, 189–92
Communist Political Association, 15, 94
Communists (American): and New Deal,
  45; FBI and, 51; early restrictions on, 52–
  54; and World War II, 54
Condon, Edward U., 80
Conference of Small Business Organizations, 100
Conference of Studio Unions, 75
Congress (U.S.): and loyalty issue, 63, 69–
  70; investigates communism, 73
Congress of Industrial Organizations (CIO):
  and Communists, 12–13, 66, 73, 86,
  99–100, 151–52; anti-Communist
  charges against, 47, 57; conflict in, 95–
  96; and civil rights, 164
Congress of Racial Equality (CORE), 165
Conservatives, and threat of subversion, 47

Index

Cooper, Gary, 76
Copland, Aaron, 132
Coplon, Judith, 91–92
Corcoran, Thomas, 61
Costigan, Howard, 64
Coudert, Frederick R., 104
Counterattack, 78, 173
Cox, Rep. Eugene, 158
Craig, Gov. George N., 140
Cronin, Father John, 19, 85
Crouch, Paul, 177–78, 183
Cullen, Hugh Roy, 169
Custodial Detention Index (FBI), 51
Czechoslovakia, 8, 13, 84

Daily Worker, 14, 15, 54, 154
Dallas, art controversy in, 33
Daughters of the American Revolution, 162
Daughters of Bilitis, 168
Davies, John Paton, Jr., 148, 197
Davies, Joseph E., 15
Davis, Elmer, 29, 130, 144
Defense, Department of, 181
DeLacy, Rep. Hugh, 64
"Democracy Beats Communism Week"
  (Kansas City, Mo.), 98
Democratic Party: Communist charges
  against, 7; blamed for rise of McCarthy-
  ism, 8–9, 84; in 1944 campaign, 56–57;
  in 1948 campaign: 82–84; and Hiss case,
  92–93; and McCarthy, 123–24, 127–29,
  130, 133, 141; and loyalty issue, 134; and
  Korea, 144; and security program, 178–
  79, 182
Dennis, Eugene, 93
Dennis v. U.S., 93–94, 113, 114, 187
Denton, Sen. Jeremiah, 199–200
Detroit, anti-communism in, 32, 109–10
Dewey, Gov. Thomas E., 57, 82, 194
Diamond, Sigmund, 103
Dickstein, Rep. Samuel, 46, 47
Dies, Rep. Martin: anti-Communist probes
  of, 47–49, 50, 52, 56; and Hollywood,
  73; and Communist Control Act, 172;
  and nativism, 188

Dies Committee, 47–49, 52, 55, 56, 105
Dirksen, Sen. Everett M., 116
Dmytryk, Edward, 76
Dodd, Bella, 153
Dondero, Rep. George, 31, 35
Douglas, Rep. Helen Gahagan, 129
Douglas, Melvyn, 77
Douglas, Sen. Paul, 93, 196
Douglas, Justice William O., 163
Du Bois, W. E. B., 165
Dulles, Foster Rhea, 34
Dulles, Sec'y of State John Foster, 148
Duran, Gustavo, 125
Durante, Jimmy, 57
Durr, Clifford and Virginia, 177–78

Easley, Ralph, 45
Eastland, Sen. James O., 145, 176–78, 185
Education, and Communist issue, 100–
  103, 153, 162–63, 172–73
Eisenhower, Dwight D.: era of, 5, 6; and
  Nixon, 22; on Communists in schools,
  103; and McCarthy, 132–36, 138, 141–
  42, 145; and Oppenheimer, 179–80; and
  Supreme Court, 185, 186, 187–88; and
  COINTELPRO, 189
Eisenhower Administration: and McCarthy,
  132, 133–36, 138; and security program,
  133–34
Eisler, Gerhart, 80, 158
Eisler, Hanns, 80, 158
Elections, and Communist issue: in 1948,
  8, 19, 20, 81–84; in 1938, 48; in 1944,
  56–58; in 1946, 63–64, 107; in 1950,
  129–30; in 1954 and subsequent years,
  193
Englund, Steven, 74
Espionage (Soviet), 18, 62, 90, 115
Evans, Dr. Ward, 180

Farm Equipment Workers Union, 99
Faubus, Gov. Orval, 178
Faulk, John Henry, 196–97
Federal Bureau of Investigation (FBI): and
  Hiss case, 19, 21, 62, 81; "dirty tricks" of,
  23; investigates Communists, 50–52, 55,

Index

56; Custodial Detention Index, 51; and *Amerasia* case, 60–61; and loyalty program, 67; and Smith Act case, 83; "educational" program of, 85; and Coplon case, 91–92; files of, 92; and National Lawyers Guild, 92; and Philbrick, 94; and universities, 103; and Rosenbergs 115; and second-string Smith Act cases, 115; and Lattimore, 148; and blacklisters, 156; and gays and lesbians, 167, 168; COINTELPROs, 189–92; monitors Left, 200

Federal employee loyalty program: adopted, 7, 66–69; as cause of McCarthyism, 9, 59; "reasonable grounds" standard, 68; impact of, 70–73, 84; replaced, 133; and China Hands, 147

Federal Theatre Project, 48

Feminism: and anti-Communists, 43–44, 166

Ferguson, Sen. Homer E., 145

Fiedler, Leslie, 93

Field, Noel, 26

Fieldites, 11

Fifth Amendment, 151, 154–55, 165, 172–73, 185, 187

"Fifth column" threat, 49, 50, 52

First Amendment, and Hollywood Ten, 77, 154

Fish, Rep. Hamilton, 45, 188

Fisher, Fred, 139, 216 n.17

Fisk University, 165

Flanders, Sen. Ralph E., 139–40

Flynn, William J., 41, 43

Fonda, Jane, 33

Football, 79

Ford, Henry, II, 159

Ford Foundation, 159, 160

Foreign Agents Registration Act, 52

Forrester, Rep. E. L., 176

Foster, William Z., 12, 41, 93

Foundations, and Communist issue, 158–61

Frankfurter, Justice Felix, 115

Freedom of Information Act, 23, 200

Freedom Train, 98

Freeland, Richard M., 68

Fuchs, Klaus, 62, 115, 120

Fulbright, Sen. J. William, 195

Fund for the Republic, 159–60, 181

Fur and Leather Workers Union, 152

Gallup poll, 60, 131, 138

Garfield, John, 157, 158

Garland, Judy, 57

Geer, Will, 154

Gellhorn, Walter, 112

General Electric, 5, 152

General Intelligence Division (FBI), 41, 51

German-American Bund, 47, 51

German-Americans, and McCarthyism, 8

Girl Scouts of America, 161

Gitlow, Benjamin, 112

Goldwater, Sen. Barry M., 193

Gorbachev, Michail, 200

Goslin, Willard, 100–101

Gouzenko, Igor, 62

Graham, Rev. Billy, 5

Graham, Sen. Frank P., 129

Gray, Gordon, 180

Great Depression, and radicalism, 10–13, 44ff

Green, Sen. Theodore F., 125

Greene, Graham, 163

Greenglass, David, 115

Griffith, Robert, 8

Groves, Gen. Leslie, 90

Gubitchev, Valentin, 91

Hammett, Dashiell, 34

Hand, Judge Learned, 114, 115

Hannegan, Robert, 64

Hanson, Haldore, 125

Hanson, Mayor Ole, 39–40

Harding, Pres. Warren G., 43

Harriman, Averell, 150

Hartnett, Vincent, 196–97

Harvard University, 103, 173

Hatch Act (Sec. 9C), 52, 55

Hawaii, and anti-communism, 112, 194–95

Hearst, Patty, 198

Index

Hearst press, 85, 97
Heikkila, William 189
Hellman, Lillian, 14, 155, 197–98
Hendrickson, Sen. Robert C., 140
Hennings, Sen. Thomas C., 136, 182
Hepburn, Katharine, 78
Herblock [Herbert Block], 134, 180
Heritage Foundation, 199
Hewitt, George, 112
Hickenlooper, Sen. Bourke B., 125, 127
Highlander Folk School, 177
Hillman, Sidney, 57
Hiss, Alger: case of, 17–23; and New Deal,
    17–18; mentioned, 25, 29, 112, 121,
    125, 176, 183; FBI and, 62; and 1948
    campaign, 81, 82; significance of case,
    92–93; and Carnegie Endowment, 158;
    as campaign issue, 193, 194
Hiss, Priscilla, 18
Hoey, Sen. Clyde, 167
Hoffman, Abbie, 195
Hoffman, Paul, 159, 160
Hollywood (movie industry): and anti-
    Communism, 30; investigations of, 73–
    78, 153–56; and blacklist, 77–78, 156–
    58; anti-Communist films of, 78
Hollywood Ten, 76–78, 153, 154
Homosexuality, and Communist issue,
    167–68
Hood, Robin. See Robin Hood
Hook, Sidney, 102
Hoover, Pres. Herbert C., 44–45
Hoover, J. Edgar: mentioned, 15, 45, 111;
    and Hiss case, 17, 19, 21; and first Red
    Scare, 41; heads FBI, 43; monitors subver-
    sives, 57; and PTCEL, 67, 70; power of,
    83; "educational" program of, 85, 97; files
    of, 92; and McCarthy, 121; and Fund for
    the Republic, 160; and Oppenheimer,
    179; and Jencks, 185; surveillance and in-
    filtration programs of, 189–91; and Mar-
    tin Luther King, Jr., 191
Hopkins, Harry, 90
Horowitz, David, 198
House Civil Service Committee, 63, 69
House Committee on Un-American Activi-

ties (HUAC): mentioned, 3, 144; and
    Hiss case, 19–20, 22, 81; and Brunauers,
    25; and 1959 art show, 33; and loyalty
    program, 69; and Hollywood, 73–77,
    153–56; and Jackie Robinson, 79; 1948
    activities of, 80–81; and atomic spying,
    90; and schools, 100, 172–73; and anti-
    communism in states, 112; miscellaneous
    investigations of, 150–51, 172–73; and
    Fifth Amendment, 154–55; and founda-
    tions, 160–61; and clergy, 173; and civil-
    rights movement, 174, 176; Supreme
    Court and, 184, 185; and Hawaii, 194–
    95; decline of, 195–96, 198
House Education and Labor Committee, 96
House Internal Security Committee, 196,
    198–99
Hughes, H. Stuart, 192
Humphrey, Sen. Hubert H.: in 1968, 22;
    and Minnesota politics, 66; and
    McCarran Act, 117; and McCarthy, 133;
    labor investigation of, 151; and Commu-
    nist Control Act, 171–72; and security
    program, 182, 183
Hurley, Gen. Patrick, 61
Hutchins, Robert M., 107–8, 159
Hydrogen bomb, 6, 7, 89, 120, 179, 180

Ichord, Rep. Richard, 198
Ickes, Sec'y of the Interior Harold, 57
Illinois, anti-communism in, 106–7, 110,
    111
Immigration and Naturalization Service,
    85, 188–89
Indian rights, 169
Indiana, anti-communism in, 4, 34, 111,
    114
Industrial Workers of the World (IWW),
    38–39
Institute of Pacific Relations, 126, 145–49
Interdepartmental Committee on Employee
    Investigations, 55
Interdepartmental Committee on Investiga-
    tions, 55
International Alliance of Theatrical Stage
    Employees, 75

236

Index

International Information Agency (IIA), 34, 136
International Longshore Workers Union (ILWU), 110, 112, 152
International United Electrical Workers Union (IUE), 151–52
International Workers Order, 70
Iowa, anti-communism in, 111
Irish-Americans, and McCarthyism, 8
Isolationism (also "neo-isolationism"), 8, 56, 58, 73

Jackson, Att'y Gen. Robert H., 51
Jaffe, Philip, 60, 61
Jencks, Clinton, 183, 185
Jencks v. U.S., 185, 186
Jenner, Sen. William, 22, 128, 134, 145
Jessup, Philip C., 125
Jiang Jieshi: mentioned, 34, 146–47; and *Amerasia* case, 61; fall of, 88–89; Lattimore and, 126
John Birch Society, 195
Johnson, Laurence, 196
Johnson, Lyndon B.: and McCarthy, 133; and the Durrs, 178; and security program, 182; and anti-Court bill, 186; and domestic intelligence, 190, 191; and Vietnam, 197
Johnson, Manning, 112, 175
Johnston, Sen. Olin D., 182
Jonkman, Rep. Bartel, 62–63
Jordan, George Racey, 90
Judd, Rep. Walter, 88, 89
Justice Department (U.S.): and IWW, 38; and first Red Scare, 41–42; jurisdiction of, 45; investigates federal employees, 55; and *Dennis*, 83, 115; and Rosenbergs, 115; and anti-Communist measures, 116; and Matusow, 182; and aliens, 188–89

Kanin, Garson, 162
Kaufman, Judge Irving, 115–16
Kaye, Danny, 77
Kazan, Elia, 156
Kennan, George F., 147

Kennedy, John Fitzgerald: in 1960, 22, 193–94; dating under surveillance, 51; and Vietnam, 150, 197
Kennedy, Joseph P., 51
Kennedy, Joseph P., Jr., 51
Kent, Rockwell, 187
Kenyon, Dorothy, 125
Kerr, Sen. Robert S., 166–67
Kersten, Rep. Charles, 69
Khrushchev, Nikita, 174, 190
Kilgore, Sen. Harley, 117
King, Rev. Martin Luther, Jr., 177, 191
Kinsey, Alfred, 166–67
Kinsey reports, 163, 166–67
Knights of Columbus, 97
Knowland, Sen. William, 64, 89, 141, 148
Knowles, Mary, 159–60
Kohlberg, Alfred, 89
Korean War: impact on McCarthy(ism), 26, 128–30, 142; and anti-communism, 102, 113–19, 144, 182; and civil-rights movement, 166

Labor, Department of, 42, 48
Labor unions, 16, 86, 110, 150–53
Ladejinsky, Wolf, 180–81, 183
La Follette, Sen. Robert M., Jr., 122–23
Lampell, Millard, 156, 157
Langer, Sen. William, 117
Lardner, Ring, Jr., 76, 77, 197
Larsen, Emmanuel, 61
Latham, Earl, 146
Lattimore, Owen: and McCarthy, 125, 126–27; and SISS, 146, 148–49, 216 n.4; grant to, 158; Budenz and, 183
Lawrence, David, 186
Lawson, John Howard, 76, 77
Lee, Robert E., 124
Lenin, N., 39–41, 43
Lens, Sidney, 10
Levitt, William, 5, 192
Levittown, 4, 5
Lewis, Fulton, Jr., 160
Lewis, John L., 13
Liberal Party (N.Y.), 66

237

Index

Liberals: and Hiss case, 23, 92–93; and anti-communism, 28–29, 64–66, 144, 169–70; and subversive threat, 47, 52, 55–56; and Vital Center, 65–66; and McCarthy, 133; and Lattimore, 150; and "McCarthyism," 163–64; assailed in 1980s, 201

Libraries, under attack, 34, 106, 162

Lilienthal, David E., 80, 90

Lindsay, Mayor John V., 198

Lippmann, Walter, 132

Lipset, Seymour Martin, 9

Lodge, Sen. Henry Cabot, Jr., 125, 127

Loeb, Philip, 156

Los Angeles, anti-communism in, 32, 109

Louis, Joe, 79–80

Loyalty Review Board, 68, 118, 131, 133, 147, 184

Lucas, Sen. Scott M., 116–17, 130

Luce, Henry R., 88, 89

Lyons, Eugene, 163

MacArthur, Gen. Douglas, 14, 44–45, 113, 131

McCarran, Sen. Patrick: as anti-Communist, 3; and China Lobby, 89; and McCarran Act, 116–17; death of, 142; and China inquest, 145–50; and unions, 151; and aliens, 188

McCarran Act (Internal Security Act of 1950): 116–18, 129, 171–72, 187, 189, 196

McCarran rider, 62

McCarran-Walter Act, 188, 200

McCarthy, Joseph R.: mentioned, 3, 6, 34, 47, 62, 150, 166–67, 184; and McCarthyism, 9, 145; on Hiss case, 22; and Esther Brunauer, 25–26, 29; noneconomic focus of, 35–36; discovers Communist issue, 120–21, 123; early years, 122–23; national rise of, 123–29; in election campaigns, 130, 131; and Eisenhower, 132–36, 141–42; chairs subcommittee, 134–38; and Army, 138–40; decline of, 138–42; censured, 140–41; death of, 142; opponents' weakness, 144; and SISS, 145;

148; accuses Service, 147; and unions, 151, 152; and Paul Hoffman, 159, 160; and Truman, 163; National Women's Party and, 166; significance of censure, 171, 172; and Supreme Court, 175–76, 185; and Oppenheimer, 180, and security program, 182; JFK and, 193; Nixon and, 194

McCarthy era, 3, 4, 187

McCarthyism, 131, 133, 179; explanations of, 3, 8–10, 201; effects of, 4; as more than McCarthy's activities, 9, 145; and courts, 150; exaggerated views of, 163–64; "public" McCarthyism declines, 188; impact on Left, 192; meaning debated, 198

McCormack, Rep. John, 46, 52

McCormick, Anne O'Hare, 87

McCormick newspapers, 85

McDowell, Rep. John, 211 n.5

McGohey, John F. X., 83

McGranery, Att'y Gen. James P., 149

McGrath, Earl, 102

McMahon, Sen. Brien, 125, 127, 128

Madison Capital-Times, 163

Maltz, Albert, 76

Mao Zedong, 61, 88, 146

Marable, Manning, 165

March on Washington Movement, 14, 66

Marshall, Gen. George C., 131

Marshall Plan, 7, 8

Martin, Gov. Edward, 64

Martin, Rep. Joe, 63

Marx, Karl, 10

Marxism (and Marxist-Leninism), 11, 15

Maryland, anti-communism in, 109, 110, 111, 112

Marzani, Carl, 63

Massachusetts, anti-communism in, 114

Mattachine Society, 168

Matthews, Herbert, 194

Matthews, J. B., 24, 107, 112, 136–37

Matusow, Harvey, 148, 182–83, 185

Mayer, Louis B., 75

Media, and McCarthy(ism), 123–24, 132, 135, 200

Index

Medina, Judge Harold, 93–94, 97
Menjou, Adolph, 76
Michigan, anti-communism in, 108–9, 110, 114
Military Intelligence (Dept. of the Army), 43–44
Military Personnel Security Program, 181
Miller, Arthur, 155–56, 162
Milton, Joyce, 115
Milwaukee Journal, 64
Mine, Mill and Smelter Workers Union, 13, 152
Minnesota Democratic Farmer-Labor Party, 66
Mississippi, anti-communism in, 109, 111
Modern art, and anti-Communism, 30–33, 35
Morgenthau, Sec'y of the Treasury Henry, 55
Morse, Sen. Wayne, 116, 118, 132
Mosinee, Wisc., 98–99
Mostel, Zero, 157, 197
Motion Picture Alliance for the Preservation of American Ideals, 75
Mumford, Lewis, 50
Mundt, Sen. Karl E.: and Hiss case, 22, 81, 92; and anti-Communist legislation, 73, 109, 116
Mundt-Nixon bill, 109, 116
Murphy, Frank (Gov., Att'y Gen.), 48, 49, 52
Murray, Philip, 66, 86, 99
Murrow, Edward R., 139, 178
Musmanno, Judge Michael, 152
Myrdal, Gunnar, 176

National Association for the Advancement of Colored People (NAACP), 165, 175
National Association of Manufacturers, 15
National Association Opposed to Women Suffrage, 43
National Civic Federation, 44, 45
National Committee for American Education, 100
National Education Association, 103
National Labor Relations Board, 45, 49
National Lawyers Guild, 92

National Security Agency, 191
National Women's Party, 166
Nativism, 37, 43, 47, 52–53, 188–89
Navasky, Victor, 198
Nazi-Soviet Pact, 13–14, 18, 49, 50, 54
Nelson, Steve, 115, 185
New Deal: conservative opposition to, 8; and Alger Hiss, 17–18, 21–22, 92–93; and Communist issue, 17, 19, 84; arts programs of, 30; charged with pro-communism, 45–49, 58; and HUAC, 80
New Hampshire, anti-communism in, 109, 114
New Left, interpretations of McCarthyism, 28–29, 68, 84, 97
New Rochelle, N.Y., registration law in, 114, 182
New York (state), anti-communism in, 104–5, 110, 111, 112
New York City: anti-communism in, 110; Board of Education, 153
New York Times, 15, 198
Niebuhr, Reinhold, 65
Nixon, Richard M.: as anti-Communist, 3; and Hiss case, 17, 19–20, 22–23, 81; later career, 22–23; and 1946 election, 63–64; on executive privilege, 81; and McCarthy, 121, 137, 142; in 1950 campaign, 129; "dirty tricks" of, 191; in 1954 campaign, 193; in 1960, 193–94; and SACB, 196; and China, 197

Ober, Frank B. (and Ober Act), 109, 112
Oehler, Hugo, 11
Office of Civil Defense, 89
Office of Naval Intelligence, 43
Office of Strategic Services, 60, 63
Ohio, anti-communism in, 109, 114
Oklahoma, anti-communism in, 108, 110
Oklahoma University, 108
Olson, Governor Culbert, 105
O'Mahoney, Sen. Joseph C., 198
Oppenheimer, Frank, 90
Oppenheimer, J. Robert, 90, 179–80, 197
"Organization Man," 4–5, 6
Ornitz, Samuel, 76

Index

Orozco, José Clemente, 30
Oswald, Lee Harvey, 196
Oxnam, Bishop G. Bromley, 173

Palmer, Att'y. Gen. A. Mitchell, 41–42
Parks, Larry, 154
Pasadena, education controversy in, 100–101
Paul, Alice, 166
Peace movement, 49, 168–69
Peale, Dr. Norman Vincent, 5, 6
Peek, George, 18
Peekskill riot, 97
Pennsylvania, anti-communism in, 109
Pennsylvania v. Nelson, 185
Pepper, Sen. Claude D., 129
Peress, Irving, 137–38, 172
Perkins, Sec'y of Labor Frances, 48
Peters, J., 82
Peurifoy, John, 126
Philbrick, Herbert, 94
Pillion, Rep. John, 195
Pledge of Allegiance, 5
Popular Front, 12–13; and liberalism, 65–66, 86, 93
Post, Louis F., 42
Potter, Sen. Charles, 137
President's Temporary Commission on Employee Loyalty (PTCEL), 67–69
Progressive Party, 9, 82, 65
Public opinion: on communism, 16, 59–60, 85; on McCarthy, 127, 138; and civil liberties, 201

Quill, Mike, 99

Raab, Earl, 9
Rader, Melvin, 108
Radosh, Ronald, 115
Radulovich, Milo, 178
Rand, Ayn, 75
Randolph, A. Philip, 14, 66, 164, 165
Randolph, Rep. Jennings, 64, 69
Rankin, Rep. John, 31, 77
Rapp-Coudert Committee, 104–5, 153
Rayburn, Rep. Sam, 49

Reagan, Ronald, 75–76, 199, 200, 202
Red Channels, 157
Red Scare of 1919–20, 39–43
Red Squads, 44
Reece, Rep. B. Carroll, 63, 159, 167
Reed College, 173
Rees, Rep. Edward, 69
Refregier, Anton, 32–33
Religion, in 1950s, 5–6
Remington, William, 81
Republican National Committee, 64
Republican Party: and bipartisan foreign policy, 7; divisions in, 8; and origins of McCarthyism, 8, 9; and Hiss case, 21–22, 92–93; and loyalty issue, 67, 69, 72–73; and 1948 defeat, 85; and China, 88–89; and McCarthy, 124–26, 132–42; in 1980s, 200–201
Reuther, Walter, 66, 99
Richardson, Seth, 118
Richmond, Al, 10
Rivera, Diego, 30, 32
Robeson, Paul, 79, 95, 97, 113, 165, 187
Robin Hood, attacked as Communist, 34
Robinson, Jackie, 79
Robsion, Rep. John, 53
Rock and roll, 161
Rockfeller Foundation, 158, 167
Rogers, Jane, 155
Rogers v. U.S., 155
Rogin, Michael, 166
Roosevelt, Eleanor, 80, 194
Roosevelt, Franklin D.: on USSR, 15–16; and Hiss case, 17, 18, 21, recognizes USSR, 45; and Communist issue, 46, 48; and Dies Committee, 48–49; and "fifth column," 50–51; and civil liberties, 51–52; and FBI, 51–52
Roosevelt, Rep. James, 196
Rosenberg, Ethel, 62, 115
Rosenberg, Julius, 62, 115, 137
Rubin, Jerry, 195
Rushmore, Howard, 112
Russell, Bertrand, 104
Russell, Jane, 5
Rutgers University, 173–74

Sabath, Rep. Adolph, 69
Salk, Jonas, 5
SANE (Committee for a Sane Nuclear Policy), 168–69
Saltzman, Benny, 189
Scales, Junius, 186
Schactman, Max, 11
Schine, G. David, 136, 137, 138
Schlesinger, Arthur M., Jr., 58, 65
Schneiderman, William, 54
Schrecker, Ellen, 172
Schulberg, Budd, 154
Schuman, Frederick, 125
Scott, Adrian, 76
Screen Actors Guild, 154
Screen Directors Guild, 154
Screen Writers Guild, 74
Scudder, Rep. Herbert, 33
Seattle, 1919 general strike, 39–40
Seberg, Jean, 191
Security program (federal), 72, 133–34,147; criticized, 178–84
Seeger, Pete, 33, 173–74, 197
Senate Internal Security Subcommittee (SISS): mentioned, 3, 145, 197; probes China Hands, 127, 145–49; and civil rights, 175–78; and Matusow, 183; and Hawaii, 195; abolished, 196
Senate Permanent Subcommittee on Investigations, 134ff., 172
Senate Republican Policy Committee, 139
Senate Subcommittee on Security and Terrorism, 199–200
Service, John Stewart, 61–62, 125, 147–48, 186, 197
Shapley, Harlow, 125
Sheil, Bishop Bernard, 139
Shivers, Gov. Allen, 152
Sinatra, Frank, 77
Smith, Rep. Howard W., 186. *See also* Smith Act
Smith, Sen. Margaret Chase, 128–29
Smith, Sen. Willis, 145
Smith Act (Alien Registration Act): passed, 53–54; wartime use of, 54; 1948 indictments, 83–84; 1949 trial, 93–95; mentioned, 109, 152, 171; second-string indictments, 115; and Supreme Court, 184, 185–86; use ends, 196
Socialist Party of America, 11, 12, 40
Socialist Workers Party, 190
Socialists, 38, 42
Sokolsky, George, 89, 131
Sondergaard, Gail, 153
Sons of the American Revolution, 100
Sorrell, Herbert, 75
Southern Christian Leadership Conference, 190–91
Southern Conference Education Fund, 176–77
Southern Conference for Human Welfare, 176
Soviet Union (USSR): postwar policies of, 8; and Spanish Civil War, 13; in World War II, 14–15
Spanish Civil War, 13, 49
Special House Committee on Un-American Activities. *See* Dies Committee
Stalin, Josef V., 8, 15, 142
Stalinism, 13, 50
Stander, Lionel, 74
Stamm, Tom, 11
Stanky, Eddie, 35
State Department: and Alger Hiss, 18–20; cultural programs of, 31–32; and loyalty issue, 62–63; Loyalty-Security Board (and security program), 72, 147, 148; investigated in Eightieth Congress, 73; and China, 89; and McCarthy, 123, 126–27, 134, 136; impact of purges on, 150; homosexuals fired, 167; and passports, 187
Steinbeck, John, 30
Stevens, Sec'y of Army Robert T., 138
Stevenson, Adlai E., 22, 107, 134, 193
Stratton, Gov. William, 107
Strauss, Admiral Lewis, 179, 180
Subversive Activities Control Board (SACB), 117–18, 187, 196
Summary dismissal statute: 52, 55. *See also* Security program
Supreme Court (U.S.): and Hollywood Ten, 77; and Coplon case, 91; and Oklahoma

Index

Supreme Court (U.S.) *(continued)*
oath, 108; and Korean crisis, 114–15;
and McCarran Act, 118; opposition to
civil rights decisions of, 174, 175–76; and
anti-communist programs, 184–88; and
flag, 222 *n.*10
Sweezy v. New Hampshire, 186

Taber, Rep. John, 69
Taft, Sen. Robert A., 125–26, 134
Taft-Hartley Act, 73, 96, 102, 184, 185
Talmadge, Sen. Herman, 176
Taylor, Sen. Glen, 129
Taylor, Harold, 34, 102
Television, in American life, 4, 5
Teller, Edward, 179
Tenney, Jack, 105–6, 111, 112
Terrorism, 198–200
Texas: oilmen and McCarthyism, 8; anti-
communism in, 109, 152
Texas v. Johnson, 222 *n.*10
Thomas, Rep. J. Parnell, 69, 76, 77
Thompson, Dorothy, 132
Thompson, Robert, 95
Thurmond, Sen. J. Strom, 176
Time magazine, 18, 92
Tocqueville, Alexis de, 71
Trotsky, Leon, 41
Trotskyites (and Trotskyism), 10, 11, 95
Truman, Harry S.: anti-Communist policies
of, 7, 16; 1948 election of, 8; blamed for
McCarthyism, 8–9; and Hiss case, 17–
19, 193; and McCarthy, 26, 123, 124,
127–28, 131; and loyalty program, 59,
66–70; and Wallace, 65, 82; Supreme
Court appointments, 77; and Lilienthal,
80; and loyalty files, 80–81; and Smith
Act case, 83–84; and H-bomb, 89; and
anti-Communist legislation, 113, 116–
18; executive order cited, 137; and civil
liberties, 144, 163; new loyalty standard
of, 147; and Lattimore, 149; and civil-
rights issue, 165; Velde subpoenas, 179
Truman Administration: and *Amerasia,* 61;
and *Dennis* case, 93; and Freedom Train,
97–98; and IUE, 151

Truman Doctrine: and anti-Communist
rhetoric, 9; and loyalty program, 59, 68–69
Trumbo, Dalton, 76, 77, 196
Tydings, Sen. Millard E., 25, 28, 125,
127–29, 130, 167
Tydings Subcommittee, 25–26, 29, 124–
29, 147, 149

Union of Russian Workers, 42
United Auto Workers (UAW), 13, 66, 99,
100
United Electrical Workers (UE): and Com-
munists, 13, 66, 96, 100, 151–52
United Mine Workers of America, 13, 15
United Public Workers of America, 110–
11, 152
United States Chamber of Commerce, 16,
85, 97
United States Information Agency, 33
University of California, 102, 106
University of Chicago, 101
University of Kansas, 101
University of Michigan, 173
University of Washington, 101–2, 107–8
University of Wisconsin, 101, 111, 173
Urban League, 164

Vail, Rep. Richard, 97
Vanech, A.D., 67
Velde, Rep. Harold, 173, 179
Veterans of Foreign Wars, 32, 79
Vietnam War, 22, 23, 33, 150, 181, 191,
197, 200
Vincent, John Carter, 146, 148
Vinson, Chief Justice Fred, 184
Vital Center liberalism, 65–66, 86, 93
Voice of America, 136
Voorhis, Rep. Jerry, 52, 63–64
Voorhis Act, 52
Vorys, Rep. John, 89

Walgreen, Charles R., 101
Wallace, Henry A.: redbaited, 9, 82, 84;
and Alger Hiss, 18; and Cold War, 65;
and Edward Condon, 80; mob action
against, 95; Lattimore and, 126

Index

Walter, Rep. Francis A., 33, 154, 173, 183, 188
Warner, Jack, 75
Warren, Chief Justice Earl, 175, 184–86, 188
Washington (state), anti-communism in, 107–8, 109
Washington Bookshop Association, 70
Watergate, 22–23, 81
Watkins, Sen. Arthur V., 140–41
Watkins v. U.S., 185, 186
Watt, Sec'y of the Interior James, 199
Weinstein, Allen, 18, 21
Welch, Joseph N., 139, 216 *n*.17
Welker, Sen. Herman, 79, 151, 193
Welles, Orson, 57
Wherry, Sen. Kenneth, 89
White, Harry Dexter, 81, 179
White, Walter, 165
Whyte, William F., Jr., 6
Wicker, Tom, 200

Williams, Aubrey, 177–78
Williams, Gov. G. Mennen, 114
Willkie, Wendell, 54
Wilson, Sec'y of Labor William B., 39, 42
Wirt, Dr. William, 45–46
Wisconsin, anti-communism in, 111
Women, in McCarthy era, 27–28
Wood, Sam, 75
Wright, Loyd G., 183
Wright, Richard, 11
Wyman, Louis, 186

Yalta Conference, 18, 21
Yates v. U.S., 185–86
Yorty, Sam, 105, 111
Youngdahl, Judge Luther, 149–50

Zeidler, Mayor Frank, 111
Zoll, Allen, 100
Zoning, 169
Zwicker, Gen. Ralph W., 137–38, 140

243

CPSIA information can be obtained at www.ICGtesting.com
Printed in the USA
LVOW11s1503100316

478624LV00001B/249/P